The

BIBLE'S CUTTING
ROOM FLOOR

The
BIBLE'S CUTTING
ROOM FLOOR

THE HOLY

SCRIPTURES

MISSING FROM

YOUR BIBLE

Dr. Joel M. Hoffman

THOMAS DUNNE BOOKS

ST. MARTIN'S PRESS ✖ NEW YORK

THOMAS DUNNE BOOKS.
An imprint of St. Martin's Press.

www.thomasdunnebooks.com
www.stmartins.com
www.thebiblescuttingroomfloor.com

Maps on pages 21 and 25 courtesy of the author.
Photograph on page 38 courtesy of the author.

The Library of Congress Cataloging-in-Publication Data is available upon request.

ISBN 978-1-250-04796-0 (hardcover)
ISBN 978-1-4668-4826-9 (e-book)

St. Martin's Press books may be purchased for educational, business, or promotional use. For information on bulk purchases, please contact Macmillan Corporate and Premium Sales Department at 1-800-221-7945, extension 5442, or write special markets@macmillan.com.

First Edition: September 2014

10 9 8 7 6 5 4 3 2 1

For my students

CONTENTS

ACKNOWLEDGMENTS

Some two thousand years ago, the poet Ovid wrote that the labor of writing can cause pleasure. In my own case I have been exceedingly fortunate to interact with people who augment that pleasure.

For five years now, Irene Goodman has been my agent and guide to the intricacies and quirks of publishing. She's a fun person with a kind soul, and I'm lucky to have stumbled upon such a partner. Without her, this book would still be an unpublished collection of thoughts, and I would never have been introduced to the folks at Thomas Dunne Books. Thank you, Irene.

My primary contact at Thomas Dunne Books is Peter Joseph, and working with him and his team has been delightful. The compromises demanded by the nature of publishing makes it ripe for contention and bickering, but my experience with Peter has been just the opposite. I am a better author for knowing him, and I have enjoyed every step of the publication process. Thank you, Peter.

I'm also grateful to a variety of talented people who work with Peter: Melanie Fried, his assistant; Angela Gibson, for her diligent and insightful copyediting; Rob Grom, for designing one of my favorite book covers (how lucky for me that it ended up on my own book); Elizabeth Catalano, production editor; Lisa Goris, production manager; Allison Frascatore, publicist; Laura Clark, team leader; and Karlyn Hixson, who oversees marketing. The fact that I have to refer to some of these people by title just demonstrates how much work went into this book that I don't even know about.

Tom Dunne is the one whose vision put these people together, so I'm in his debt not just for publishing my work but for doing so in a way that let me enjoy the process. Equally, I'm indebted to Sally Richardson, publisher at St. Martin's Press.

Special mention is due to Rev. Paul Raushenbush, the executive religion editor at *The Huffington Post*. A couple of years ago he surprised me by requesting some dozen drafts of a short piece I wrote for him. My writing has benefited greatly from what that process taught me.

The path that brought me to where I am has been graced by far too many people to mention by name, but I must single out a few, starting with my father, Rabbi Lawrence Hoffman, Ph.D., who, in addition to everything else he has done, has been my lifelong study partner.

I'm also particularly grateful to: Rabbi Gary Bretton-Granatoor, who helped me thrive; Marc Brettler, for his compassion and knowledge; Rabbi Billy and Cantor Ellen Dreskin, for their support, honesty, and wisdom; Jennifer Hammer at NYU Press, for publishing my first book in a way that made me want to continue; Rabbi Shoshana Hantman, a rare island of wisdom and sanity (though she'd never admit it) in an otherwise turbulent sea; Rabbi Stuart Geller, for his compassion, support, and humor; Rabbi Allen "Smitty" Smith, for believing in me; Danny Maseng, for expanding my horizons; David and Karen Frank, for their kindness and thoughtfulness, and for opening so many doors; Rabbi Jaimee Shalhevet, for her insight;

Lauren Rose, for her support and enthusiasm; Tal Varon, who by personal example reminds me to walk humbly; Janet Walton, for being clear on what matters; and Rabbi Danny Zemel, a modern-day prophet.

Finally, I am endlessly grateful to my parents, Sally and Larry, who gave me a good life.

The
BIBLE'S CUTTING
ROOM FLOOR

INTRODUCTION:
THE ABRIDGED BIBLE

The Bible you usually read is the abridged version.

Its contents were culled from a much larger selection of holy scriptures when new realities forced religious leaders to discard some of their most cherished and sacred books, resulting in what we now call the Bible.

Some writings were left out for political or theological reasons, others simply because of the physical restrictions of ancient book-making technology. At times, the compilers of the Bible skipped information that they assumed everyone knew. Some passages were even omitted by accident. For these reasons and more, your Bible doesn't give you a complete picture.

The Book of Genesis in the Bible tells you about Adam and Eve in the Garden of Eden, but not what happens to them after they get kicked out for disobeying God. It presents Abraham, the father of monotheism, but doesn't explain how he came to reject idolatry and leave his father's idol factory. It introduces you to Noah, who walked with God but, except for the briefest of mentions, not to his grandfather

Enoch, who also walked with God and, in addition, learned the secrets of the universe. Other books that were left out of the Bible detail the fascinating second part of Adam and Eve's life, the intriguing first part of Abraham's, and Enoch's mysterious saga.

Your Bible contains only 150 Psalms, but it's clear from other books that there used to be more.

The Gospel of Matthew refers to "the time of King Herod," when wise men came to Jerusalem from Bethlehem. But it doesn't tell you who King Herod was, why that Roman ruler is so important to readers of the New Testament, how he came to be in charge of Jerusalem in the first place, or about the amazing connection between the Maccabees and the forced conversion of Herod's family that made it possible for Herod to reign in the first place. Modern readers cannot fully appreciate the message and value of the Gospels without this background information, but they have to look outside the Bible to find it.

The Book of Esther describes the famous story of the Jews' near destruction at the hands of the Persians and how the Jews were saved by heroes named Mordecai and Esther. Though you can read most of it in your Bible, the story opens with a dream in which Mordecai frames the struggle between the Jews and the Persians in terms of two serpents that are ready for battle. That dream is missing from your Bible.

Christians know they have the Book of Revelation, about the end of times and what happens when God's plan for earth is fulfilled, because Revelation is in the New Testament. Jews had similar books, also about the end of times, which offered different answers to what eventually happens to the earth. But those books were left out.

At the heart of these omissions—and many more like them—is the very nature of the Bible. While we now consider it a single book, it began as a diverse set of writings, remarkably similar to a "best of" collection, a college literature course, or a suggested reading list.

Two thousand years ago there were hundreds of religious documents that were important to the Jews and early Christians. Some of these lie at the heart of both religious and secular Western life to this day: Genesis (with stories that almost every child learns), Exodus (the focus of more than one major motion picture and also a source for the Ten Commandments), Leviticus (with its laws about homosexuality), Psalm 23 ("The Lord is my shepherd"), the Book of Isaiah ("beat their swords into plowshares"), Ecclesiastes ("To everything there is a season"), the Gospels (with their descriptions of the virgin birth), John ("For God so loved the world"), Revelation (the sign of the beast), and so forth. But these parts of the Bible represent only some of the central writings from that influential time period.

Even today's word "Bible" means different things to different people. For Jews, it's the collection of writings often known as the Old Testament or Jewish Bible. The Hebrew term for this set is a three-consonant acronym—*TaNaK*—that reflects the tripartite division of the Old Testament into the Five Books of Moses (*Torah,* in Hebrew); the Prophets (*Nevi'im*), which includes the prophets and some historical books; and the catchall Writings (*K'tuvim*), with things like Psalms, Proverbs, and Job.

For Christians, the "Bible" includes the entire Old Testament as well as the New Testament: the Gospels, Corinthians, Revelation, and others. For some Christian readers (Catholics, primarily), the "Bible" also includes books like Maccabees, which form a category known technically as the Apocrypha or commonly as "noncanonical" books. These writings earn their common name because they are Old Testament–like books that are not part of the official Jewish canon. Their technical name derives from the Greek for "hidden away" and reflects a Christian judgment that they are unsuited for public reading, not being part of the official canon.

Two other technical names demonstrate the controversy about these books. Catholics call them deuterocanonical, that is, "part of the second canon," specifically including them in a canon. The Orthodox churches call these books "worthy of reading," taking an even stronger position about their value. These same Orthodox churches introduce even more books into "the Bible," with, for example, two additional books about the Maccabees.

In the end, correct answers to the question, How many books are in the Bible? range from thirty-three to seventy-eight. Yet even with seventy-eight books, more material was left out than was included.

Additionally, different groups of people order the books of the Bible differently. The modern Jewish order is different from the traditional Jewish order. Christians put the Old Testament books into a third order yet. (For instance, Christians put Daniel near the other famous prophets like Ezekiel and Isaiah, to underscore his centrality. Jews marginalize Daniel by grouping him with the other "writings.") The Apocrypha, too, appear variously as part of the Old Testament, as an addition to the Old Testament, or—as we just saw—not at all.

Underlying all of these differences is the simple fact that there used to be lots of holy writings, and different groups of people compiled different collections of them to form a single book.

As with so many other important historical changes, the move from collection of books to single book was made possible by new technology. Originally books were written on scrolls, which could only practically hold so many words. Then technology progressed, and it became possible to bind leaves of parchment together to form longer volumes. This new type of compilation, called a codex and practically the same as our modern book, made it possible to gather a collection of scrolls into one set. The Bible was the first major collection of scrolls.

This fact is reflected in the very word "Bible," which comes from the Greek word *biblia,* the plural of *biblos.* And *biblos* is Greek for "papyrus," the plant that was used to make one of the three common ancient writing surfaces. Parchment was the second. The third was wood, or, in Latin, *caudex*. This became the Latin *codex*, which is also our modern English technical term. The more common Latin word for "book," *liber*, originally meant "bark." All of this reflects the close connection between bookmaking technology and the Bible.

But even though a codex could be longer than a scroll, its length was still limited. This meant that even though scrolls could be collected to form the Bible, not all of the scrolls could be included. So the "Bible" as an abridged collection of scrolls was formed.

But the Bible was never meant to exclude the other writings completely. Just as a permanent collection at a museum doesn't imply that the items in storage have no value, and just as a window display at a store isn't intended to devalue the rest of what the store offers, the Bible was meant to highlight some contents, not to reject all the others. In fact, many of the scrolls were excluded simply because there wasn't enough room for them in a codex.

This could have been the rationale behind the omission of the Life of Adam and Eve (the subject of chapter 5), which picks up the story of Adam and Eve just as things get interesting. What happened to the couple after they left the Garden of Eden? Did Adam forgive his wife? Did they stay married? (Adam lived to be 930 years old. That could be a lot of bickering.) What was it like for them when one of their sons killed the other? And so on.

The Life of Adam and Eve also addresses the nature of good and evil: Why is there evil in the world? Why did Adam and Eve suffer? Why did the snake trick them? Was Satan involved? And what are the lessons for our own lives? Christianity is clear that humans live in a state of fallenness stemming from the Garden of Eden. Judaism asks and answers the question of evil in a different framework, also dealing with the general notion of an imperfect world. The Life of Adam and Eve explores these same themes.

Similarly, the Apocalypse of Abraham (covered in chapter 6) puts

Abraham's life into context: his early life with his parents, his father Terah's idol factory, Abraham's rejection of idolatry, and even Terah's violent, fiery death in front of his young son. What was it like for Abraham to watch his father die? Did Abraham wonder if he could have saved Terah? Did he feel responsible? How did Abraham's youth impact his later life? And how does this help us read the Bible with more insight?

The Apocalypse of Abraham also deals with the nature of good and evil, even focusing on the fascinating question of whether evil people who remain unpunished in this world are necessarily punished in the next. In other words, is there a hell? Is there a heaven? And who goes there? But the story of Abraham's early life and of what he learns isn't in your Bible, even though later mainstream extrabiblical sources refer to it.

Noah may be one of the most famous characters in the Bible—who hasn't heard of the great flood, Noah's ark, the rainbow, and so forth?—but Noah and the flood mark the end of a story that began three generations earlier with Enoch. And Enoch is so important that he has his own book, but even though the New Testament quotes it, it's not in your Bible.

The intricate Book of Enoch (explored in chapter 7) explains who Enoch was and why he was so important. It recounts an argument between God and a group of angels known as the Watchers, who got in trouble for violating God's trust and for mating with humans instead of watching over them.

Like the Life of Adam and Eve, the Book of Enoch explores the nature of living life as a human here on earth. Among other things, the book offers bold answers to the universal question of why people suffer, which is one reason it was so popular two thousand years ago. But these same courageous theological positions pushed the book into near obscurity a few hundred years later as the focus of religion shifted.

This popular book was certainly written before the Book of Daniel. Daniel is in everyone's Bible, so no one can say that Enoch was written too late to be included in the Bible, just as no one can claim that it was too obscure. It was just left out.

These three—the Life of Adam and Eve, the Apocalypse of Abraham, and the Book of Enoch—represent just a tiny portion of the books that didn't make the final cut into the Bible. I choose to focus on them in chapters 5–7 because they all deal directly with good versus evil and the human condition, asking the same timeless questions and offering different insightful answers to them. In this regard, they are very biblical. They also offer a sense of the different kinds of literature that ended up on the Bible's cutting room floor.

The Apocalypse of Abraham, as the name suggests, is an "apocalypse." Though we now think of that word as referring to a major disaster, it originally meant "disclosure," as in a work that discloses or reveals something. The most famous example is the final book in the New Testament, called variously the Revelation of Saint John the Divine or the Apocalypse of John. Those two titles were supposed to mean the same thing, because an apocalypse was supposed to be something that revealed secrets.

As a literary genre, apocalypses tend to be written in the name of someone other than the actual author ("pseudonymous"), to feature otherworldly symbols, and to deal with heavenly bodies and the end of time. The biblical Book of Daniel is, therefore, an apocalypse. So too, of course, is the Apocalypse of Abraham, along with Apocalypses of Adam, Daniel, Elijah, Ezra, Zephaniah, and others. But unlike Revelation and Daniel, these were all excluded from the Bible.

Other literary genres, too, were excluded, among them stories (like the Life of Adam and Eve), poetry (including some psalms that got left out), oracles, biblical summaries, legal codes, and more.

Because so many of these should-have-been-biblical books are apocalypses, and because apocalypse authors tend to sign someone else's name to their work, part of this grand collection is often called the "pseudepigrapha," that is, "written with a false superscription," or, more plainly, "written in the name of someone else." These pseudepigrapha are the most famous documents left on the Bible's cutting room floor, though "famous" here is, of course, relative, and compared with the text of the Bible, all of these writings are, unfortunately, obscure.

But for historical reasons, the collection called the "pseudepigrapha" completely omits the Dead Sea Scrolls (the focus of chapter 2)—perhaps because the term was already in common use when the scrolls were discovered—as well as other writings from two thousand years ago. So even though there are pseudepigrapha on the Bible's cutting room floor, there are other kinds of texts as well, most important, alternative traditions, translations, and histories.

This is why I include the Dead Sea Scrolls here. They represent our most expansive knowledge about a religious tradition that never became mainstream. Usually such countercultural movements are suppressed, but in this case an entire trove of documents was buried in the desert, beyond the reach of revisionist historians. I include the Septuagint (the subject of chapter 3) because it is the most influential ancient translation of the Bible, though calling it a "translation" is already misrepresenting it somewhat. Modern translations are supposed to be as accurate as possible, while in antiquity translation and interpretation were intermeshed in ways that go beyond what is usually accepted today. The Septuagint is both a translation and a commentary.

And I include Josephus (the hero of chapter 4), because he is far and away the most comprehensive historian of the time whose work survives. His writings help us put the Bible in its proper context, by giving us background information that the authors of the Bible didn't bother to include because it was common knowledge in Jerusalem two thousand years ago, for example.

Taken together, these apocalypses, stories, traditions, translations, and histories represent what was left out of the Bible as we now know it, conveying the flavor and nature of what's missing.

But your Bible isn't just incomplete. It's also inaccurate in some places.

For example, Matthew quotes Isaiah as talking about a virgin giving birth to a boy who will be called Emmanuel. But Matthew is quoting the Greek translation discussed in chapter 3, which got Isaiah's Hebrew wrong in this case (and in many others). Isaiah wasn't talking about a virgin. It's this same Greek translation that puts the Book of Esther into context with Mordecai's dream—a dream that got left out of the Bible.

All of these works were composed in and around ancient Jerusalem, an area scholars call the Ancient Near East, which is where King David established the Israelite monarchy approximately three thousand years ago and where the First Temple and Second Temple were built. (Archaeological evidence of the First Temple was just unearthed recently.) And it is where Jesus was born and later crucified. These events, and many more, are detailed in the Bible.

But what about the political infighting among the different groups of Jews, some of whom would eventually found Christianity, others of whom would create Judaism as it is now practiced? What about the role of Rome in all of this? How did the founders of Christianity see their own lives? What did citizens of Jerusalem two thousand years ago think about the Bible? What did they think about the Jewish sacrificial cult, soon to come to an end (though they did not know it)? What about the blossoming cultures that gave the world Christianity and rabbinic Judaism? The Bible is largely silent on all of these matters.

Fortunately, other texts fill in the gaps, shedding light on the culture and context that gave the world the two (and later three) great mono-theistic faiths.

The following pages introduce you to these captivating writings from the Bible's cutting room floor. As you read on, you'll discover what's missing from your Bible, who left it out, and why it is so important.

We start in chapter 1 with an overview of the fascinating thousand-year-long chain of upheaval that created the Jerusalem in which many of the documents were written and which paved the way for the life of Jesus and for the Rabbis that would revolutionize Judaism. Then in chapters 2–4 we turn to three comprehensive sources of background material. Next we explore how all of this paints some of the most familiar characters from the Bible in a new light (chapters 5–7). Along the way, we'll uncover different answers to the most fundamental and universal questions people ask about their lives. Finally in chapter 8, we examine the lessons we learn from the intriguing writings that are missing from your Bible.

So your exploration of the writings found on the Bible's cutting room floor starts in ancient Jerusalem and ventures through a wide variety of texts to bring you back to modernity with a renewed appreciation for the Bible, an awareness of what's missing from it, a better understanding of some of the forces that were most influential in shaping Western society, and an uncanny sense that the past has a surprisingly urgent message for the present. Enjoy the journey.

1

JERUSALEM: AN ETERNAL CITY IN CONFLICT

Very few things happen at the right time, and the rest do not happen at all: the conscientious historian will correct these defects.
—MARK TWAIN, ON HERODOTUS, THE FIRST HISTORIAN

Let others praise ancient times; I'm glad I was born in these.
—OVID, FIRST CENTURY A.D.

By local reckoning, the year was that of Roman consuls Antonius and Cicero, during the 179th olympiad cycle. Only later would we date the events to 63 years before the birth of Christ, or to the 3,697th year of Creation.

It was three months into the siege.

In Jerusalem, the hot summer sun had yet to give way to the relative cool of winter—Jerusalem's weather fits nicely into three seasons, not four—and the sacrificial rites of the first millennium B.C. had yet to mutate into more modern forms of worship. So following a thousand years of tradition, Jewish priests in the great temple oversaw the slaughter of animals for God twice each day, in the morning and again around the ninth hour.

The menu for sacrifice was varied. A wealthy man, thankful for a particular stroke of good fortune, brought a bull. Another arrived with a lamb for the same reason. For a third denizen of Jerusalem, a lamb was to atone for a wrongdoing. The poor brought doves when they couldn't afford mammals.

The cacophony of so many animals in one place—bulls, lambs, goats, and even pigeons—combined with the general hubbub of the masses: bellows and bleats, merchants and middlemen, sacrificial incantations and everyday conversations. It was a spectacle, part circus, part sacrament, and part barbecue.

The stench of animals both living and dead mixed with the smoky aroma of burnt flesh and blood. The blood from the sacrificial animals was considered particularly important, for in it was the sacred power of life. The priests collected the blood from the slain animals, saving it to be sprinkled by hand on the altar.

This particular day, the priests' job was made incomparably harder by the onslaught of an invading Roman army as part of the siege. The world's mightiest fighting force had set its sights on the holy city of Jerusalem, leaving human blood running alongside that of the animals.

That same year, some 1,400 miles to the northwest, a Roman woman named Atia gave birth to a sickly son whom she called Gaius Octavius. Though his poor health would work against him, his grandmother was Julia, sister to Julius Caesar. This family connection would later help Gaius Octavius earn the title Augustus and become Rome's first emperor.

In the same year that Gaius Octavius was born, Caesar himself—Gaius Octavius's great uncle—was elected pontifex maximus, high priest of the Roman College of Pontiffs. Later he would be called a god. Though in retrospect the signs of Rome's decline are clear, Caesar was apparently unaware of the violent upheavals just around the corner, and equally unaware that he would be assassinated within two decades.

Similarly, the Jewish priests' power in Jerusalem was dimming, and, like Caesar, they did not know it. The siege in Jerusalem was only part of the problem. The more significant threat to the priests' power was internal Jewish turmoil. Sacrifice had been the binding force behind Judaism for nearly a millennium. Now that approach to serving God was being called into question. Maybe, some said, God didn't want sacrifices after all. And maybe the priests weren't as holy as they claimed.

A few decades earlier, the Roman Republic's greatest times were waning as that world power struggled through military defeat, political upheaval, and civil war.

In 82 B.C., a dictator named Sulla ruthlessly took power. (In one particularly gruesome gesture, he publicly posted the names of his political opponents, signifying that anyone who was able should kill them.) Sulla had a protégé named Pompey, who began his own military career at the young age of seventeen. By the time Pompey was in his twenties, his mentor was ruling Rome. This is how Pompey came to command an army, which he took to Damascus—part of modern-day Syria—in 64 B.C.

Pompey had been sent to conquer the region. And with so few armies able to stand up to the fighting force that he had at his disposal, currying favor with the Roman general was seen as a hugely important diplomatic task among the soon-to-be-conquered. Ambassadors from Syria, Egypt, and the Jewish province of Judea (which contained Jerusalem) came to greet Pompey.

In fact, two Jewish kings arrived in Damascus. The first was Hyrcanus II, who claimed to be ruler of Jerusalem and king of Judea. The second was his younger brother Aristobulus II, who also claimed to be ruler of Jerusalem and king of Judea.

In a not atypical situation for Jerusalem at the time, even as both brothers claimed the holy city as their own, they were utterly despised by the Jews they presumed to rule. Though Hyrcanus and Aristobulus hailed from a priestly family, and though they were descendants of the great Hasmonean Maccabees who revolted against the Syrian Greeks a century earlier to establish an independent Judea, they had both become increasingly Roman in their ways, adopting the lifestyle of pagan monarchs instead of comporting themselves in the familiar Jewish fashion. The Jewish population saw them as representing too sharp a break with tradition. The Jews served priests, who in turn served God. Kings were for other nations.

Unable to achieve a popular victory at home, both brothers tried to enlist the help of Pompey. Hyrcanus explained that, as the older brother, he was the rightful king. The younger Aristobulus countered that Hyrcanus was too placid a ruler. Aristobulus explained that he was forced to overthrow his older brother in order to prevent other, nonpriestly forces from wresting control of Jerusalem and pulling it completely out of Jewish hands. It was sibling rivalry playing out on a world stage.

In the end, Pompey condemned Aristobulus's behavior as a coup d'état but urged both men to exercise restraint. Pompey promised to come to Jerusalem at a later date to settle things. But, bypassing his brother, Aristobulus ignored Pompey and rallied an army. He marched it into Judea, a provocation that infuriated the Roman general with whom he and his brother had just met.

In response, Pompey marshaled his legions and set out for Judea himself. Along the way, he took command of a fortress in a place called Corem. Atop a mountain named Alexandrium, due east of Jerusalem and just a dozen miles north of Jericho, Corem was an ideal staging point for an assault on the Jewish capital. From there, Pompey offered Aristobulus one last chance for peace. But Aristobulus, worried that Pompey would give Judea back to his older brother Hyrcanus, refused the peace offer and, instead, prepared for war.

So Pompey pitched camp in Jericho and from there marched two dozen miles west into Jerusalem. Seeing the Roman troops, Aristobulus pleaded for peace, surrendering Jerusalem and offering Pompey money. Pompey called off his attack. But Aristobulus reneged. Enraged, Pompey imprisoned Aristobulus and ordered a full assault on Jerusalem.

The population of Jerusalem, now left completely without leadership, split into two camps. Some people, fearing Rome's might in the form of Pompey's army, were glad that Aristobulus was out of the picture. This way, they thought, a peaceful settlement with Pompey could be negotiated. Other people feared Rome's rule more than its wrath and hoped to forcibly keep Pompey out of Jerusalem.

Jerusalem at the time was fortified on the east, south, and west by walls—the north side was more vulnerable—and encompassed by a defensive ditch. The Temple itself was also surrounded by walls.

Amid the power vacuum and confusion in Jerusalem, Pompey was let into the city from the north, but soon afterward the bridge he had used to enter was destroyed. Even though Pompey was near the Temple, his all-important battering rams and catapults were stuck beyond the ditch, outside Jerusalem. Pompey couldn't yet take the Temple—the Jewish seat of religious and political power. But the siege had begun.

Pompey's army had to slowly raise a bank, gathering rocks and whatever else they might find to fill in the massive ditch and gain access to Jerusalem from the north. In the meantime, the Jews had not only a tactical problem but a religious one as well. Jewish law at the time prohibited work on the Sabbath. An exception was made for active defense, but not for more general meddling in the enemy's preparations—for war or for anything else.

The Romans used this to their advantage. While they attacked Jerusalem for six days a week during the siege, on the seventh they ceased all active hostilities, devoting their energies instead only to bridging the ditch. And the Jews, in religious observance, did nothing to interfere. So even though it is usually easier to knock down a hastily built bank than to build one up, the Romans had one day each week during which their progress was essentially unimpeded.

Eventually Jerusalem fell. Pompey took the city, brought Aristobulus back to Rome as his captive, and restored the older Hyrcanus to power. Pompey once again made Judea part of the province of Syria (basically the same political power from which the Hasmonean Maccabees had fought for freedom less than a hundred years earlier but now under Roman control). The tax revenue formerly earmarked for the priests was now paid to Rome.

Jerusalem had become a pagan city.

It was the beginning of the end. The Temple itself—the very core of over a thousand years of Jewish service to God—would soon be destroyed by Roman forces, never to be rebuilt (to date). The Jews would be exiled. The practice of sacrifice would end.

It was also the start of a new beginning. Scripture, already a focus from the first exile of 586 B.C., would take on new importance as the only remnant of pre-exilic Judaism: a sacred souvenir, as it were.

Other seeds had been planted in Roman Jerusalem, perhaps most important the precursors of Christianity and of rabbinic Judaism.

In short, the thousand-year tradition of Temple-based Judaism was about to end, simply because Hyrcanus and Aristobulus couldn't get past their petty sibling rivalry, prompting Rome to invade.

This story of the people and events leading up to the fall of the Temple is well known, even if it seems in some ways unsatisfactory. Of all of the problems presented by this narrative—and, certainly, there are many—the biggest is this: We don't know how much of it is true.

Our fundamental issue is that most of our knowledge about these events comes from a man named Joseph ben Mattityahu, better known simply as Josephus, and his evidence, as we discuss in chapter 4, is suspect for a variety of reasons. He sometimes made things up, for example. So even though we have a compelling and detailed narrative, we also have reason to doubt almost all of it.

We do know the broad strokes, though, not just starting in 63 B.C., but even going back to about 1000 B.C., when King David reigned over the fledging nation of the Hebrews in Jerusalem. The short version is that over the next thousand years, Jerusalem would be ruled by Jewish kings; Babylonians, who would exile the Jewish people; Persians; various Greeks based in Greece, Egypt, and Syria; the Jews themselves, in the form of the spectacularly incompetent Maccabees; Romans; Persians again, very briefly; and finally Romans again, who would exile the Jews for the second time.

We also know a lot of the particulars.

We start around the year 1000 B.C., because we have very little reliable historical evidence for anything earlier, but we have good reason to believe that King David established the Israelite capital right around the start of the first millennium B.C. We also essentially skip over the first four hundred years of his kingdom. They are fascinating in their own right, exhibiting intricate power balances among kings, prophets, and priests, for example, and admitting no small degree of palace intrigue. But ultimately these years have little to do with what Jerusalem looked like at the end of the millennium.

So we skip to the year 605 B.C., about four hundred years into the reign of King David and his descendants; the Israelite King Jehoiakim was on the throne, and the great prophet Jeremiah walked the streets of Jerusalem. And we jump to a city on the Euphrates River called Carchemish, by the modern-day Syria-Turkey border, not far from the modern Turkish city of Kargamiş.

For several hundred years, the major force in the region had been the Assyrian Empire, ruling from their capital of Nineveh, across the Tigris River from modern-day Mosul. Around 705 B.C., the Assyrian king Sargon II had established Carchemish as an Assyrian province.

The Babylonians, to the south of the Assyrians, had their own empire, which dated back at least to the days of Hammurabi from the first half of the second millennium B.C. He had established Babylon as the capital of southern Mesopotamia. While the Babylonians had once been the primary power, their power had waned in comparison with the Assyrians.

Around 612 B.C., a group of Babylonians joined forces with other local armies in an alliance against the ruling Assyrians. They sacked the Assyrian capital of Nineveh, pushing the Assyrians westward to Harran (in modern-day Turkey), then finally to Carchemish.

In 605 the Babylonian ruler Nebuchadnezzar II (whose name is also spelled Nebuchadrezzar, with an *r* instead of an *n*) set out to defeat the Assyrians in Carchemish. Unfortunately for Jerusalem, Egypt had been allied with the Assyrians. Egypt lies to Jerusalem's south, and Carchemish roughly to its east. Or to look at things differently, Jerusalem lies between Egypt and Carchemish. So when Pharaoh Necho II of Egypt set out to help the Assyrians in Carchemish, he had to pass by Jerusalem.

When Pharaoh Necho, along with the Assyrians, lost the famous battle of Carchemish, Nebuchadnezzar II reestablished the primacy of the Babylonian Empire, in what is commonly called the Neo-Babylonian Empire, to distinguish it from the original Babylonian Empire of the second millennium B.C.

Having emerged victorious, Nebuchadnezzar set out to annex all of Egypt to his growing Babylonian Empire. Again unfortunately for Jerusalem, the path from Babylonia back to Egypt, obviously, also runs almost directly through the holy city. This is how David's descendants got caught in the middle of a struggle to rule the world, establishing a pattern that would repeat itself many times.

As the Egyptians fought back against the invading Babylonian Empire, they used Jerusalem as a proxy: They urged the Jewish capital to rise up against Babylonia.

A few years later, according to both Babylonian and biblical records, Nebuchadnezzar therefore replaced the ruling king in Jerusalem (who at this point was Jehoiakim's son Jeconiah) with a monarch who would, he hoped, be more friendly to Babylonia. His name was Zedukia. And he was Jehoiakim's younger brother. But, perhaps influenced by Pharaoh Psametichus II, Zedukia sided with Egypt, or, at least, refused to side with Babylonia.

So around 587 B.C., Nebuchadnezzar, no longer content to play the role of puppet master in Jerusalem, conquered the city, put an end to Zedukia's rule and with it the Davidic monarchy, exiled the Jews, and destroyed the Temple that had served as the symbol and center of Jewish life for nearly half a millennium. This is commonly known as the first exile.

One primary destination for the exiled Jews was Babylonia (modern-day Iraq). This is why we have a biblical lament (from Psalm 137), now immortalized in song, about lying down to weep by the waters of Babylon. The weeping was prompted by forced exile from the holy land. This is also why Jews in modern-day Iraq trace their lineage in that country back over 2,500 years.

Less than forty years later, in 549, a man named Cyrus ("the Great" or "Cyrus II") was building his own empire some thousand miles east of Jerusalem. He took over Persia (modern-day Iran) from a people called the Medes and then set his eyes both westward, toward Babylonia and Jerusalem, and eastward, toward what is now Afghanistan. He was successful in the west, and as part of his victory he eventually put an end to Babylonian rule in Jerusalem.

Cyrus's predecessors in Jerusalem had thought that an empire should impose a uniform culture. So Jerusalem under the Babylonian Nebuchadnezzar was supposed to be a Babylonian city. Cyrus disagreed with this approach and conceived of an empire in terms of a pluralistic union of different cultures. It was perhaps this mentality that helped Cyrus's Persian Empire grow larger than anything the world had seen before. It was also this mentality that, in 538, led Cyrus to promote the return of the Jews from exile and to encourage the rebuilding of the Temple.

Jerusalem thrived under the Persians. The Second Temple was rededicated in 515. The great leader Ezra, described in the biblical Book of Ezra, starting reading the Bible publicly in the city in 458. Nehemiah, who also has a biblical book, built new city walls in 445.

The next major influence on Jerusalem would come not from the east but from the west.

The Mediterranean Sea that forms Israel's western coastline has two large northern bays. The bigger and westernmost one, farther from Israel, has two parts, the Ionian Sea just north of the Mediterranean, and, north of that, the Adriatic Sea. The Ionian Sea gives southern Italy its Eastern coast, and Greece its western coast. The Adriatic does the same for northern Italy and the Baltics. Closer to Israel, the smaller Aegean Sea to the east lies between modern-day Greece and Turkey. (See map opposite.)

While the Egyptians, Babylonians, and Persians had been fighting over Jerusalem, various groups of people around the Aegean Sea had been building their own form of civilization since at least the middle of the eighth century. They would eventually become the hugely influential Greeks, giving the world Aristotle and Zeus, the *Iliad* and the *Odyssey,* the Olympic games and the Hippocratic oath, euclidean geometry and platonic love, and even politics and democracy.

As it happens, the Greeks shared the Persian approach of admit-

Land and water geography of Ancient Near East

ting diverse cultures into their empire. But even so, a clash between the two growing powers—Greece to Jerusalem's west and Persia to its east—was inevitable. Greece was expanding eastward from Europe, and the Persians had already annexed land to their west.

The kingdom of Lydia (in modern-day Turkey) proved to be the flash point. As early as the seventh century, a Lydian king named Croesus got the idea that wealth could be represented symbolically in the form of money. So he started what is widely believed to be the first central bank. (Though unrelated to Jerusalem's saga, coinage and central banking were also being invented in China, at almost the same time.)

Until Croesus, commerce was generally only possible between people who trusted each other to repay debts. If I wanted meat from one of your cows so I could feed my family long enough to raise chickens and give you eggs, you had to trust me when you gave me the meat. You could rely only on my personal promise that I would give you eggs later. Or, still before Croesus, I could give you gold, which you would have to carefully weigh and perhaps analyze. Indeed, this is why we find biblical passages like Deuteronomy 25:13–15 that emphasize the importance of fair weights. But in the end, unless you were an expert metallurgist in addition to a farmer, you would have no way of knowing exactly how much gold I was giving you unless you trusted me personally.

But Croesus minted standardized units of precious metal, stamping each coin with a mark that both indicated the value of the metal and, more important, put his kingdom's full faith and credit, as we might now say, behind the value of the money. As controller of the money, Croesus would amass a huge personal fortune. (This is where we get the expression "as rich as Croesus.") And his central government would make it possible for strangers to conduct business. Now, when I bought your meat, you didn't have to know me or know anything about the gold I was giving you. Croesus himself was guaranteeing my bona fides, and the proof was the stamp on the coin I was holding.

As a result of this new system, Lydia became a natural center of commerce. And as a result of its location at the far western part of Asia or, alternatively, the far eastern part of Europe, it was geographically convenient. What better place to put a bank?

Around 540 B.C., the Persians continued their westward march and overthrew Lydia. Then they crossed into Europe, further threatening the Greek Empire. Greece fought back, and hostilities continued in the form of battles and minor skirmishes for some time. The importance of these conflicts is underscored by the way some of them have become part of popular culture. For example, in 490 B.C. the Athenians successfully repelled a Persian invasion at a place called Marathon, whose distance from Athens set the standard marathon length.

By 449 the wars had ended and a peace between Greece and Persia had been established, paving the way for Greece to become the next major influence on Jerusalem, though it would take some time and come only through a double intermediary.

Greece at the time was in fact a coalition of various cultures, among them the famous city-states of Athens and Sparta. Athens proved to be the most successful and influential, though its success would ultimately catalyze its own downfall. As Athens grew, other city-states, feeling threatened, became envious and rebellious. Sparta and Athens, which had always enjoyed an uneasy combination of brotherly cohesion and sibling rivalry, ended up in prolonged conflict, in the famous Peloponnesian War.

The connection between these events and Jerusalem begins with a kingdom in northern Greece called Macedon. In 359, the Macedonian ruler Philip II saw three things. The Persian Empire was weakening. Athens was not as strong as she had once been. And Macedon had always had a tradition of military might.

The last quality meant that it wasn't hard for Philip to build and train an impressive fighting force, which he used at first to solidify control of Macedon. Then he turned his army on the injured Athens, and, after his victory over them, he directed Athens to join an attack on Persia.

Philip didn't live long enough to see things through, but he left his son and successor, Alexander III (now almost universally known as Alexander the Great), everything he needed to change the map of the ancient world, including Jerusalem.

Alexander, after first putting down some minor revolts, set out, quite simply, to conquer the world. And he nearly succeeded. He defeated the Persians at the battle of Issus, marched through Syria, and conquered Egypt. (This is why Egypt has a city named Alexandria, though Egypt is, of course, not the only such place. Two thousand miles away, Kandahar, Afghanistan, also bears his name, as do numerous cities in between and elsewhere.) In both a figurative and literal marriage of East and West, Alexander took as a second wife the daughter of the defeated Persian ruler Darius III.

In 332, a year before defeating Darius, Alexander offered an ultimatum to the Persian-aligned leaders of Jerusalem: fight or surrender. Jerusalem chose the latter, and switched from being a Persian city to a Hellenistic one.

But the real story lies not in what Alexander did but rather in what he did not do. He did not plan for his own succession. He can hardly be blamed. The year was 323. Alexander was a young man, only thirty-two years old. In just ten years he had conquered the world, becoming the most powerful person the region had ever seen. And his first wife, Roxana, was seven months pregnant with his first child, a son, they hoped. Everything was looking up for Alexander the Great. How could he know that he wouldn't live to see the birth of his child?

Illness took his life shortly thereafter. And with Alexander's death came enormous instability. By the time his son was born two months later, his first wife, Roxana, had already murdered his second, Persian wife. Roxana and her son with Alexander were soon killed, too, and the newly conquered world was left without any prospect of a recognized leader. So Alexander's generals and other power brokers fought for control.

To understand what happened next we have to know not only the physical layout of the area around the Ancient Near East but also the conceptual geography, which forms a slightly crooked and ill-proportioned capital letter T (see opposite). The long top of the T runs from Greece in the west to Persia (Iran) in the east. Along the way are, from west to east, Turkey, Syria, and Babylonia (Iraq). The shorter vertical line of the T connects Syria in the north to Egypt in the south. A straight line on the map from Jerusalem to Tehran, Iran, runs practically right through Baghdad, Iraq. But it also runs through the inhospitable and largely unnavigable desert that forms the Arabian

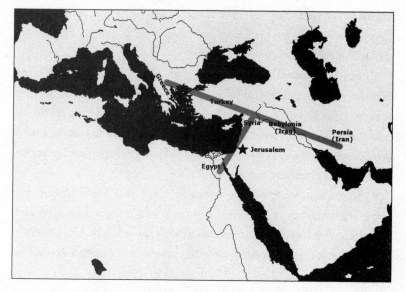

Conceptual geography of Ancient Near East

Peninsula in what is now Saudi Arabia. So in antiquity, Baghdad was not directly between Tehran and Jerusalem but rather between Tehran and Aleppo, Syria, to Jerusalem's north, because a journey from Jerusalem to Tehran had to start to the north to avoid the desert. Similarly, even though Kandahar is actually about half a degree south of Jerusalem, it lay to the northeast for Alexander, because Alexander had to go north, then east, to get there.

Likewise, running north to south along the coast of the Mediterranean Sea are Tripolis (now Tripoli, Lebanon), Byblos, Sidon, and Tyre. But even though it runs north-south, this line also forms part of the conceptual west-to-east path from Greece to Persia.

Jerusalem is just barely farther south of Tyre, not quite on the west-to-east path but very close to the north-to-south journey toward Egypt that naturally runs through Gaza, on the Mediterranean. This put Jerusalem nearly on the path from Greece to Persia, and even closer to the path from either of those places to Egypt, all of which is why Jerusalem ended up being drawn in to almost any conflict in the Ancient Near East.

This conceptual configuration has three natural end points: Greece, at the western end of the top bar of the T; Persia, at the eastern end; and Egypt, at the southern end of the vertical line. It also has a fourth point of unique interest: Syria, where the lines meet. This is why Greece, Egypt, Persia, and Syria keep popping up as power centers, both in antiquity and now.

This is also why, when Alexander the Great died, strongholds were first established in Greece, Egypt, Persia, and Syria. And understanding what happened to Jerusalem after the death of Alexander the Great entails understanding what happened in those four central locations.

We start with Egypt, where a general by the name of Ptolemy Soter immediately grabbed power. He and his descendants, in the form of the Ptolemaic dynasty, would keep Egypt until the death of Cleopatra III in 30 B.C. It was Ptolemy's son (Ptolemy II) who would be credited with commissioning the Greek translation of the Bible known as the Septuagint. Under the Ptolemaic dynasty, Egypt enjoyed a few hundred years of relative stability and power.

The easternmost parts of Alexander's empire were taken over by an Indian ruler, leaving little Greek influence or control in those regions. And off to the west, Athens and Macedon for some time would remain too busy with internal conflict to impact Jerusalem directly.

But the middle region, the vast swath from Persia to Syria, continued to be influential. A general by the name of Antigonus briefly unified that huge stretch of land, including Jerusalem. But one of Alexander's friends, a noble named Seleucus, also wanted the region.

Seleucus's uneven rise to power is complicated. The highlights are that he fled from Babylonia to Ptolemaic Egypt, then conquered first the eastern and then western halves of what Antigonus had just recently claimed.

This complex power struggle was taking place just north of Jerusalem, which thus found herself surrounded by three new and sometimes unstable leaderships: Ptolemy and then the Ptolemaic dynasty was to the south. To the north were the quarrelsome Antigonus and Seleucus.

As Seleucus was battling Antigonus to the north of Jerusalem, Ptolemy of Egypt came from the south and took Jerusalem from Antigonus.

Seleucus eventually prevailed over Antigonus, by the year 300 unifying the region from Syria to Persia. Seleucus established his capital in Antioch, Syria, and, like Ptolemy, became the first ruler in a dynasty.

Antigonus was banished to Europe, where he also established a dynasty, to rule Macedon and Athens. This left three people in charge of three dynasties around Jerusalem: Ptolemy, to the south in Egypt; Seleucus, to the north in Syria; and Antigonus, to the west in Greece.

Amid these rapid power shifts that reshaped the future of the Middle East and the world, Jerusalem in one generation went from being a Persian city ruled by Darius to a Macedonian city ruled by Alexander to a vaguely Greek city ruled by Antigonus to a vaguely Greek city ruled by Seleucus to an Egyptian city ruled by the vaguely Greek Ptolemy.

The phrase "vaguely Greek" reflects the complicated combination of a Macedonian conqueror, Macedonian successors, Greek language, and Greek thought. The term "Hellenistic" is often used to express this kind of Greek influence, and it is in this sense that Jerusalem became Hellenistic, a flavor she would retain solidly until the year 63 B.C.

This rapid succession also leads to other potentially confusing terms. The inhabits of Antioch, Syria—the capital of Seleucus's new empire—are known as Syrian Greeks, but also, more briefly, sometimes just as Syrians and sometimes just as Greeks. (This is why the Jews' foes in the Maccabean revolt are to this day variously called either the Syrians or the Greeks. They were Syrian Greeks.) Similarly, back in Europe, the Greeks and Macedonians were at war. But the "Greek" Syrians had more in common with the Macedonians than they did with the Greeks. And for that matter, the Ptolemies in Egypt declared themselves pharaoh in most of the land, so the Egyptian pharaoh for a long while was a Macedonian Greek. This is also why it was in Egypt, not Greece, that the Bible was first translated into Greek.

At any rate, Greek or "vaguely Greek" or Hellenistic influence was firmly entrenched in and around Jerusalem, with the Ptolemies in Egypt to the south and the Seleucids to the north.

The families of Ptolemy, Seleucus, and Antigonus—originally all part of Alexander the Great's fighting force from Macedon—remained in touch, even as they built their own fiefdoms. Over the next few hundred years, they would fight, join forces, conspire, and betray one another. This was bad news for Jerusalem's stability.

Jerusalem remained under Egyptian Ptolemaic rule for about a hundred years.

Then, around 200 B.C., a conspiracy of sorts shook things up yet again. The descendants of Seleucus and the descendants of Antigonus ganged up on the descendants of Ptolemy. Antiochus III (Antiochus the Great), the sixth king of the Seleucid dynasty in Syria, plotted secretly with Philip V of the Antigonid dynasty back in Macedon to attack Ptolemy V in Egypt—which is essentially a detailed way of saying that Syria and Greece waged war on Egypt. Antiochus III of Syria won Jerusalem, making the holy city a (Greek) Syrian province.

At some point around this time, a group of people from the region of Jerusalem set up a society in the desert, northwest of the Dead Sea. We don't know exactly when, we don't know exactly why, and we don't know exactly who the people were. What we do know is that they would live in the desert for just over two centuries, creating a society of Jews similar to the one developing in Jerusalem, though sometimes also at odds with it. For many years details about this curious group of people were completely unavailable. Then, starting in 1947, their writings started to surface, as I describe in chapter 2.

Elsewhere, Philip V (of the Antigonid dynasty in Macedon) was also trying to enlarge his territory. But he didn't fare as well at battle as his Syrian coconspirator Antiochus III, and, facing defeat, he turned to his secret partner in Syria for support. But Antiochus had other plans and refused to help. Philip V was left on his own, a turn of events that, as we'll see, may have indirectly led to the downfall of Jerusalem a few centuries later.

Philip's next move was to turn to a group of people whose background is, to this day, unclear. We know that they came to Europe sometime in the first half of the first millennium B.C., but we don't know exactly when, and we don't know for sure from where. We do know that early in the first millennium they had writing, sophisticated art, considerable societal organization, skilled traders, and, notably, an advanced military. It also appears that women enjoyed an unparalleled degree of equality with men.

To understand them better we turn to twin springs high up in the Apennines in the Italian Peninsula. Water from those springs forms the river Tiber that meanders down to the Tyrrhenian Sea, which in turn connects to the northwest portion of the Mediterranean Sea. Either through foresight or luck, some of these talented people of unknown origin chose to dwell on this particular river's southern bank, not far from the sea. In addition to its obvious maritime qualities, the spot would soon be home to the world's most influential force. The people were the Etruscans.

The Etruscans had clearly had some early contact with the Greeks, though details remain obscure. After settling in and around the Tiber River, they continued to interact with Greece, at first as trading partners, when Greece established its first colonies in the section of the Tyrrhenian Sea known as the Bay of Naples, some 150 miles south of the Tiber. Then, as both the Greeks and the Etruscans grew in power, the two became rivals and, eventually, military adversaries. By the end of the sixth century, the Greeks and the Etruscans had battled more than once, and the Etruscans had lost.

Weakened, the Etruscans also lost their influence even in their own town on the Tiber River, and the place reverted to local control by the then-indigenous Latins. Though these locals managed to expel the Etruscans, they held on to much of the Etruscan culture, including their system of writing, their religion, and their military prowess. These Etruscan innovations gave this Latin city a huge advantage over nearby, and otherwise similar, settlements. The city is Rome, and in 509 B.C. its inhabitants combined their local culture with what they had learned from the Etruscans to form a republic that would last until 31 B.C., and that would continue to exert influence far beyond that.

At the dawn of the second century B.C., Rome was nearing the height of its power, exactly when Philip V of Macedon needed help because his secret partner, Antiochus of Syria, had abandoned him. So Philip turned to the mighty western power. Unfortunately for Philip, Rome intervened not with him but rather against him, defeating him decisively and conquering much of Greece in 197.

This was just one step in Rome's ultimate involvement in Jerusalem.

The next came in a roundabout way through a northern African city known in Phoenician as Kart-Hadasht ("new village") or, in English, as Carthage. It was established in an ideal spot for a military power: Situated in the Gulf of Tunis (in modern-day Tunisia), it was easily defensible; and as the northernmost spot in Africa, it was ideal for projecting might into Europe.

Carthage and Rome had fought a major war in the middle 200s over control of the islands of Corsica and Sicily. Located off Europe's southern shore, and therefore off Africa's northern shore, these islands were a natural focus of dispute between the northern African power and the southern European one. Not surprisingly, the Iberian Peninsula (Spain), lying even closer to Africa, was also a source of contention during the war.

Rome won the war, and as part of the peace treaty between the two powers, Carthage agreed to limit its influence to the southern shore of the Erbo River in northern Spain, which is to say, Carthage could have most of the Iberian Peninsula but couldn't cross the Pyrenees to encroach any further on Europe.

In 221, a twenty-six-year-old Carthaginian living in Spain became the Carthaginian commander in chief. His name was Hannibal. He attacked an independent Iberian city called Saguntum, which was geographically south of the Erbo—so Hannibal wasn't technically in violation of the peace treaty with Rome—but the Romans nonetheless saw this as an act of war, perhaps because of their cultural ties to Saguntum. In response, Rome declared open war on Carthage.

This is how Hannibal ended up taking a force of infantry, cavalry, and elephants across the Pyrenees, through what is now France, and then over the Alps toward Rome. The journey exhausted his troops, though, and in the end his campaign against Rome ended in defeat in 195.

These two wars, and a third one after it, are generally called the Punic Wars, because the Romans called the Carthaginians "Poeni," reflecting the city's founding by the Phoenicians.

None of this would matter for our story except that in the midst of this Second Punic War, Hannibal, in 215, joined forces with Philip V of Macedon. Then once he had lost the war, Hannibal fled to Syria to advise Antiochus III, where, it would seem, he convinced Antiochus to take up arms against Rome.

Not surprisingly, Antiochus lost. In the year 190, as part of his surrender, the Romans demanded hostages, including Hannibal and Antiochus III's own son, Antiochus IV. Hannibal managed to escape, but Antiochus IV wasn't so lucky. He ended up a Roman prisoner.

So the next leader of the waning but still powerful Syrian Greek Empire was not Antiochus IV, who was in Roman captivity, but rather his brother Seleucus IV. He took power in 187.

Then in 175, in an odd choice of family loyalty, Seleucus IV traded his own son Demetrius to secure the return of his brother, Antiochus IV. Antiochus IV was thus back in Syria when a man named Heliodorus, Seleucus IV's chief minister, staged a coup d'état and killed Seleucus IV. Antiochus IV in turn took power from Heliodorus and found himself in charge of Syria.

While Antiochus III was nicknamed "the Great," his son and eventual successor, Antiochus IV, was called "the Mad." Not surprisingly, this would not bode well for Jerusalem, still under Syrian control.

Whereas Antiochus III had adopted a charitable posture toward Jerusalem, granting it special rights, Antiochus the Mad saw it largely as a source of revenue. Also, probably because of his close contact with the Romans, he seems to have abandoned the Greek mentality that encouraged different cultures to thrive within an empire. Rather, in keeping with Roman doctrine, the younger Antiochus wanted everyone to adhere to a common culture and religion, though in this case the common culture was not Roman but his own Greek ways of life.

Details are unclear as to who first got the idea to turn Jerusalem into a Greek city like any other. It may have been Antiochus the Mad, or it may even have been Jason, the Jewish high priest from 175 to 172, who may have hoped to curry favor with Antiochus. Either way, in what was tantamount to a civil war, Jason in Jerusalem was replaced by an even more ardent Hellenist, Menalaus, who was closely aligned with Antiochus. (In 169, Jason would successfully mount a bloody counterattack.)

Around 170 B.C., on his way back from a failed attempt to take over Egypt, Antiochus and his army stopped by the great Temple in Jerusalem and despoiled it of all its wealth. Two years later, after his failure in Egypt became clear to him, Antiochus stepped up his oppression of the Jews in Jerusalem, exacting taxes and forbidding even the most central aspects of local religious practice, among them circumcision and celebration of the Sabbath.

In 168 B.C., he rededicated the great Jewish Temple to the Greek god Zeus.

At this point a Jewish priest named Mattathias from the city of Modein comes into the picture. Unlike the priests Jason and Menalaus, Mattathias and his family were firmly opposed to hellenization, and the sacking of the holy Temple pushed them into outright rebellion. Mattathias and his sons—most notably, Judah—fled to the hills, from where they mounted a guerrilla offensive against Antiochus the Mad.

In 165, Judah "the Maccabee" (his father, Mattathias, had died in 166) succeeded in recapturing the Temple and rededicating it to the Jewish God. This triumph is still celebrated in the form of the Jewish holiday of Hanukkah.

The disorganized state of the Seleucid empire and leadership make it hard to determine exactly when the Maccabean victory was complete. Antiochus the Mad died in 164. His son Antiochus V took the reins, but not for long, partly because he was just a boy when he took the throne, but mostly because Demetrius (the son of the recently deposed Seleucus IV, who had been sent to Rome as a prisoner in order to secure the return of Antiochus IV) managed to escape in 162. He, too, wanted the throne. And he managed to get it by force, giving

Syria, and therefore Jerusalem, the dubious distinction of having twice been ruled by escaped Roman prisoners.

In the meantime, a local Seleucid leader had granted the Jews the right to worship as they wished, but simultaneously, pagan practices were encouraged even among the Jews. Judah took to battle again, eventually losing his life in a confrontation with one of Demetrius's generals and depriving Jerusalem of her last hope for unification. The city was left with no coherent policy of government, and she was subject both to ruthless leadership from afar and violent rebellion from within.

In an example of the complex interplay between the power struggles in Syria and the chaos in Jerusalem, it was an attempted coup in Syria that ended up giving the Maccabees official recognition in Jerusalem. More specifically, a man named Alexander Balas, who in 153 wanted to wrest control of Syria from Demetrius, gave Judah's younger brother Jonathan the office and title of high priest. After Jonathan's death, Simon—the next brother in line—took over, establishing the precedent of a Hasmonean dynasty. (The name "Hasmonean" comes from Josephus, who reports that Mattathias had an ancestor named Hasmoneus. Josephus also reports that he himself was descended on his mother's side from these same Hasmoneans.) Simon convinced Syria to let him mint coins and secured an exemption from paying taxes to the Seleucids in Syria.

It seemed like good news. The anti-Hellenistic revolt was a success. The Syrian Greeks had been repelled. The Temple was Jewish again. And local Jewish high priests ran Jerusalem.

However, the Maccabees, though priests, were not descended from Zadok, who had established the original high-priest dynasty hundreds of years earlier. Accordingly, some people saw the rise of the Maccabees as a coup against the real high priests. Even worse, the Hasmoneans proved to have as little governing skill as the Seleucids.

So Jerusalem's apparent victory was in fact only a shift from one inept ruling family to another and, worse, served to exacerbate internal strife among the Jews.

Of Simon's three sons, John Hyrcanus I was the next in line, ruling from about 135 to 104. The reason that Hyrcanus was next, rather than one of Simon's other two sons, is that Simon's son-in-law had murdered them, along with Simon himself. Even in the face of invasions from the Syrian empire, now on its last legs, Hyrcanus managed to successfully defend Jerusalem and shore up his own power. He also redoubled the military expansion that his father and uncles had begun, forcefully and forcibly insisting that the entire region was part of the Jewish heritage. Jerusalem had become both a military target and a military provocateur.

Among the places Hyrcanus occupied was Idumaea, the site of the biblical Edom, southeast of the Dead Sea. There, as was his practice, Hyrcanus forced Judaism on the locals. He had no way of knowing that, in doing so, he was paving the way for one of Jerusalem's most viciously tyrannical rulers.

Hyrcanus had intended for his wife to succeed him, and she did, very briefly. But his son, Aristobulus, seized power from her in 104 and ruled briefly until 103. Coins from the day indicate that he called himself the high priest, but some reports put his title not as "high priest" but rather as "king." This was a matter of some importance, because the high priests were considered Jewish, and kings, Greek. The point of the Maccabean revolution had been to keep Jerusalem Jewish, and any ruler calling himself king could have been seen as betraying the original cause.

Next in line in the dynasty was Hyrcanus's brother, Alexander Jannaeus, who reigned viciously from 103 to 76, a period marked primarily by even more war and tension. On some coins from his reign he is clearly called King Alexander. In just two generations, the same

Hasmoneans who had thrown off the yoke of Greek rule had themselves become Greek in character—and Greek aggressors, at that.

Alexander Jannaeus's widow, Salome Alexandra, succeeded him upon his death in 76. She tried to reverse some of her husband's disastrous decisions, but she didn't live long enough, and, at any rate, the turmoil and internal strife in Jerusalem made the city virtually ungovernable at this point.

When the widow died in 67, both of her sons aspired to the throne. They are Aristobulus II and Hyrcanus II, who, as we saw at the outset, went to Syria to meet Pompey in the year 63, and whose inability to get along with each other prodded Pompey to lay siege to Jerusalem.

So it wasn't just that two brothers were fighting. Jerusalem, once the peaceful, prosperous center of Jewish worship and practice, had fallen steadily, suffering blows at the hands of warring Greeks from both the south and the north, enduring religious oppression, and succumbing to forced hellenization at the hands of a Greek ruler. In response, a revolution had been mounted, the success of which only intensified the hellenization and increased the bloodshed. Jerusalem had become a chaotic city marked by internal strife and violence, and even her original mission as the capital of the Jewish people was in doubt.

And things were about to get much worse, because the Romans were on the way.

In 63, Pompey conquered Syria, and, with it, Syrian-ruled Jerusalem. Syria became a Roman province. Even though Jerusalem, as part of the region of Judea, retained some autonomy, Jerusalem's power was greatly diminished, and she lost the independence that the Hasmoneans had fought for. Hyrcanus II defeated his brother, Aristobulus II, but he was not the king. Jerusalem no longer had a local monarch. Hyrcanus was just the high priest. And though this might seem like a victory against hellenization, it was not, because in place of a local king were Roman rulers.

Before long it would be clear that Jerusalem had been taken over by a world power that wasn't just mighty but also unstable. Fifteen years later, Rome was engulfed in a civil war that primarily pitted Pompey against Julius Caesar, and the future of Jerusalem was less certain than ever. Julius Caesar emerged victorious as he put a violent end to the centuries-old Roman Republic, replacing it with a dictatorship. Jerusalem, therefore, was now in the hands of a dictator.

At this point we return to Idumaea, near the Dead Sea. This was one of the places that Hyrcanus I had annexed to his Judean empire during his campaign of forced conversion. As it happens, a power broker by the name of Antipater lived there. He had helped Hyrcanus II, the older of the widow Salome Alexandra's two sons, regain the throne from his younger brother Aristobulus before Pompey came in and took over.

With Pompey now out of the picture (thanks to Julius Caesar), the government of Jerusalem was again up for grabs. Hyrcanus II and his patron, Antipater, sided with the victorious Julius Caesar in order to secure their own political future.

In return, Caesar named Hyrcanus the high priest and "ethnarc"— that is, ruler of the local ethnicity—of Jerusalem, a position that turned out to be largely symbolic and devoid of actual power. More important, one of the rewards Caesar bestowed on Antipater was to give powerful posts to Antipater's two children. His older son, Phasael, was put in charge of Jerusalem, and his younger son, Herod (the tyrant we discuss later in the context of his importance for understanding the New Testament), was given Galilee. Antipater, Phasael, and Herod were technically Jewish, but only because Hyrcanus I had forced the Idumaeans to convert.

Rome declined into further chaos with the events of 44–42, including Caesar's assassination, violent internal strife, and Mark Antony's ascension to power. Jerusalem followed Rome down its vortex of deepening chaos.

Fallen stones in Jerusalem from the destruction of the Second Temple in A.D. 70. In the background on the wall, the ancient remnants of an arch are still visible.

Amid the turmoil in the West, an eastern empire known as Parthia managed to take Jerusalem. Based in what is now Iran, the Parthians had had considerable success reaching eastward toward China and conquering much of what is now Iran, Afghanistan, and Pakistan, but they'd done less well moving westward. They had never liked Alexander the Great or his successors the Seleucids, and they certainly had not liked Rome. In the year 40, they mounted a successful, if short-lived, occupation of Jerusalem.

With Hyrcanus and his family firmly aligned with Rome, Aristobulus's son Antigonus Mattathias saw an opportunity to regain control of Jerusalem. He sided with the Parthians, who appointed him high priest and king. Because he was a descendant of the famous Hasmoneans, he had immediate legitimacy and even popular support.

Antipater, on the other hand, had been aligned with the now-ousted

Romans, which was bad news for him and his sons Herod and Phasael. Phasael is reported to have killed himself, which had the long-lasting effect of creating an eventual power vacuum in Jerusalem. Herod fled to Rome, where he set his sights on the holy city.

Herod worked out a deal with the Romans. If they would support him in his bid for power in Jerusalem, he would support them against the Parthians. Herod was an unlikely choice for this task. He had no army. Unlike the reigning Antigonus (who was descended from the Hasmoneans), he had no legitimate claim to the throne. And his family had only recently adopted Judaism. However, Herod was a skilled politician, and he managed to win over the Romans, who, for their part, saw in him an ally against the Parthians. Though Jerusalem was still in the hands of those Eastern rulers, Rome declared Herod king of Judea.

Herod tried to take Jerusalem back and failed. Then, as the Parthians' local power waned, he tried again, this time enlisting the help of Roman legions. Success came in the year 37, putting Jerusalem in the charge of the Roman crony Herod, who was not a high priest and was only nominally Jewish. In a poignant symbol of where Herod stood, a Roman legion was tasked with guarding Herod in Jerusalem, primarily to protect him from the Hasmoneans, who were popular folk heroes with legitimate claims to the throne.

As it happened, this was the same year that Octavius declared war on the newly married Mark Antony and Cleopatra in Egypt. Octavius eventually beat Mark Antony and reconquered Egypt, putting an end to hundreds of years of Ptolemaic rule there. Rome's civil war was over, and the imperial power emerged stronger than she had ever been. Octavius was the man in charge. Within a few years he would earn the title Augustus ("great" or even "sacred"), then Pontif Maximus ("high priest"). With such a power firmly behind him, Herod could do as he wished in Jerusalem.

Herod ruled with an iron fist, oppressing the population and doling out favors only to keep himself on the throne. He was a builder, largely for his own glory, and he built huge edifices and even whole cities in the Roman style, physical reminders of his power, but also of his self-styled image as a Roman citizen. He paid for his massive projects by taxing the people. Life in Jerusalem was not demonstrably worse than in many other Roman regions, but the inhabitants of Jerusalem were unaccustomed to this oppressive and heavily taxed style of life. To this day Herod is remembered as a vicious and cruel outsider, both in such mainstream works as the Talmud (e.g., Baba Batra 3b) and in more obscure material (e.g., Testament of Moses 6) and is used as a symbol of misery in the New Testament.

When Herod died in the year 4 B.C., he left a population of Jerusalem that was overtaxed, underserved, oppressed, and alienated. This was the Jewish world into which a man named Jesus would be born and, not long after, crucified.

With Herod's death, the population of Jerusalem demanded changes in the form of lower taxes and better government. Herod had bequeathed Jerusalem to his son Archelaus, who was unable to maintain order amid the growing uprisings, and before long the streets of Jerusalem were filled with riots and other violence. The Syrian leader Varus, representing Rome, had to step in with his own army to restore order.

Then Augustus himself, even as he recognized the legitimacy of Archelaus's rule, restricted his power, stripping him of the title "king." Archelaus, who seems to have learned his father's cruelty but not his skill at governing, served as ethnarc for about a decade, until unchecked growing opposition made his rule untenable.

In A.D. 6, Augustus removed Archelaus from power and reorganized the region of Jerusalem into a Roman province like any other, calling it the Latin "Iudaea." Herod, who was a local in name only, had begun the process by which Jerusalem came to be part of the Roman Empire. In deposing the local ruler, Augustus had finished it.

Jerusalem, though still standing, was a walking corpse. Augustus and his family would rule Rome until the death of Nero in A.D. 68. Two years after that, Roman troops would sack Jerusalem and raze the great Temple that had stood, in one form or another, for a thousand years.

Not surprisingly, the denizens of Jerusalem and the surrounding areas in this hugely turbulent time reacted in various ways. Some yearned impotently for a return to the past, while others worked actively to restore what had once been. Some embraced the Roman variety of Hellenism; others eschewed anything modern. Some awaited an otherworldly influence that would bring back some sense of sanity; others taught that sanity would come only to those who left this world. Some people strove to understand the past; others planned for a better future.

Two groups in particular emerged from these chaotic days and their aftermath.

Most obviously we have Christianity. Jesus walked the earth during this time period, as did the writers of the Gospels, the apostle Paul, John the Baptist, and the other people who shaped the emerging new religion. The story of Christianity is the story of Jerusalem.

Less widely appreciated are the changes that took place within Judaism. The Jews were about to abandon a thousand years of sacrifice in favor of prayer services, for example. They would soon compose the Midrash and the Talmud, the great guiding compilations that continue to define Judaism to this day. In fact, most of what people now think of as Judaism comes from changes that began around two thousand years ago and that are recorded in the Talmud: the details of prayer services, keeping kosher, Sabbath customs and so on. This time period saw the relegation of the priesthood to largely ceremonial functions and the rise of a new class of leaders: rabbis. It was these rabbis who wrote the Talmud. (They were no longer in Jerusalem but were still living very much in the spirit of a movement that had begun there.) For this reason, it is helpful to refer to "biblical Judaism" and the "rabbinic Judaism" that replaced it. The story of rabbinic Judaism is the story of Jerusalem.

In this sense, both the Christianity of today and the (rabbinic) Judaism of today were born at roughly the same time in roughly the same place and in response to roughly the same conditions. Both traditions asked the same questions, even as they recorded and lived by different answers.

But there were in fact a great variety of groups asking these questions and grappling with the same issues. It is only in retrospect that we divide them into "Christians," "Jews," and "everyone else." A more accurate demographic accounting recognizes diverse and sometimes vague associations with a complex array of partially overlapping writings, opinions, and beliefs.

Certain themes recur with various nuances and interpretations among the disparate factions: the value of the past and the end of times, the battle between good and evil, a savior and his nemesis, and the ways in which human behavior might interact with all of these. In other words, the population of Jerusalem focused on the human condition: What is the nature of the universe and what is our role in it? What are we supposed to do with our lives? Is there an absolute right and wrong? Where did we come from? And what happens next?

Our great fortune is that so much of the brilliantly penetrating writing from the waning days of Jerusalem's glory has survived: The Bible is the most well-known collection, but there are myriad others. Some were well known at the time, having faded into relative obscurity over the years. Others, as we see next, remained obscure until they were rediscovered only recently.

Like the Bible, the lesser-known writings explore the nature of good and evil, ask why people suffer, debate the role of God, and offer advice about how to live our lives.

We now turn to buried textual treasure as we begin our exploration of these remarkable gifts from the past.

2

THE DEAD SEA SCROLLS: HOW A LOST
GOAT CHANGED THE WORLD

Do not sow seeds in the sand.
—LATIN PROVERB

It's almost as if the most expansive and impressive library of texts from the Bible's cutting room floor wanted to stay hidden, trying time after time to thwart modern efforts to bring them to light. Though once widely read, a massive collection of scrolls hid in desert caves some two thousand years ago. When they finally revealed themselves, it was not to archaeologists or historians but to children who could not read the writing. Then some of the scrolls changed hands under false pretenses, and many more made their way to a group of scholars so secretive as to earn the nickname "the cartel."

But they have all been exposed and published, and they give us a uniquely clear window into the Jerusalem of two thousand years ago, the forces that created rabbinic Judaism and Christianity, and the texts that both groups of people held holy: They do more to authenticate the text of the Bible than any other source, though they also highlight at least one clear scribal error in the Hebrew text of the Five Books of Moses. They shed light on what life was like two thousand years ago, though they also raise new, challenging questions. They fill in gaps in the Bible and explore the questions that the Old and New Testaments set out to answer. Reading the Bible without taking them into consideration is like reading a book report instead of the whole book.

These are the famous Dead Sea Scrolls from the region just outside Jerusalem known as Qumran. The full story of their discovery starts in 1947 with a lost goat and the bedouin children who couldn't find it. Then the tale incorporates corrupt clergy in Jerusalem and malicious merchants in Bethlehem, with starring roles for a general and for a photographer who shared a love of archaeology, and guest appearances by a Christian preacher from Virginia and the Chase Manhattan Bank, of all things.

As a novel or summer movie, this story would be so patently ridiculous and so obviously full of contrivances that no one would take it seriously. It has unlikely coincidences, like the scrolls from Qumran being translated by a Mr. Qimron. It has enigmatic sensationalistic elements, like a treasure map that otherwise has no place in the main story. It has unbelievable plot twists, like animals that lead people to hidden wonders. And it has cliché villains (like the researcher who told the world that Judaism was a horrible religion) who battle cliché heroes (like the archaeologist who took time off work to literally save his nation from destruction). In fact, the only thing saving the otherwise absurd tale is the bizarre fact that it happens to be true and well documented.

The key figures involve some combination of an unscrupulous antiquities dealer, an archaeologist with military training, a graduate student with a camera, a televangelist, three young bedouin shepherds, a partridge, and a lost goat.

The goat belonged to the three young bedouins, who were members of the Ta'amireh tribe and who lived not far from Jerusalem. One day in 1947, they found themselves in the hot Judean Desert looking for the lost member of their herd. The unique terrain, with its pock-marked chalky hills, dry riverbeds, and uneven, constantly shifting landscape gave the goat the advantage. Hiding was easy.

As they were looking for the lost animal, the boys found themselves doing what boys do: throwing stones, perhaps as a show of prowess, perhaps out of boredom, maybe out of frustration. After some time, one of the boys tossed a stone toward the top of one of the many small mounds typical of the area. But rather than the expected "thump" that a stone normally makes when hitting the desert floor, the boys heard a surprising "ping."

But the sound a rock makes in the desert wasn't their first priority. They had to find their goat.

And eventually they did. Still, the "ping" had made the boys curious, and a few days later they returned to the site of the odd-sounding stone.

The small mound turned out to be hollow, with an opening at the top that formed a natural skylight, and potential entrance. But while the hole atop the cave might let the boys in, there was no guarantee they'd be able to get out if they dropped through from above. They wisely resisted the temptation to enter. They did, however, continue exploring and they eventually found what looked like a ground-level entrance that had long ago been blocked by stones. They cleared the fallen rocks out of the way and entered the cave.

Inside, they found ten jars made of pottery. Eight of them were completely empty. A ninth contained only dust. Inside the final jar were three leather scrolls, two of which were wrapped in cloth and a third exposed to the elements. The boys took the jars and the scrolls back to their tent.

Not long after, a few other members of the Ta'amireh tribe returned to the cave and found four more scrolls. These, too, were brought back to the bedouin camp, where along with the first find, they were kept as a curiosity. But it was only a mild curiosity, because the bedouins couldn't read what was written.

Someone got the idea that the pots and scrolls might have some value on the open market, so they set out for nearby Bethlehem to find a buyer. The task proved more difficult than they had thought, but eventually they found a shady character named Jalil "Kando" Iskandar Shalim. A cobbler by trade and a self-declared "dealer in antiquities," Kando purchased the scrolls from the bedouins.

Kando wasn't a collector but rather a merchant, and his plan was to sell the scrolls, at a markup. His first success combined clergy and duplicity. He approached Metropolitan Athanasius Yeshue "Mar" Samuel, the archimandrite (like an abbot) of the Syrian-Orthodox monastery of Saint Mark in Jerusalem. Mar Samuel paid 24 liras (about $110 at the time, or roughly $1,000 in 2014 dollars) for four of Kando's seven scrolls. But like Kando, Samuel's interest in the scrolls was financial.

As a prominent leader of a Jerusalem monastery, Samuel was in a position to pretend that the scrolls, instead of coming from the desert outside Jerusalem, had actually been found in the holy city itself. While Kando was still trying to sell his other three scrolls, Samuel set out to sell what he called the Jerusalem Scrolls from the holy ancient city of Jerusalem.

Kando found a buyer for the remaining scrolls in one Eliezer Sukenik, a professor of archaeology at the Hebrew University and director of the University Museum of Jewish Antiquities. Sukenik secured the purchase of Kando's last three scrolls, along with two of the jars in which they had been stored.

So at this point a lost goat had led three bedouins to a hidden cave. Seven scrolls from that cave had been sold and resold. Four were still on the market under false pretenses, and three were in the custody of the Hebrew University.

Then the war for the independence of the State of Israel broke out.

As with so many parts of the Dead Sea Scroll saga, we have two versions of what happened next. Everyone agrees that a man by the name of John Trever at the American School of Oriental Research (ASOR) was involved. Everyone agrees that he was approached by Mar Samuel. Everyone agrees that Trever photographed three of the "Jerusalem scrolls," as Samuel was calling them. And everyone agrees that Trever helped the scrolls make their way to the United States, though he didn't buy them. But while some insist that Samuel and Trever were working to ensure the safety of the ancient writings, others claim that the scrolls were illegally smuggled out of the country amid the hostilities.

Either way, the scrolls had been discovered by bedouins in the Judean Desert that had been Palestine and that was now part of the fledgling state of Jordan. They had been sold to a man of dubious repute in Bethlehem, then deceitfully passed off as having been found in Jerusalem, before being removed from a war zone on the continent of their discovery and brought to the United States. Their legal status was, at best, unclear, and Samuel was unable to find a buyer for his scrolls.

Trever made more progress with his photos than Samuel did selling his scrolls, because even though Trever's hobby was photography, his profession was antiquities and the Bible. The scroll Trever had seen was huge, almost a foot high and twenty-four feet long. And it was beautifully preserved. The ink was clear, and the leather still flexible. With the help of the scholar William Albright, Trevor recognized the writing on the scroll.

At the start of the first millennium B.C., Hebrew was written in a script called paleo-Hebrew. Then, gradually, the older script was replaced by a version of what's still in use today, the "square" script.

Trever and Albright saw that the writing on the scroll was an early version of the newer square script. The forms of the letters themselves, which hung from a top guideline instead of rising from a baseline, tentatively suggested that the scroll was about two thousand years old. And the words were the text of the biblical Book of Isaiah!

At the time, the oldest known physical copy of any book of the Bible dated back only about a thousand years. Trever was in awe. It was possible that he had just seen the world's oldest known copy of part of the Bible, predating anything anyone else had seen by a full millennium. It was even possible that he alone knew the significance of the scroll.

So on April 11, 1948, Trever sent out a press release and then published his photographs. This, combined with a press release that Sukenik (at the Hebrew University) issued fifteen days later regarding his own scrolls, set the worlds of archaeology and biblical studies on fire: How old were these scrolls? Who wrote them? What were they doing in Jerusalem (according to Mar Samuel and Trever) and in the desert? What was in the scroll Trever hadn't identified? Were there more scrolls to be found?

Though they didn't know it at the time, the scroll Trever recognized as the Isaiah scroll was only part of the reason these scrolls would change the way we view the Bible.

Even more important was a scroll that Trever described as "a manual of discipline of some comparatively little-known sect or monastic order" and that is now variously called the Manual of Discipline or the Community Rule. As we'll see below, this describes a previously unknown religious community. Its members lived through the tumultuous downfall of Jerusalem, the birth of Jesus, and the early stages of Christianity, but its customs, religious documents, and general outlook remained in obscurity until the discovery of the Dead Sea Scrolls last century.

Like the early Christians and rabbinic Jews, the people described in the Community Rule revered the Old Testament, and, also like both groups, they felt the need for changes. The Community Rule describes a third response to Jerusalem's waning days, similar to Christianity and Judaism yet different from both.

Other scrolls found along with Isaiah would turn out to be the War Scroll, about the end of days; a book of biblical commentary; a collection of religious hymns; and fragments of an expanded book of Genesis that includes the mysterious Watchers (discussed in our chapter 7), Noah's great-grandfather Enoch (also in chapter 7), and Enoch's grandson (and, therefore, Noah's father) Lamech.

None of this was the focus of attention when the scrolls were first unearthed, though. Rather, one question above all occupied researchers: Were the scrolls authentic? After all, at the time it was difficult to date antiquities even under the best of circumstances, because carbon dating was still in its infancy and its more accurate and less destructive relative, accelerator mass spectrometry, wouldn't be invented until the 1980s.

Back in 1883, Moses Shapira, another "dealer in antiquities," this time not from Bethlehem but actually from Jerusalem, had announced that he possessed an ancient copy of the Book of Deuteronomy. Scholars had similarly been enthralled by the possibility of a book of the Bible that significantly predated the thousand-year-old copies that they had. But after expansive publicity, Shapira's discovery had proved to be forged. Archaeologists in the 1940s were reluctant to embrace another unauthenticated ancient find.

Without any reliable way to connect the chemical makeup of the ink or the parchment to any particular date, scholars had only two methods of determining the age of the scrolls. They could examine the physical environment in which the scrolls had been found. And they could compare the handwriting in the scrolls to other ancient handwriting.

The first option was unavailable to the researchers for two reasons. The Ta'amireh bedouins had become aware of the hoopla surrounding their discovery, so they refused to tell anyone where they had found the scrolls. Additionally, the hostilities resulting from the 1948 war made excavations for Jewish scrolls in Jordan difficult.

And for that matter, in removing the scrolls from the cave, the bedouins had upset what archaeologists call the "strata," that is, the layering of the ground that helps determine the age of a find. Even if they knew where the cave was and even had they been granted access, archaeologists at the time might not have been able to date the scrolls accurately.

So that left the handwriting analysis, more technically known as paleography. Though this was an inexact and still-unproven combination of science and guesswork, an analysis suggested that the scrolls were probably approximately two thousand years old, making them potentially the most important biblical find of the millennium.

But even as the legal status and authenticity of the scrolls were being questioned, scholars were at work studying Trever's photographs. The scrolls looked real. They seemed to be very old. And no one knew for sure what they were. In addition to the Book of Isaiah, they had a scroll that looked like a previously unknown commentary on the biblical Book of Habakkuk, and a third scroll that described life in an unknown community. The contents of Samuel's fourth scroll, which Trever had not photographed, were still a mystery.

Archaeologists and other researchers devoted considerable energy and resources to trying to find more scrolls in this magic area of the Judean Desert. But the desert is not an easy place to look for things. The climate is hostile and unforgiving, and even to the trained eye, many places look remarkably similar. Without local guides (and without modern GPS equipment, obviously), even basic navigation was a challenge. And, equally, the tense political climate remained a daunting obstacle.

In 1923, under British rule, the Department of Palestinian Antiquities was established to see to the safekeeping of any local artifacts of historical significance. In 1936, a man by the name of G. Lankester Harding assumed leadership of that department. So in 1949, just after the war, Harding was well positioned to look for more scrolls.

In consultation with the Jordanian military (technically the Arab Legion of Jordan), Harding managed to locate the bedouins' cave. He formed an archaeological expedition with Father Roland de Vaux of the École Biblique et Archéologique Française (the French Biblical and Archaeological School) and set out for the desert to explore the cave. When they arrived, they discovered that the cave had already been excavated ("raided," as the archaeologists phrased it), not only by the bedouins but also by monks from the nearby Syrian monastery of St. Mark.

But the team was able to find more pottery and pieces of more scrolls, including, most important, fragments that had once been part of the seven original scrolls. This was enough for the team to declare conclusively that the scrolls were authentic and very old.

Because scholars now knew that all seven scrolls had, in fact, been found in the area of the Judean Desert around the Dead Sea known as Qumran, they started calling the scrolls either the Qumran Scrolls or the Dead Sea Scrolls.

It seemed as though the world of scholarship had gained an invaluable window into history, in the form of these seven scrolls that were the only known significant physical writing to date back to the days of Jesus. Before the Dead Sea Scrolls, scholars had only fragments and copies.

Then in 1952, the bedouins again surprised the world by finding more scrolls. These new scrolls came from an area known as the Wadi Murabba'at, south of the original cave, and once they surfaced, archaeologists rushed to the Wadi Murabba'at, hoping to excavate the area before the bedouins were able to take anything. So excavations were hastily set up, and a few hundred documents, mostly from the Bar Kokhba revolt (the rebellion led by Bar Kokhba against the Romans in the early second century A.D.), were found, cataloged, and analyzed. But these proved a disappointment compared with the original seven scrolls because they had little to do with the Bible or with the Jerusalem of Jesus' day.

In the meantime, though, the bedouins were embarking on their own searches back in Qumran. Armed with local knowledge, they found it much easier to navigate and explore the area, and before long they had discovered another cave, just south of the first one. With more than one Qumran cave, scholars now needed a way to distinguish one from the other, and they cleverly called the first one Cave 1; the second was Cave 2. The bedouins found more than thirty scrolls in Cave 2.

As word leaked of the new cave, archaeologists from the École Biblique et Archéologique Française, with the American School of Oriental Research and the Palestine Archaeological Museum, decided to explore the entire Qumran region, starting with the bedouins' Cave 2, where they found a few remaining fragments, the bedouins having taken most of the scrolls.

Northeast of Cave 1, the archaeologists found a third cave ("Cave 3"). Overjoyed that they had beaten the local bedouins, the scholars rushed to explore the cave, carefully cataloging what they found. They had the usual plethora of fragments that, in this case, seemed to come from at least a dozen different scrolls.

They also unearthed something completely unlike anything that had been discovered in the area, or, for that matter, any other area. They discovered a scroll of thin copper onto which writing had been beaten. This copper scroll, still open to a middle passage, as though it had been buried before its reader had a chance to roll it back to the beginning, was at once fascinating and frustrating. It was a find of a completely new sort, but the copper was too brittle to unroll, and the archaeologists had no way of reading the scroll.

It wasn't until four years later, in Manchester, England, that re-searchers got their first glimpse of the contents of the Copper Scroll (as scholars cleverly dubbed it). Using a fine-toothed saw of the sort usually reserved for brain surgery, technicians managed to cut the scroll into tiny strips, which they then reassembled.

Any good adventure story needs buried treasure, and to the astonishment of the researchers, this is exactly what they found as they read the copper strips. The Copper Scroll was a verbal treasure map, pointing the reader to the location of hundreds of thousands of pounds of gold and silver, stashed in and around Jerusalem. The scroll has the flavor of a code, with Greek letters and other oddities mixed in with Hebrew directions like, "under the steps leading east, sixty feet," you will find "a chest of silver."

Though the quarter-million pounds of booty described in the scroll exceeds even the most generous estimate of how much precious metal even existed in the ancient world, the fascinating combination of intrigue and riches embodied in a copper scroll has prodded more than a few diviners to look for the buried treasure. But none has been found (to date). And the caves' best archaeological finds were still to come.

If the mascot of Cave 1 is the lost goat, the mascot of Cave 4 has to be the partridge. De Vaux, the French archaeologist who, with Harding, led the first organized exploration of Qumran, tells the story of sitting with the Ta'amireh bedouins one evening around a campfire. They were talking about all manner of things, including, obviously, the Dead Sea Scrolls. When one of the older men heard about the financial value of the scrolls, he told de Vaux about his life growing up in the desert and about hunting for food in the Qumran region.

In addition to climate, the geology of Qumran works against the local hunter. The sedimentary rock of the area forms cliffs technically known as marl terraces. These cliffs, like much of the region, are bone dry for most of the year. Then, usually about once or twice a year during the rainy season, they are exposed to sudden, massive quantities of water. (This meteorological pattern prods the sudden blossoming of the otherwise barren desert, a striking phenomenon that is immortalized in Psalm 126, also numbered 125, which compares the restoration of Israel to the streams of the Negev desert.) This copious rainfall on otherwise dry ground also creates the famous wadis (dry riverbeds) of the area, as well as numerous cavities and clefts in the rocks.

In particular, there are hundreds of small holes in the marl terraces. Since they are largely inaccessible, de Vaux and his team had made the reasonable decision not to search these pockmarks. But as they were sitting around the campfire, this old bedouin man told de Vaux that, in his youth, he had chased a wounded partridge into a hole in a wadi wall. Inside, the old man recalled, he had found a passage that led to a room full of old pieces of pottery and even a lamp. The man had left the pottery behind but kept the lamp.

De Vaux decided to search the holes immediately. But, of course, the bedouins had the home-team advantage again, and a few bedouin youths used the old man's description to find the exact spot he had in mind. The kids rushed in to find the pottery and whatever else might be there.

De Vaux didn't want yet another trove of scrolls to be destroyed by amateurs, so in this case he sent the police to keep the bedouins out. But he was too late. By the time he and Harding arrived at what was now known as Cave 4, only about a thousand fragments of the astonishing fifteen thousand that had been inside remained.

It took six years—until 1958—for all of the pieces to be sold by the bedouins and collected and cataloged by scholars. One reason for the delay was the sheer number of fragments, which essentially demanded fifteen thousand transactions.

The second reason was financial. The Jordanian government was the most likely purchaser of the scrolls, but it couldn't afford to buy everything that had been found. In a move that would eventually end up thrusting the Dead Sea Scrolls into major media outlets, Jordan turned to the Vatican Library and major universities for financial assistance. These institutions helped purchase the contents of Cave 4, but only in return for the exclusive right to publish the results of what they found.

Even with graduate students, it is a daunting task to piece together fifteen thousand fragments of ancient parchment, some of them so small that they can only be manipulated with tweezers. So for a while, de Vaux oversaw a huge project in Jerusalem that bore remarkable resemblance to a massive jigsaw-puzzle party. By the time they were done assembling the pieces, they had parts of over five hundred manuscripts.

What had started as seven scrolls only a decade earlier was now an impressive and substantial collection of ancient documents.

While the bedouins were negotiating prices and terms with Jordan, the Vatican Library, and the other institutions, Samuel—the religious leader of the Syrian-Orthodox monastery in Jerusalem—was still trying to sell his original "Jerusalem scrolls." They were in the United States, but, both because of their dubious legal status and because photographs of three of them had already been published, Samuel couldn't find a buyer.

Finally, in 1954, Samuel got the idea to advertise his scrolls in *The Wall Street Journal,* next to an offer for a time share, as it would turn out. His copy read, "Biblical manuscripts dating back to at least 200 B.C. are for sale. This would be an ideal gift to an educational or religious institution by an individual or group." Interested parties were directed to reply to "Box F 206" at *The Journal.*

As it happens, Professor Sukenik, the archaeologist who had purchased three of the original scrolls for the Hebrew University, had a son in the United States who had planned to go into the family business. The son's name was Yigael Yadin.

Yadin's career in archaeology had been interrupted when he joined the Hagganah, the pre-Israel paramilitary organization that eventually became the Israel Defense Forces (IDF). (As part of his service, he took a nom de guerre, which is why he doesn't share his father's surname.) Yadin rose through the ranks first of the Hagganah and then the IDF, eventually serving as the IDF's chief of staff before retiring in 1954. With his retirement, Yadin wanted, finally, to return to archaeology. He saw Samuel's advertisement, raised $250,000 (over two million dollars in the economy of 2014) to buy the four scrolls, purchased them, and immediately sent them to Jerusalem.

So in less than a decade, the original seven scrolls that had sat patiently in the desert for almost two thousand years had been discovered by bedouins, sold to a shady dealer in antiquities in Bethlehem, resold to an archaeologist and an unscrupulous religious leader, photographed, separated as some were smuggled abroad, advertised in a mainstream newspaper, and finally reunited after being purchased by father and son.

Back in Jerusalem, the scrolls were deemed so important that the Israel Museum had a new hall built to house them, the Shrine of the Book, where they still sit to this day.

While none of the gold or silver from the Copper Scroll has ever been found, both the bedouins and the archaeologists realized that the scrolls themselves were like treasure, and even as they negotiated the sale of the contents of Cave 4, both sides continued the battle to be the first to find new caves with scrolls.

In September of 1952 the archaeologists found Cave 5 and, in it, a handful of scrolls with primarily biblical texts.

Then the bedouins found Cave 6, also with a handful of scrolls.

A few years later, de Vaux found some stairs in the area. It turned out that they led to three collapsed caves: Cave 7 yielded scrolls written in Greek, rather than the Hebrew more commonly found in the Dead Sea Scrolls; Cave 8 offered scrolls and some religious artifacts; and Cave 9 produced some miscellaneous fragments.

Cave 4 had a mat of sorts. Under it was Cave 10, which didn't house any scrolls but did have a decorated lamp and a bit of pottery inscribed with letters that might or might not spell "Jesus" in Hebrew.

In 1956, the bedouins discovered Cave 11, the last of the Dead Sea Scroll caves (to date). In addition to the usual variety of scrolls and fragments, Cave 11 had a huge scroll, dubbed the Temple Scroll, that appeared to be a replacement for Deuteronomy or perhaps an additional book of the Bible. Like Deuteronomy, which retells stories from the previous three books of the Bible, the Temple Scroll similarly summarizes material from those books, and it also includes summaries of otherwise unknown biblical material.

At twenty-five feet in length, the Temple Scroll was (and is) the longest of the Dead Sea Scrolls, longer even than the scroll of Isaiah found in Cave 1. It was also beautifully preserved. Kando, the Bethlehem merchant who was still helping the bedouins market their finds, figured that these qualities would help the Temple Scroll fetch a higher price than usual. So rather than approach Jordan, Kando tried, unsuccessfully at first, to find deeper pockets.

At this point we turn, surprisingly, to one of the first and most successful television evangelists, a man from Virginia named Rev. Joseph Uhrig, who introduced Jerry Falwell to television, paving the way for his *Old Time Gospel Hour.*

The year was 1960. Uhrig had been to Israel and Jordan five years earlier and, while there, had met a wonderfully helpful guide who called himself Marcos Hazou. When Hazou decided to leave Israel and move to America, he enlisted the help of the reverend. Uhrig agreed, sponsoring Hazou and his family as they made their way to the New World. Uhrig even housed and employed Hazou, further cementing their friendship. Then in 1960, the grateful Hazou told the reverend about a brother, Aboud, who still lived in Bethlehem. Aboud knew someone who had some ancient manuscripts, and Hazou wanted to know if Uhrig was interested in them.

Uhrig decided to return to Bethlehem to see the manuscripts. When he got there, he met Hazou's brother, Aboud, who in turn introduced him to the man with the manuscripts. The man's name was Kando.

Uhrig returned to the United States and set about trying to broker a sale. The obvious place to start was with the prominent Dr. William Albright, who had helped Trever authenticate the first Isaiah scroll. After a few conversations about the material, and especially the considerable possibility that it might be fake, Albright put Uhrig in contact with Yigael Yadin, who just a few years earlier had raised $250,000 to buy Samuel's scrolls.

Uhrig wrote to Yadin, now living in Jerusalem, and also started making more trips to Bethlehem.

Kando was hoping that his huge scroll would fetch at least one million U.S. dollars (with the buying power of nearly eight million in 2014). He also had a handful of fragments available for lesser sums. But executing a purchase, even for some of Kando's smaller items, was tricky, in part because of the culture clash between a Virginia clergyman and a Middle Eastern merchant, and in part because Bethlehem at the time was part of ferociously anti-Israel Jordan, while Yadin had convinced Uhrig that the scrolls belonged in Israel's Shrine of the Book. The unstable and contested Israel-Jordan border was a significant obstacle to commerce.

While Yadin wanted Kando's scroll, he flatly refused to pay the huge price that Kando was demanding. But Uhrig stayed in touch with Kando, who by this time had been nicknamed "crazy Kando" by the reverend.

At one point, partly to demonstrate his bona fides as a legitimate buyer, Uhrig bought one of Kando's fragments for $2,500. Back in the United States, Uhrig wondered what to do with his new purchase. After a few months, he got the idea of sending it to Yadin in Jerusalem. So he simply wrapped the thing in a paper napkin, put it in an ordinary paper envelope, and mailed it off, without even an asking price.

It turned out that the fragment Uhrig had purchased from Kando was part of the Psalms Scroll from Cave 11. The rest of that scroll had been purchased by the Rockefeller Museum in Jerusalem, and Yadin had access to it. So Yadin now knew that this man in America who was brokering for the man in Bethlehem who was brokering for the bedouins in the desert had access to authentic Dead Sea Scrolls. Yadin mailed back a letter and a check for $7,000. We don't know what Yadin thought of the fact that a fragment from only a few miles away had traveled more than eleven thousand miles to reach him.

We do know that Yadin decided to try to buy the Temple Scroll.

We know that Yadin gave Uhrig $10,000 in cash, which the reverend carried in a sock to Bethlehem. And we also know that the scroll was never purchased and remained with Kando. But beyond that we have conflicting information, depending on who tells the story.

Yadin seems to have believed that a firm price had been agreed to for the scroll: $130,000. In addition to the $10,000 in cash he gave Uhrig, Yadin put $120,000 into an account in the Chase Manhattan Bank. He gave the deposit slip to Uhrig, who in turn could show the slip to Kando as proof that sufficient funds were available to purchase the scroll.

Kando seems to have had no idea what a deposit slip was. He wanted cash.

Uhrig in the meantime was having personal financial woes, and he seems to have hoped that he might earn enough of a profit as a broker to help him stay solvent. He recalls throwing the $10,000 at Kando in Bethlehem and begging the merchant to sell the scroll. Kando refused. Frustrated at being so close to completing such an important sale—the scroll was actually right in front of his eyes at this point—Uhrig tore off a scrap of the scroll to show Yadin. And then he left, without his $10,000 and without the rest of the scroll.

Somehow Yadin got Uhrig's scrap, though the two men differ on how. Yadin, now out $10,000, seems to have played down the significance of Uhrig's scrap, perhaps as a negotiating tactic. Uhrig—who insisted that his motivation was helping Israel recover the scroll— gave up on ever retrieving the precious artifact; he even began to doubt its worth.

Because of Uhrig, Yadin knew exactly where the scroll was and, because of the scrap, knew it was authentic. But he had no way to get it, so, like Uhrig, he gave up.

And the scroll might have remained in Kando's hands forever were it not for the 1967 Six-Day War.

The months leading up to the start of the war on June 5, 1967, saw an increasing cycle of violence between Israel and her neighbors. Egypt had closed the Straits of Tiran to all Israeli shipping, which had the result of cutting off Israel from her only supply route with Asia and her main supplier of oil. (In a sign of how much has changed, that supplier was Israel's friend Iran.) Egyptian troops were preparing for battle in the Sinai desert to Israel's south, and Syrian troops were doing the same in the Golan Heights, to Israel's northeast. Russia was sending arms and support to the Arabs. Two months earlier, Syria had attacked Israeli kibbutzim, and, in a retaliatory attack, Israel had shot down six Syrian MiGs.

On June 4, 1967, Yigael Yadin, who had mostly left archaeology for politics, was recalled to military service and asked to serve as military adviser to the Israeli prime minister, Levi Eshkol. This is how it happened that three days later, on June 7, when the IDF captured Bethlehem from Jordan, Yadin was able to secure the services of a lieutenant colonel in the IDF. Yadin gave this soldier an order, "Go get my scroll from Kando!"

The lieutenant colonel complied, forming an expedition to Bethlehem.

By June 8, 1967, over a decade after the discovery of Cave 11, Yadin finally had the scroll. To his huge dismay, though, fully one third of it had rotted away as it sat in a shoebox under a flooring tile in Kando's home.

Though Kando had no legitimate claim to the scroll, which, after all, he was keeping in violation of both Israeli and Jordanian law, the State of Israel nonetheless agreed to pay Kando over $100,000. And the scroll joined the other Dead Sea Scrolls in the Shrine of the Book.

But while the Temple Scroll was now publicly available, the fifteen thousand fragments from Cave 4 were still in the hands of the multiorganizational consortium that had purchased them almost ten years earlier in 1958. And the consortium seemed to be in no hurry to make anything public.

The first Dead Sea Scrolls were found in 1947, and they were published eight years later in 1955. By contrast, the finds from Cave 4 were still unpublished in 1967. It would take a media campaign and a graduate student who dabbled in computer programming to make these scrolls public.

The political tensions in the area had crept into the academy. In 1965, the official Oxford University journal devoted to publishing the Dead Sea Scrolls had been renamed from *Discoveries in the Judaean Desert* to *Discoveries in the Judaean Desert of Jordan,* a title which, after the Six-Day War, was no longer accurate, at least according to some, but, either way, there is only one "Judaean" Desert, and everyone knows where it is. The addition of "of Jordan" to the title was purely a political gesture. And we have already seen that the archaeologists and the bedouins were in constant competition, too. These controversies would be augmented by a bitter debate about publishing the finds from Cave 4.

The problem, according to most people, was that the original purchasers of the material were taking too long to publish it. How was it possible, they wanted to know, that the consortium had had the material for nearly a decade and nonetheless published nothing?

In 1968, the consortium published their first results, but they still refused to grant access to the scrolls to anyone but a limited group of thirty scholars, dubbed "the clique." This not only antagonized non-clique scholars who couldn't see the scrolls, but raised suspicions in the minds of the broader public. Only Christians were part of the clique. This led some people to believe that parts of the scrolls were purposely being concealed because they would undermine Christianity.

These tensions simmered and grew for nearly twenty years. In 1985, a man named Hershel Shanks took up the cause of freeing the Dead Sea Scrolls from their academic captors. As editor of the popular *Biblical Archaeology Review,* he had a ready-made platform, and it wasn't long until his pleas made their way to more mainstream American media. Soon after that, the consortium of scholars earned the title of "cartel," a moniker usually reserved for groups of violent outlaws.

In an attempt to pacify the increasingly vocal protesters, in 1988 the cartel agreed to a compromise. They wouldn't release the scrolls or grant anyone else access to them, but they would release something called a concordance, which lists each word in the scrolls and the context in which it appears.

A concordance is a useful linguistic tool, because knowing the contexts in which a word appears is one of the best ways of determining what a word means. And even though the Dead Sea Scrolls were mostly written in Hebrew, they were not written in the same dialect of Hebrew as the Bible or as later rabbinic writings. So just figuring out what the words meant was an exciting challenge, and one of the first things the cartel had done was to compile a concordance to facilitate their own work. As part of the compromise with the rest of the academic world, one copy of this compilation was sent to Professor Ben Zion Wacholder at Hebrew Union College—Jewish Institute of Religion in Cincinnati.

As Wacholder was looking at the concordance, the cartel and people associated with it were inadvertently fanning the fire of controversy. A man named John Strugnell had taken over as chief editor of the cartel's Dead Sea Scrolls in 1987. In 1991 he called outside scholars who wanted access to his scrolls "a bunch of fleas who are in the business of annoying us." This wasn't nearly so bad as when he said later that year that Judaism was a "horrible religion," a misstep he might have survived had he not been talking to Avi Katzman, an Israeli journalist.

The previous year, a man named Emanuel Tov had joined Strugnell as coeditor. Strugnell was forced to leave after his media gaffe, and he was, in fact, replaced by two people, with the result that three people were now in charge. But it was Tov who took the next step toward facilitating the publication of the scrolls.

Tov had a graduate student named Martin Abegg. Tov didn't hide his displeasure at the pace of publication from his student, and, in fact, Tov had even sometimes given Abegg and his other students unpublished Dead Sea Scrolls material to work on. As Abegg was getting ready to leave Tov, his mentor cautioned the young student not to tell anyone about the contents of the scrolls.

Abegg happened to decide on Cincinnati as his next destination, because he wanted to work with Professor Wacholder. From Tov, Abegg had learned that the Dead Sea Scrolls' slow pace of publication was decidedly unacademic and secretive. And Wacholder just happened to have a concordance.

Most important, Abegg, a generation younger than Wacholder, knew something that his teacher did not. He knew how to program a computer. And he also knew that it wasn't hard to write a computer program that would analyze a concordance such as the one Wacholder possessed and that would use the analysis to re-create the original text from which the concordance was produced.

Abegg did just this, and while the cartel was still keeping most of the material from Cave 4 secret, Abegg and Wacholder published the material in September 1991.

Finally, with the proverbial cat out of the bag, the Dead Sea Scrolls were scientifically dated, using a procedure known as accelerator mass spectrometry (AMS). Normal carbon dating, which had been available almost since the first Dead Sea Scrolls were discovered, suffers from the unfortunate technical drawback that in order for something to be dated, it has to be burned. Archaeologists were quite reasonably unwilling to burn a scroll just to determine its age.

AMS, on the other hand, involves the destruction of much less original material. In 1992, a team in Zurich applied the new AMS technique to fourteen of the Dead Sea Scrolls. With only one exception, the results from Zurich agreed very closely with dates that had previously been established, mostly from handwriting analysis, but also from a tiny handful of scrolls that were independently datable based on their contents. These results were widely considered the final verification of both the authenticity and antiquity of the Dead Sea Scrolls.

It took almost half a century, a cobbler from Bethlehem who fancied himself a dealer in antiquities, a dishonest cleric in Jerusalem, thousands of hours of painstaking labor, clandestine excavations, scrolls smuggled to America and a scroll hidden under a floor tile, a preacher from Virginia, a team of IDF soldiers, and an unauthorized computer reconstruction—to say nothing of the goat and the partridge—but finally the Dead Sea Scrolls are available to anyone with access to a library, bookstore, or computer.

The scrolls describe a communal, devout, ascetic society. The group, most commonly known as the Dead Sea Sect or the Qumran Sect, probably numbered in the hundreds, certainly not more than the low thousands, and lasted from approximately the Maccabean revolt in the second century B.C. to the Roman destruction of Jerusalem in A.D. 70.

Who wrote the scrolls? What do the scrolls contain? And what do we learn from them?

The answers to these questions shed new light on the Old Testament and the New Testament, on the early rabbinic Jews and on the early Christians. They show what it was like to serve God in the context of holy scrolls before there was a Bible and demonstrate that the simplistic division of the ancient world into Jews, Christians, and others glosses over internal conflicts and more widespread similarities. And they exemplify how the turbulent times that we saw in the last chapter influenced the way people thought.

The scrolls also take us on a meandering and sometimes uncertain path, offering answers that pose a whole new set of questions. Almost every aspect of life at Qumran and of the sect that lived there is like a riddle, and while some clues are clear, others are vague or even contradictory. In the end, we will be left knowing more about antiquity, but also will be aware of newly found ignorance on our part.

We start with the people who lived there, as they describe themselves in one of the original scrolls found in 1947. First known as the Manual of Discipline, then later as the Community Rule or Rule of the Community, the scroll describes life at Qumran for the Dead Sea Sect.

A word about nomenclature is in order before we start reading the Community Rule, because, as with all the scrolls from the Dead Sea, the document also enjoys a more technical name: 1QS. The 1 indicates that the scroll was found in the first Qumran cave. The Q is for

"Qumran." And the S is from the Hebrew *serech,* which means "rule." Similarly, 1QM is a scroll from Cave 1 at Qumran. The M stands for the Hebrew *milchama,* which means "war." That scroll is nicknamed the War Scroll.

Once scholars realized how many scrolls there were in Qumran, they started numbering them instead of using final letters. So, for instance, there's a 1Q28, which is the twenty-eighth scroll (according to an arbitrary enumeration) from the first Qumran cave. As it happens, 1Q28 is a second copy of 1QS. 4Q491 is the 491st scroll from Cave 4 and just happens to be another edition of the War Scroll.

The word "rule" in the English title Community Rule, is a technical term that usually refers to a description of life in a monastic society, for example, the Rule of St. Benedict from about fifteen hundred years ago that, to this day, forms much of the basis of Benedictine life. Similarly, the Community Rule from Qumran describes various aspects of life at Qumran, including the theology, worldview, political stance, and daily routine of the society's members.

The general flavor of Qumran is established at the outset in what might be considered a preamble of the Community Rule. The community is for "seeking God" with "all one's heart and all one's soul," language reminiscent of the famous text from Deuteronomy 6:5 ("love the Lord your God with all your heart and all your soul"), which Christians recognize as, according to Jesus, the "most important commandment" (Matthew 22:37–38 and elsewhere) and which Jews to this day keep written on entranceways in religious markers known as *m'zuzot.*

Right from the start, then, the community places itself firmly in the biblical Old Testament tradition, but it also focuses on an aspect of the Old Testament that would remain central in the New Testament and rabbinic Judaism.

The Community Rule could have begun with a reference to "serving

God in accordance with the laws of levitical sacrifice," for example, which also would have been in keeping with the Old Testament, but which would have been in opposition to the New Testament and to the rabbis that would re-create Judaism after A.D. 70. Or the Rule could have begun, as the Gospel of Matthew does, with genealogy, an option that would connect the document to the Old Testament in yet a different way.

The choice to quote Deuteronomy 6:5 is typical of the community, which seems, like early Christianity and rabbinic Judaism, to have been grappling with how to reinterpret the Old Testament. Christianity ended up creating the New Testament and assigning at least as much value to that new work as to the older parts of the Bible. Rabbinic Judaism kept the primacy of the Old Testament, supplementing it with the Midrash and the Talmud. Though different than both of those groups, the Dead Sea Sect seems also to have been reevaluating the Old Testament in a world marked by upheaval.

The goal of the community, according to 1QS, is "to do what is just and right according to God," which is to say, that which God commanded "Moses and his servants the prophets." Equally, the goal is to eschew everything evil, which is to say, that which God rejects. The world according to the Community Rule is thus divided into two opposing camps, which in typical Dead Sea Scroll language are the "children of light," representing God, and the "children of darkness," representing God's Qumranic foe, called Belial in the Dead Sea Scrolls. (Belial also appears as God's foe in the Old and New Testaments.)

This focus not only on good but more specifically on good versus evil is, of course, known from the Bible. The tree in the Garden of Eden that provides the fruit for Adam and Eve's downfall is, after all, the "tree of knowing good and evil." Similarly, prophets such as Amos exhort the people to "hate what is evil and love what is good," while Micah condemns unjust rulers who "hate what is good and love what is evil." And the psalmist enjoins the people to "turn from what is evil and do what is good." But the primary emphasis in the Bible is God's commandments and what is good, not on the battle between good and evil.

The Community Rule, by contrast, focuses intensely on a cosmic duality of good and evil. (And as we'll see below, the War Scroll details a war between the two sides.) The leader of the community is supposed to teach the "children of light" about the nature of the "children of humanity." In particular, God "created humans to rule the world" and "put within them two spirits" so that God could walk among humans until something called God's "appointed time."

The matter is so important that it warrants a detailed discourse in the scroll about these two spirits and what they represent: good versus evil; light versus darkness; honesty versus deceit; justice, patience, generosity, and understanding versus injustice, impatience, greed, and foolishness. The world as described by the Community Rule is one in which good and evil play equal and complementary roles. For example, not only are "acts of injustice" anathema to truth, but "paths of truth" are similarly anathema to injustice. Good and evil exist side by side, battling things out, as part of God's plan for humankind and the universe.

But even as the Community Rule puts good and evil side by side, the document makes it clear that the coexistence of good and evil is a temporary state, to be remedied when God helps good conquer evil. (One particularly interesting detail notes that the "spirit of truth" will be "sprinkled like water" to cleanse people of evil, a concept reminiscent of the baptism that would help define Christianity.) This world of good and evil waiting for God's intervention is the context in which the members of Qumran gathered to bolster the forces of good through their own lives, freely "returning from evil," as they enigmatically put it.

In deference to its biblical allegiance, the society is specifically ordered with priests first, then levites (another privileged biblical class), and finally everyone else. That general population is organized by "thousands, hundreds, fifties, and tens," a description that mirrors the organizational scheme in Exodus 18 by which Moses is to arrange the fledgling Israelite society: "Moses chose capable men from among all of Israel and appointed them as heads over the people, as officers of thousands, officers of hundreds, officers of fifties, and officers of tens." This nod to the traditional text seems more symbolic than practical, though, because two thousand is near the upper limit of how many people were likely to have lived at Qumran, so there were probably no "thousands" at all.

One intriguing and still unanswered question is who exactly these people living in Qumran were. They were obviously living according to some Jewish tradition, and equally obviously concerned about which parts of that tradition should be continued and which parts should be revised. Though they ultimately came to different answers, these are the same issues that occupied the early Christians and rabbinic Jews.

These people living according to Jewish tradition were, apparently, involved in internal Jewish debate.

According to the Community Rule, those who have returned from evil are supposed to follow in the path of the "sons of Zadok" and separate themselves from the "people of injustice." The Rule explains that the "sons of Zadok" are the "priests who keep the covenant." This matches what is described in the Bible (e.g., 2 Samuel 8:17), where Zadok is the high priest, so it is tempting to equate the "sons of Zadok" with "the descendants of the high priest."

Similarly, the Dead Sea Scrolls use the Hebrew word for "nations" (*goyim*) to mean non-Jews. So we potentially have three groups: the "sons of Zadok," the "people of injustice," and the "nations." If the "people of injustice" are different from the "nations," they would have to be Jews, but not the group of Jews who follow the tradition of Zadok.

If so, the Community Rule would have pitted legitimate high priests against other interpreters of Judaism, a worldview that would dovetail nicely with what was happening in Jerusalem during the second century B.C. The Syrian Greek Antiochus IV ("the Mad") had begun meddling in the high priesthood, and then the Maccabees, who were priests but not descended from Zadok, had taken power as they overthrew Antiochus's government.

So one way of understanding the people of Qumran as described in the Community Rule (and elsewhere) is that they were Jews who rejected the new power structure in Jerusalem.

Unfortunately, the name Zadok comes from the Hebrew root for "righteous," and the "sons of Zadok" could also be more generally "the righteous people." Or the attribution of the community to "Zadok" could be, like its division into "thousands," no more than a metaphorical incorporation of tradition. Or, also reflecting tradition, the "sons of Zadok" may refer to Ezekiel 40:46, where the "sons of Zadok" will be the ones who approach God in the rebuilt Temple.

In short, it's not clear if the Community Rule is meant to describe a general position of piety in contrast to people who have strayed, or more specific religious and political tensions. One problem in particular arises because the "sons of Zadok" in the Community Rule, in contrast to the new Jewish leaders, would be priests insistent on keeping the old traditions alive, most prominently sacrifice. But the Community Rule seems to have given up sacrifice in favor of prayer. The Rule itself looks forward to a day without the flesh of burnt offerings, when the offering of the lips will be like the "aroma of justice" and when walking the "perfect path" will be like the "freewill offering." Equally, the Community Rule stresses "praying" or "blessing" (the

Hebrew might mean either) as a group, in particular after a communal meal. So this seems to be a community that has if not already moved away from sacrifice toward prayer, then at least taken most of the important steps. This position seems at odds with the cult's insistence that they are the keepers of tradition.

We have other clues about this group's theology.

We have already seen phrases like "all your heart and all your soul." The Rule also directly introduces quotations from the Bible with phrases like "as is written" or "in accord with what is written" (*ka'asher katuv* in Hebrew). An alternative form of this phrase (*kakatuv*) was commonly used by the Rabbis who reinvented Judaism with the Talmud and the Midrash. The Rabbis use the phrase to make a connection—often tenuous—to a biblical passage. The New Testament uses the Greek word *pliro-o* for the same purpose (though it's harder to see, because many English translations get this word wrong, incorrectly rendering it as "fulfill" in English). So we learn that the Dead Sea Sect was quoting the Bible in the same way that early Christians and rabbinic Jews did: as part of an agenda to incorporate Scripture into a new form of religious practice.

For example, the community is supposed to "walk to the desert" and there walk God's path, in accord with what is written (in Isaiah 40:3): "In the desert clear a path for the Lord." Like the New Testament and the Midrash and Talmud, the Community Rule cites Scripture as the rationale for religious behavior.

There's something else striking about this reference to Isaiah. The full quotation is, without punctuation, "The voice of one crying in the desert clear a path for the Lord." Two possible interpretations of this line present themselves. The voice might be crying in the desert, "clear a path for the Lord." Or the voice might be crying, "in the desert clear a path for the Lord." The Community Rule assumes the latter. There is a voice. And the voice is crying about what should happen in the desert. But the voice could be anywhere.

What's striking is that Matthew also interprets Isaiah 40:3, and his interpretation of the passage differs from the way the Community Rule understands it. Matthew (3:3) assumes the voice is in the desert, and he equates that desert voice to Jesus. John does the same.

There are well over twenty thousand verses in the Old Testament. While many of them do not readily lend themselves to deep theological interpretation, there are still thousands of verses that do. Just for example, Obadiah 1:1 refers to "rising up to do battle" in favor of the Lord. One might imagine that that line would figure prominently in the literature of the Dead Sea Sect or some other religious cult focused on good versus evil. But it does not.

When we see the same passage—Isaiah 40:3, in this case—used centrally in two different traditions, we have reason to believe that the traditions were culturally connected. And the line ended up in the Jewish liturgy, too. Once again, it seems as though the Dead Sea Sect, the early Jews, and the early Christians were all asking the same questions in the same context, even focusing on the same texts, though they didn't always arrive at the same answers.

In addition to such lofty issues as theology and the battle between good and evil, the Community Rule addresses more practical matters, including, for meetings, an early parallel to *Robert's Rules of Order* (which are designed to facilitate equitable and efficient meetings) and some legal codes.

Communal meetings, called "the sessions of the Many" in Hebrew, were to be strictly hierarchical, with people sitting according to their rank: priests first, then elders, then ordinary people. Similarly, they were to speak in that hierarchy. No one was to talk when someone else was talking or, enforcing the notion of hierarchy, before someone of higher rank. There appears to have been a meeting chair, often translated as "inspector" (*maskil*), who was the only one who could say things that the Many "didn't like," though this "liking" could have been a technical notion, more limited than mere general dissatisfaction. To raise a new point, someone had to "stand on his feet and say, 'I have something to say to the Many.'" And so forth.

Punishments generally took the form of exclusion from the community. Among the most severe crimes was breaking even a single word of "Moses's *Torah*" (which probably means any part of Jewish law, even though the word *Torah* also refers more narrowly to the Five Books of Moses) through haughtiness or carelessness, the punishment for which was outright expulsion so that the offender could never return.

Interestingly, the Rule differentiates between haughty or careless breaking of Moses's law and accidental violations. The second category was punished with a two-year probation of sorts, during which the offender was cut off from the congregation and the food and drink it provided. This distinction between willing and accidental violations suggests that the Rule was supposed to be practical in addition to symbolic.

Other crimes that resulted in expulsion were uttering the "honored name," that is, the name of God; defaming the Many; and complaining against the foundation of the Many. There are presumably details and nuances we don't understand anymore: What exactly was defaming? How was defaming different than complaining? What was the foundation? But the point seems clear. The statutes seem designed to protect God's law, God's name, and the integrity of the Qumranic society, often in ways that may seem particularly harsh to modern readers.

Lesser sentences were prescribed for other crimes. The punishment for defaming a member of the society was a one-year probation;

for deception, six months; baseless animosity, either six months or one year (the text has "six months" corrected to "one year"); causing a loss to the community's property, sixty days; interrupting someone else, ten days; sleeping during the session of the Many, either ten or thirty days; public nakedness, six months (though a curious provision exempts people who have a valid reason to go naked, raising the obvious if unanswered question of what that valid reason might be); and so forth.

The Rule also contains provisions for initiation into the society, along the lines of modern immigration and naturalization law. In fact, much of what we find in the Community Rule has modern parallels. We have already seen rules for communal debate, akin to *Robert's Rules of Order.* Now we see initiation qualifications. Similarly, the Rule's prohibition against defaming a member of the community is similar to modern slander laws. Like the Dead Sea Sect, we still grapple in modernity with what to do with accidental acts of violence. And so on.

One difficult question is whether there were any women or children around Qumran. Complicated grammatical aspects of Hebrew make it difficult to distinguish between "men" and "people," between "children" (in the metaphoric sense) and "sons," and so forth. So for example, while we've used the phrase "children of light" here, the point may have been more narrowly "sons of light." The Rule provides that a priest be present at any gathering of ten or more, but the text may refer to ten people or ten men.

In the entire Rule, we find only one reference to a woman, and there she simply serves the poetic role of giving birth to a man (or a person). So even though the Hebrew is ambiguous, there don't seem to have been any women or children. (By contrast, both the Old and New Testaments contain women.)

All told, the Rule paints a picture of a group (probably of men) living together in the desert, sharing their meals and their resources, living in strict hierarchy and strictly according to some version of Jewish law.

Unfortunately, this picture contradicts another detailed source of information about Qumran, the Damascus Document.

Jewish custom demands that texts that bear God's name be treated with reverence and, instead of simply being discarded, be kept in a room, buried, or otherwise cared for in ways generally reserved for corpses. The storage location for these holy documents is called a *genizah*.

Toward the end of the ninth century A.D., a synagogue was built in Fustat, which in 641 had become the first Arab capital of Egypt. In keeping with Jewish custom, anything God's name was written on was not discarded but instead put into a *genizah* in Fustat.

For reasons that remain unclear, the practice in this particular synagogue in Egypt was to extend that care to any text written in Hebrew letters, a fact that would come to light only in 1896, when the Romanian-born Cambridge scholar Dr. Solomon Schechter traveled there and found the huge trove of documents: prayer books, property deeds, Talmudic collections, personal correspondence, Bibles, legal codes, and more. Many of these were in Hebrew, others in Arabic and written in Hebrew letters (a common practice), others yet in various other languages, sometimes tossed in apparently by accident, sometimes included because they had been reused to write Hebrew.

The collection, dubbed the Cairo Genizah, was the first modern window into ancient documents, the first time modern scholars could look at actual documents from antiquity. For example, among the finds there was a Hebrew copy of the Wisdom of Ben Sira, a book from the early second century B.C. that, until then, had been preserved in Greek and, therefore, not considered part of the Jewish canon.

Also among the documents discovered in the Cairo Genizah was the Damascus Document. Because it was discovered in Cairo and not at Qumran, its technical abbreviation is CD ("Cairo Damascus"). But it turns out that the Damascus Document is probably a copy of a Dead Sea Scroll. The language and contents are similar to other Dead Sea Scrolls, and, more importantly, fragments of another copy of the Damascus Document were found in Qumran, primarily in Cave 4. So in addition to CD, we have, for example, 4Q266 (the 266th fragment found in the fourth Qumran cave), which is also called 4QD^a, because its text matches CD. (The *a* means that it is the first Damascus Document fragment; 4Q267, for example, is called 4QD^b.) The document gets its more colloquial name, Damascus Document, from the repeated, probably metaphorical, references to Damascus in it.

The Damascus Document, like the Community Rule, describes life at Qumran. It refers to the "children of Zadok," the priests, Belial, a division into "thousands, hundreds, fifties, and tens," etcetera, all similar to the Community Rule. Unfortunately, though, the two documents are at times incompatible.

One huge difference is that the Damascus Document specifically includes women, while, as we saw, the Community Rule seems to have excluded them. For example, the Damascus Document has specific provisions for the introduction of a woman into the society (she must be sexually pure, according to a variety of criteria) and specifically extends the laws of incest to apply to women, even though in the Torah they are "written from the point of view of the males." The Damascus Document also contains laws about childbirth, specifically including children and, obviously, women.

Secondly, the Damascus Document has provisions for private property, including what to do with objects whose owners are unknown (the priests keep them) and how many witnesses are required to demonstrate theft (two).

Thirdly, the Damascus Document seems to accept at least a limited role for the Temple, while the Community Rule seems to reject the Temple completely.

Fourthly, the Damascus Document makes reference to what one can and cannot do inside and outside the city, which seems inconsistent with the Qumran desert environment, in which there were no cities.

In fact, this fourth inconsistency suggests the most common way of reconciling the Damascus Document with the Community Rule. There may have been two kinds of people living under the auspices of the Dead Sea Sect: some in cities (to which the Damascus Document would apply) and others who removed themselves completely and left for the desert (to whom the Community Rule would apply). The Damascus Document seems to be compatible with this division, referring to some people who live in "holy perfection" and apparently contrasting them with those who live "in camps, according to the rule of the land, and who take wives and become parents."

Even so, the discrepancies are widespread and troubling, leaving us—as is so often the case with the Dead Sea Scrolls—suspicious that we have missed something fundamental about the nature of the Dead Sea Sect, and urging us to seek clues elsewhere.

One thing we see clearly from the content of the Dead Sea Scrolls, not just the Community Rule and Damascus Document, is a representation of the major themes of the day. We have already observed how the Dead Sea Scrolls quote some of the same texts as, for example, the New Testament and Jewish liturgy.

They also address some of the same debates.

It appears, for instance, that one important question back then concerned how to celebrate the Sabbath. The Bible forbids any work but doesn't spell out exactly what counts as working (though many people don't appreciate the Bible's silence in this regard, because Jewish tradition, primarily as codified in the Talmud much later, offers much more detail). It seems that all the Jews in the final centuries of the first millennium B.C. were grappling with this question, and they came to different answers.

A passage in the New Testament from Matthew 12 pits Jesus against the Pharisees. (The Pharisees were one mainstream group of Jews at the time. The other was the Sadducees. Though it's obviously a gross simplification, the Pharisees are often credited as the precursors to rabbinic Judaism, while the Sadducees are known for trying to preserve the priestly caste and its ways.) As part of the dispute, according to Matthew, Jesus rhetorically asks a group of people in a synagogue if they would rescue a sheep that had fallen into a pit on the Sabbath. The assumption is that of course it's the right thing to do, and that even on the Sabbath, one should rescue an animal from a pit.

The Damascus Document offers a contrary opinion, warning that it is specifically forbidden to raise an animal out of a pit on the Sabbath.

The Talmud, recording the legacy of the rabbinic tradition of Judaism, also weighs in on this issue, in Shabbat 128b. There the claim is that the goal of preventing pain to animals supersedes prohibitions against work on the Sabbath, because the prohibitions come from the Rabbis, while the commandment to care for animals dates back further, to the Torah. Despite the rhetoric, though, the Rabbis actually invented both prohibitions, and the reasoning seems to have been created to justify the result they wanted.

While animals and pits were more common in antiquity than they are now (at least, in and around modern cities), it can hardly be a coincidence that the Damascus Document, New Testament, and Talmud all offer a specific answer regarding what to do when an animal falls into a pit on the Sabbath. Rather, as with the quotation from Isaiah about the voice and the desert, these three—the Dead Sea Sect and its authors, the New Testament and early Christians, and the Talmud and the Rabbis—all seem to have been doing the same thing. They were adapting the Old Testament to what they saw as changing times. As part of their task, they were asking the same questions, though they often didn't come to the same answer.

In this particular case, the Rabbis and authors of the New Testament agree that it's permitted to rescue an animal on the Sabbath, while the Dead Sea Sect dissents. In the case of the Isaiah quotation ("the voice of one crying in the desert clear a path for the Lord"), the Dead Sea Sect agrees with the Rabbis that "in the desert" describes the path but not necessarily the voice, and the New Testament is the dissenting voice. Other cases exhibit other combinations of agreements and disagreements.

These persistent common themes are one reason that the Dead Sea Scrolls are so useful for understanding early Christianity and rabbinic Judaism.

Perhaps the biggest issue from the days of the Dead Sea Sect can be generalized to, What happens next? After we die, is there an afterlife? And if so, is it the same for everyone? Is it good ("heaven")? It is bad ("hell")? Do people continue to inhabit the earth roughly the way we do now, or will there be a dramatic change? And again, if so, will it be for the better or for the worse? These questions fall under the category of eschatology, and discussion of them is generally called eschatological literature.

The Old Testament is largely silent on all of these questions. It doesn't mention heaven or hell, the closest to the former being an idiom that equates death to meeting up with relatives, and the closest to the latter being a representation of death as a "pit," the Hebrew word for which is *sh'ol*, which gives us the English Sheol (the abode of the dead). Equally, the Old Testament doesn't directly refer to the Messiah, though Isaiah and some other prophets allude to the idea.

But these ideas—heaven, hell, the Messiah, and other eschatological matters—weighed heavily on the minds of people living in Jerusalem toward the end of the first millennium.

So the Dead Sea Scrolls flesh out these issues, most clearly in the War Scroll, a detailed description of the final cosmic war between good and evil.

The War Scroll describes two evenly matched opponents. On one side are the "sons of darkness," led by Belial, on the other, the "sons of light," led by God. This division mirrors the general mind-set at Qumran that we saw above in the Community Rule. Good and evil are equal, complementary forces in the world. One focus of the Community Rule was directing the inhabitants of Qumran toward the good. Here in the War Scroll, we find the two forces pitted directly against each other.

The entire ordeal is predestined, with the opening lines laying out a three-stage battle, complete with place-names, as if the sons of light and the sons of darkness are engaged in a real-world battle for real estate.

In the first stage, the sons of light conquer Judea ("Edom") with neighboring Moab and Syria ("Ashur"). Then, in the second stage, they conquer Egypt. Finally, they conquer the north. This division of the world into Syria, Egypt, and "north" mirrors the power structure of the day. The sons of light conquer the major world powers one by one.

The War Scroll describes the details of the battles in great, earthly detail. We read about the different kinds of trumpets used to sound the battle cry, including even the slogans that are written on them: "the people God calls," "God's secrets for destroying evil," "God's princes" among others. We also read about the banners carried into battle and what is written on them: "God's truth," "God's justice," "God's glory," as well as things like "God's families" and "God's tribes," in addition to much more.

The text is equally specific regarding the battle formations, including how the troops are to be deployed. (Scholars use these details to learn about the military culture in which the scroll was composed, on the assumption that the strategy was taken from real military doctrine. The descriptions in the scroll seem most consistent with Roman warfare.)

And we learn about the weapons, such as the shiny bronze shields, 10-foot spears (assuming a Roman cubit of about 1.5 American feet), and 2.5-foot pure iron swords. One battalion will carry a shield and spear, the next a shield and sword. Then there's the cavalry, composed of seven hundred on each flank, riding stallions that are quick-footed, soft-spoken (presumably they don't bite), long-winded (so as not to tire), and trained for war.

With so much of the text seemingly based on real places, real tactics, and real weaponry, some scholars wonder if the War Scroll was meant to describe a real war, either planned for some future date, or at least hoped for.

Of particular interest in this regard is the word *kittim,* a plural noun in Hebrew apparently used to represent a group of people, perhaps a nationality. The first round of the war involves the "*kittim* of Ashur," and the second, the "*kittim* in Egypt." Who were the Kittim? Were they a real people, or were they used symbolically to represent evil in general?

The word *kittim* appears a handful of times in the Bible. And though it doesn't seem to have been used consistently for one people, it often looks like it refers to Cyprus. Because Rome ruled Cyprus for some time and even used Cyprus as a major administrative center, "Cyprus" could in fact mean "Rome" (the way, for example, "Washington" often means "the U.S. in general"). In fact, in Daniel (11:30), the Hebrew word *kittim* becomes "Rome" in the Greek translation called the Septuagint.

Furthermore, the obvious candidate for a real enemy of the Dead Sea Sect is Rome. So some people think that *kittim* in the War Scroll are the Romans and that the War Scroll is really about defeating the evil Romans. And perhaps *kittim* was used instead of a more readily obvious word so that Romans reading the War Scroll wouldn't know that they were the intended object of God's wrath.

More likely, though, *kittim* is a general word for "enemy." Even though the phrasing "*kittim* in Egypt" suggests a particular occupying power, no candidate—not even Rome—is completely consistent with all the details in the War Scroll. And this would not be the only time that the word for a specific nation was generalized to refer to any enemy.

Either way, it's clear that the Kittim represent all that is wrong with the world, much like "sons of darkness." This battle between good and evil is not merely a matter of mundane politics or borders, which is why the battle for "God's might" will occur amid the sound of a great multitude and involve "gods and people."

In keeping with the general approach that we saw in the Community Rule, the War Scroll cites the Bible, connecting military details with religious doctrine and providing quotations for the purpose of putting the War Scroll into the biblical tradition. So the priests who sound the trumpets must do so at a distance once the enemy starts to fall, because priests, according to the Old Testament, are not allowed near corpses. Similarly, regarding God's certain victory, the text quotes passages ranging from Numbers 24:17–19 ("a star will depart from Jacob. . . . It will smash the temples of Moab") to Isaiah ("Ashur will fall by a non-mortal sword, a non-human sword destroying it").

Much of the scroll deals with the final battle of this war, which has seven engagements. After the first six, the sides of light and dark emerge equally ranked, with three wins apiece. Finally, God's own hand intervenes, effecting a decisive victory over Belial. Though the details (including a final prayer that addresses God as "God of gods") are interesting, more important is the way God's intervention reflects the central theme of the book: God will make things better.

This hope for God to improve life has at least two crucial parts to it. The first and more obvious element is the existence of God, and that had always been part of Judaism. The second element is dismay or even despair with the current situation. The end of the first millennium B.C. was a profoundly unhappy time in many ways, not just for the Jews in Jerusalem—who suffered a series of blows, starting, ironically, with the Maccabees' victory—but, it would seem, also for the Jews at Qumran. Similarly, we'll see in chapter 4 that the context of Jesus' arrival in the New Testament is one of suffering at the hands of an oppressor.

This zeitgeist of dissatisfaction gave us the War Scroll and, some decades later, Revelation in the New Testament. That book, like the War Scroll, combines the cosmic and the quotidian: visions and symbolic sevens mix with horses and trumpeted battle cries. Parallel to God and Belial in the War Scroll are Christ and Satan in Revelation, represented in that book by the lamb and the beast. Where the War Scroll uses the Kittim to represent oppression at the hands of outsiders, Revelation has Babylon, also commonly equated with Rome, though, like the Kittim, Babylon represents outsiderness in general. In this sense, both Revelation and the War Scroll incorporate current events.

Finally, both Revelation and the War Scroll promise victory to a righteous minority amid a more powerful majority. In the War Scroll, it's the Dead Sea Sect, and in Revelation, those whose names have been written in the "book of life," judged "according to what they had done." (Curiously, Revelation doesn't quote the Old Testament, though theologians are quick to find references and other connections.) Both books, then, are eschatological. They ask, What will happen in the end? And the fundamental answer in both cases is that good will emerge victorious over evil.

But beyond that the War Scroll and Revelation offer very different answers. Primarily, Revelation ends with what is commonly called "the New Jerusalem," or, more generally, a rebuilding of the world only after it has been completely destroyed. The War Scroll, by contrast, concludes with the same old world made better.

The biblical Book of Daniel, too, is eschatological in nature and was probably written around the same time as the War Scroll. Daniel also refers to current events, evil rulers (Antiochus IV in particular), the plight of the local people, and the promise of better times. And there are other, similar works as well, as we saw in the introduction.

In other words, the Dead Sea Sect was not unique in hoping for better times. With all of these eschatological works floating around, the War Scroll stands out not because of the primary question it asks (what will happen in the end?) or its genre (a cosmic battle) but because of the details of its answer, which set the Qumran community apart: Good and evil are evenly matched in the world, eventually God will help good prevail, and this will happen in this world.

These various eschatological works created more than a little controversy. The Book of Revelation, with its imagery of the New Jerusalem, barely made it into the New Testament (and it's not in the Old Testament). Even a cursory look at the book reveals how it seems to conflict with the generally pacifistic nature of the rest of the New Testament. For example, regarding the leader of heaven's army riding on a white horse, the Book of Revelation describes, "From his mouth comes a sharp sword with which to strike down the nations . . . he will tread the wine press of the fury of the wrath of God the Almighty. He has a name written on his cloak and on his thigh, 'King of kings and Lord of lords.'" Striking down nations and the fury and wrath of

God are a far cry from the Gospels, as, for example, the famous passages from Matthew and Luke about "turning the other cheek," in which Jesus insists that his followers offer no resistance to evil.

And we've already seen that the Book of Daniel has been appropriated differently by Jews and Christians. Christians see messages in the book that are consistent with Christ, resurrection, and the end of times. So in the Christian canon, Daniel is a major prophet, on a par with Isaiah and Jeremiah. Jewish tradition does not see Daniel as a prophet at all, and the book is placed along with Esther (which, in the Jewish version, doesn't even have God's name in it) and other more clearly historical books, like Ezra.

The Dead Sea Sect, like the early Christians, saw Daniel as a prophet. And in addition, fragments of a work known as "The New Jerusalem" were found in Caves 4 and 11. These texts mirror the New Jerusalem in Revelation. This broad collection of eschatological works is one more way in which the inhabitants of Qumran demonstrate their unique form of early Judaism that was similar in some ways to what the Rabbis were building but also to what the early Christians had in mind.

The Community Rule and Damascus Document tell us directly about the Dead Sea Sect. The War Scroll gives us information about one issue that was important to them. Other Dead Sea Scrolls expand our knowledge in other ways, such as giving us better insight into the original text of the Bible.

For example, the text of Samuel as we have it in our current versions of the Bible is clearly incomplete. 1 Samuel 11:1 starts with a particularly violent passage:

Nahash the Ammonite went up and besieged a place called Jabesh-Gilead. All the men of Jabesh said to Nahash, "Make a pact with us and we will serve you." But Nahash the Ammonite said, "This is how I will make a pact with you, by gouging out your every right eye. . . ."

This eye gouging comes seemingly out of nowhere. This is our first introduction in the text to Nahash, and we read only that he is an Ammonite. Then he's suddenly gouging out eyes. Why? And why do the men of Jabesh want to make a pact?

It turns out that there's a whole passage missing from our text in the Bible. Fortunately, we find it in the Dead Sea Scrolls, in particular in 4QSam^a, which contains the text of the book of Samuel. There, 1 Samuel 1:11 starts as follows:

> Nahash, king of the children of Ammon, was the one who se-verely oppressed the children of Gad and the children of Reuben, and gouged out their every right eye and visited terror and dread on Israel; not one man among the children of Israel was left beyond the Jordan whose right eye was not gouged out by Nahash, king of the children of Ammon. Only 7,000 men left the children of Ammon and came to Jabesh-Gilead. And it was after roughly a month that Nahash the Ammonite alighted and besieged Jabesh-Gilead. All the men of Jabesh said to Nahash the Ammonite, "Make a pact with us and we will serve you." But Nahash the Ammonite said, "This is how I will make a pact with you, by gouging out your every right eye. . . ."

Unlike the biblical account, the Dead Sea Scrolls introduce us to Nahash as an oppressive ruler. Then we read details of his cruelty, so it makes perfect sense that the people of Jabesh feel the need to make a pact with him, and it is similarly in character that he in turn re-sponds by menacing them.

Furthermore, if we look carefully, we can actually see a remnant of the missing text in the Bible. Chapter 10 in the traditional Hebrew ends with the bizarre, "he was like a silent one." The line is so out of place that some translations simply ignore it.

A complex bit of Hebrew explains what's going on. By changing one Hebrew letter in "he was like a silent one" to an almost identical one (a *resh* to a *daled*) we get "it was after about a month." (Though these two phrases seem unrelated in English, they are almost the same in Hebrew, because: "he" and "it" are the same in Hebrew; "like" and "about" are the same in Hebrew; and the difference between the roots that form "silent" and "month" is only one letter, a *resh* versus a *daled*.) The phrase "it was after about a month" comes from the full version of the story, the one we find in the Dead Sea Scrolls.

In short, the biblical text is missing a few lines and, in addition, has a mistaken substitution of one letter for another similar one. We find the original in the Dead Sea Scrolls. (As it happens, the Septuagint, which we turn to in the next chapter, translates this line from the original, uncorrupted line as "after about a month.") But for the Dead Sea Scrolls, we might never understand this passage in Samuel.

Like other groups of people—most notably the Jews who would create the collection known as the Old Testament and the Christians who would do the same for the New Testament, the members of the Dead Sea Sect had to decide which documents they wanted to highlight. What did they choose?

Except for Esther, we have found copies of all or part of every book of the Old Testament at Qumran, and we don't know if the exclusion of Esther is happenstance or if the sect didn't know about it. But we also have found much more.

Particularly interesting is the Temple Scroll, which IDF soldiers recovered from under Kando's floor on behalf of the archaeologist/

military adviser Yadin. The Temple Scroll reads like an account of God talking directly to someone, presumably Moses. (Hebrew grammar makes it possible to know that it is a single male person, not a woman and not a group, that is being addressed.) And it covers much of the same material as Deuteronomy, summarizing material from Exodus, Leviticus, and Numbers, as well as offering new information about how the Temple should be built and operated.

Many of the concepts and much of the language in the Temple Scroll are clearly reminiscent of Deuteronomy. For example, Deuteronomy (16:18–19) teaches, "You shall appoint magistrates and officials for your tribes, in all the gates that the Lord your God is giving you, and they shall govern the people with due justice. You shall not pervert justice: you shall show no partiality; you shall not take bribes, for bribes blind the eyes of the discerning and upset the plea of the just." And the Temple Scroll has the similar, "You shall appoint magistrates and officials in all your gates and they shall govern the people with due justice. They shall show no partiality and they shall not take bribes and they shall not pervert justice, for bribes pervert justice." Both texts follow up with the famous line, "justice, justice shall you pursue" and then move on to the prohibition against a Canaanite religious object called an Ashera. (The reason to pursue "justice, justice" in both books is "so that you live." But the Temple Scroll, unlike Deuteronomy, expands on this theme, "The one who takes a bribe or perverts due justice shall be put to death. Do not be afraid of killing him. Do not behave in your land in the way that the nations do," establishing an Ashera and otherwise behaving in pagan ways.)

It is tempting to see this as a book that is "similar to but not part of the Bible." But while it is certainly that for us, it may have functioned exactly like Deuteronomy, maybe even instead of Deuteronomy, for the Dead Sea Sect, among other possibilities. It could have been no different from Numbers. Scholars still disagree about what the Temple Scroll was in its time.

Other books, too, are similar to what we now have in the Bible, and they raise similar questions. For example, the Old Testament has exactly 150 Psalms, organized into three sets of fifty. But many more psalms were found in Qumran. For instance, 11Q5 contains parts of many of the final fifty psalms from the familiar Book of Psalms but also new psalms that are not in the Bible. This raises the interesting possibility that our current collection is a "best of" compilation chosen from a wider collection. For example, one psalm newly discovered in Qumran, now called the "Hymn to the Creator," starts off, "Great and holy is the Lord, the Holy of Holies, from generation to generation. Before him walks glory and after him the roar of many waters. . . . He separates light from darkness. He created the dawn . . . and when all the angels saw it, they celebrated, because he had showed them something they had not known. . . ." Another new psalm begins, "It is not the maggot that praises you, and your kindness cannot be extolled by a worm. The living, the living praise you . . ." (It is perhaps easier to understand why this one didn't make it into the top 150.)

Some of these "noncanonical" psalms were already known from elsewhere, such as "Psalm 154," found in the ancient Greek translation of the Bible called the Septuagint. Others, like the two we just saw, are known only from the Dead Sea Scrolls.

In general, though, the distinction between "the Psalms" and "noncanonical psalms" reflects modern bias more than ancient reality. They simply had more psalms in Qumran than we do now.

More generally, the Dead Sea Sect seems to have had a lot of holy books, only some of which made their way into what we now call the Bible. Some of these books may have been specific to Qumran, but some may have been read more widely and only through accident left out of the Bible. We already know that some of the material from Qumran (like Psalm 151, which, until Qumran, was only known from its Greek translation) was popular outside the desert community.

This is more confirmation that there was a broad collection of holy writings in the centuries leading up to the creation of the Bible, and only some of those writings made the cut. Sometimes political or theological considerations were at play, but other times it was simply a matter of chance.

Through its writings, we've learned a lot about the Dead Sea Sect. Its members were Jews who were devoted to Judaism as they saw it. They lived in the shadow of tyrants and were unhappy with the power structure in Jerusalem.

It is common to equate the Dead Sea Sect with a group of people known as the Essenes (a generally enigmatic group of Jews), among others, but none of the ancient writers describes the Essenes in detail. So the claim that the Dead Sea Sect are the Essenes is mostly just a matter of equating two unknowns with each other.

Despite what we do know, then, we are left with a vexing set of questions: What was the connection between the inhabitants of Qumran and more mainstream schools of thought? Did they compose the scrolls they kept? Why were these people living in the desert? Or did some of them live in cities?

So on one hand the scrolls are both fascinating in their own right and instructive about the state of monotheism in the years leading up to the birth of Jesus and the destruction of the Second Temple. But in solving some mysteries, they have also created new ones. Though who knows? Perhaps at this very moment an animal in the desert is leading a child to a whole new window into the past.

Either way, the Dead Sea Scrolls represent an alternative biblical tradition that was all but unknown for about two thousand years. Next we look at another alternative, which is similar since it reveals debate and internal conflict about what the Bible should be but also different since it has been front and center since it was first composed.

3

THE SEPTUAGINT: HOW SEVENTY SCHOLARS TOOK SEVENTY DAYS TO GET IT WRONG

As with many matters of importance from the last few centuries of the first millennium B.C., the story of the first great translation of the Bible begins with Alexander the Great.

And also as with many matters from that time period, part of Alexander the Great's contribution was to die.

Alexander rose to power in his home kingdom of Macedon, north of Greece. Next he conquered Greece, defeated the Persian rulers of Jerusalem, marched through Syria, and conquered Egypt. Then he died.

The ensuing power vacuum let opportunistic generals divvy up Alexander's newly formed empire. One of those generals, Ptolemy Soter, took Egypt. Ptolemy Soter then had a son, Ptolemy II ("Philadelphus"), who ascended to the throne in 283 B.C. and who became convinced during his reign that the "laws of Jews"—that is, the Five Books of Moses—were of value. He decided that his royal library needed a copy, but not in the original Hebrew. In Greek.

So King Ptolemy II asked his librarian to summon Jews from Jerusalem to translate the Five Books into Greek. The librarian wrote to the Jewish high priest in Jerusalem, asking for translators and an authoritative scroll with the Five Books, which Jews called (and still call) the Torah.

The high priest in Jerusalem complied, sending six men from each of the Twelve Tribes of Israel, or seventy-two men in total. While modern readers might find six an unusual number for the high priest to have selected, it made much more sense in antiquity, when the Babylonian system of mathematics based on 6's as well as 10's was still prevalent. (We see remnants of this ancient system in our reckoning of sixty seconds to a minute and sixty minutes to an hour.)

The Jews arrived in Alexandria, Egypt, with gifts for the king and were then treated to a royal banquet, a grand working lunch, as it were. They dined on royal food and discussed their new project. What would the translation look like? How would they translate the Hebrew? And so forth.

The city of Alexandria, named for Alexander the Great, who created it, is cleverly located not right on the Nile delta, but rather some ways away, near a lake called Lake Mareotis. Alexander the Great chose the site carefully, hoping to avoid the navigation problems that come from silt that piles up in the Nile. Alexander then dug a canal to connect the lake to the Nile, creating a city with convenient water access both to the Nile and the Mediterranean. The city continued to grow under Ptolemy II's father, Ptolemy Soter, who built a lighthouse on the nearby island of Pharos to help coordinate navigation. A mirror and fire atop a structure of some six hundred feet, or maybe more, directed ships to Alexandria. (The lighthouse, the first of its kind, was called the Pharos Lighthouse and then, as it became more famous than the island on which it had been built, just the Pharos. To this day, the word for "lighthouse" in most Romance languages is some variation on the word "faro.")

This island of Pharos was chosen as the spot where the high priest's seventy-two translators would work on their translation.

As chance would have it, the translators finished their task exactly seventy-two days later. Upon its completion, the translators read their work to the elders and other leaders of the Jewish community, who gave it an enthusiastic and universal endorsement. It was so good, they said, that not a single word should ever be changed. In fact, it turned out that every translator, working in isolation, had come up with exactly the same perfect translation. This was proof of the validity of the work.

Details of the story differ from account to account. Not all variations emphasize the isolation of the translators. According to some, there were only seventy translators working for seventy days, a figure that survives in the name of the translation, the Septuagint (sep-TOO-a-jint), which comes from the Greek word *septuaginta,* "seventy." It also survives in the common abbreviation for the work, LXX, which we will use here. (It is particularly scholarly to use a Roman numeral to represent a Greek word.)

Though the original account only concerns the Torah, the terms Septuagint and LXX refer more broadly to Greek translations of the entire Hebrew Bible, a topic we return to below.

Our primary account of this story—Ptolemy II, the librarian, the high priest in Jerusalem, the seventy-two men from the Twelve Tribes of Israel, all of it—comes from something called the Letter of Aristeas, also known as the Epistle of Aristeas. The lengthy document, preserved through numerous medieval copies, has the form of a personal letter from a man who calls himself Aristeas to his friend or brother Philocrates.

But a third name for the document, Pseudo-Aristeas, reflects the fact that it was probably not a personal letter, probably not written by Aristeas, and probably not written during the reign of Ptolemy II.

One problem is the number of copies floating around. If this was really simply a letter from Aristeas to his friend, why did so many people make copies? Equally, the letter has the flavor of having been written by a Jew, though Aristeas claims that he is Greek.

A more fundamental problem has to do with the Twelve Tribes. Aristeas lists not only the tribes but the names of the six representatives from each one. However, the tribes of Israel had long since been dispersed, and they no longer functioned as the primary association network of the Jewish people. At best, the notion of the Twelve Tribes would have been symbolic. More likely, people living in Jerusalem at the time wouldn't even have known which tribe they were from unless they were Levites (who retained a privileged role).

Scholars suspect that the letter was written as much as one hundred years after the translation of the Septuagint, and that its purpose was to defend the legitimacy of the Greek translation, because all of the details of the Letter of Aristeas seem to point ardently in that direction. The involvement of the high priest shows that the translation was officially sanctioned. The inclusion of all twelve tribes suggests universal support for the project. The unanimity of opinion about its success suggests quality work. The Septuagint, as described in the Letter of Aristeas, is an official, universally approved translation of the highest caliber, a God-inspired work.

The vehemence with which the author defends the Septuagint suggests that it was under attack. If so, there were probably two camps, one in favor of the Septuagint and one opposed to it. While it has been proposed that the Letter of Aristeas was designed to support the Septuagint over other Greek translations, most scholars agree that the battle lines were drawn over whether to use a Greek translation at all. If so, this debate was part of the broader conflict in the final centuries of the first millennium B.C. regarding the hellenization of Judaism.

One detail in particular cries out for scrutiny. The author of the letter—let us call him Aristeas for convenience—describes a letter he wrote to King Ptolemy II of Egypt. In that letter, he notes that Jews worship "the same god . . . that we [the Greek rulers of Egypt] do, Your Highness, though we call him . . . Zeus." In other words, says Aristeas, we're all basically the same, whether we worship the Greek Zeus or the Jewish Adonai ("the Lord"). It seems unlikely that the high priest in Jerusalem in the third century would sanction this position. (On the other hand, as we saw above, the second-century priests Jason and Menalaus, who were aligned with Antiochus IV, might have been more sympathetic to such a view.)

Aristeas seems to represent a Hellenistic branch of Judaism, probably based in the Greek-speaking Hellenist city of Alexandria. This in turns suggests that, a hundred years after its creation, the Septuagint was being used by some Jews, while it was condemned, or at least frowned upon, by others. Certainly we know that some Jews in Jerusalem were concerned about the increased hellenization of their capital and, with it, their religion. Perhaps some Jews in Alexandria were, too.

So the Letter of Aristeas probably tells us more about the state of Judaism in the second century B.C. (when it was most likely written) than it does about the creation of the Septuagint in the third. We have no reason to think that Aristeas (or whoever wrote it) had any of the details right.

Aristeas's letter isn't the only external information we have about the Septuagint, but later writers tend merely to embellish and emend the story of its creation. The idea that the translators were working in isolation comes from Philo (a Jewish philosopher who lived in Alexandria around the time of Jesus), who may have been reporting an earlier tradition. The Talmud (middle of the first millennium A.D.), in Megillah 9, repeats Aristeas's story with Philo's innovation. But in another part of the Talmud, Soferim 1, the story is that there were only five translators, not seventy-two or seventy.

The confusion over whether the translators numbered seventy-two or seventy may stem from using "70" as a shorthand for "72," or it may reflect a deliberate attempt to equate in some vague way the seventy translators with the seventy members of the Sanhedrin that served as arbiters of all things Jewish in Jerusalem (though in fact there's some evidence to suggest that the seventy-membered Sanhedrin had seventy-one members).

But even if Aristeas is unreliable on the details, it seems as though the Torah was translated into Greek in the third century B.C. and that that translation formed the beginning of what we now call the Septuagint. The rest of the Bible was translated later.

What we don't know for sure is who commissioned and created the translation. Aristeas may be right that the Greek king of Alexandria was involved, but it seems unlikely.

Another quirk of Aristeas is that he doesn't seem to distinguish between Hebrew writing and the Hebrew language. One reason a Greek translation was needed, according to Aristeas, was that the Torah was written in Hebrew characters. His approach is evidence of the fairly primitive understanding of translation typical in its day.

Both in antiquity and now, it was common to use a writing system for more than one language: French and English, for example, both use the Roman alphabet; Hebrew and Aramaic are both written in Hebrew letters. Though it's less common, there are also languages that are written in more than one script: Jews often wrote Arabic in Hebrew letters during the golden age of Spain, and the Serbo-Croatian of the former Yugoslavia was written in both Roman and Cyrillic letters.

Linguists know that it's easier to convert from one script to another (commonly called transliteration and technically called transcription) than it is to convert from one language to another (translation).

But if Aristeas was aware of this important difference, we see no evidence of it. In fact, even as late as the Talmud, around the middle of the first millennium A.D., we see this same confusion between language and script (Megillah, chapter 2). All of this serves to remind us how far we have come in the fields of linguistics and translation. So we should hardly be surprised that, even though the Septuagint was highly praised in antiquity, it actually proves frustratingly deficient by modern standards.

Despite the uncertainty regarding its creation, though, and the relatively poor quality of the translation, the Septuagint is both an invaluable window into alternative biblical traditions and a source of joyful surprises.

For example, the Septuagint gives us unicorns.

There's a Hebrew word, r'em, and though we don't know exactly what it means, it was clearly an animal of some sort. It seems that the r'em had more than one horn (presumably two), because Deuteronomy 33:17 mentions the "horns of the r'em." It's true that the phrase might mean "horns such as are found on the species r'em," but, even so, there's no reason to think that the r'em had only one horn—any more than a phrase like "the horns of the antelope" in English would mean than an antelope has only one horn. So the r'em doesn't seem to be a unicorn.

Still, the Septuagint takes the Hebrew word r'em and translates it as monokeros, from the Greek mono ("single") and keras ("horn"). This is why Psalm 29:6, for example, involves Sirion (probably Mount Hermon) skipping "like a young unicorn" in the four-hundred-year-old King James Version translation, which takes its cue from the Septuagint. The more modern Jewish Publication Society and New Revised Standard Version translations, relying more closely on the Hebrew, refer instead to "a young wild ox."

The closest mention of a unicorn in the Hebrew of the Bible is Daniel 8:5, which specifically speaks of a goat of some sort with one horn between its eyes. But it's clear from context that that animal and its horn are meant to be symbolic. The next lines talk about a battle between this single-horned goat and a double-horned ram. The one horn proves more powerful than the two, but then the goat with its horn becomes haughty, which precipitates its downfall, in the form of a broken horn that is replaced by four new horns. Then Daniel 8:20–21 spells out the imagery. The two horns of the ram are the kings of Media and Persia, and the one horn of the goat is the original king of Greece. This is an allegory about the downfall of Greece. It's not about a real unicorn. But the Septuagint text is about real unicorns. (We talk more about real and imaginary animals in the next chapter.) In short, we see two biblical traditions, one in which there are unicorns, the other in which there are not.

In Isaiah 34:7, we again find the Hebrew word *r'em*, this time in the plural. Here, though, the Septuagint does not have "unicorns" but rather the seemingly unrelated "mighty ones" or "exalted ones."

What's going on?

This is an example of a common kind of pattern in the Septuagint. It offers us information about the state of the Bible in antiquity, but only in the form of a puzzle that we have to solve. Here the puzzle is why a Hebrew word that seems to refer to an animal gets translated as something completely different.

A bit of Hebrew explains the discrepancy. Hebrew has a letter, Aleph, which by and large serves only to mark vowels and syllabification. We find this letter Aleph in the Hebrew *r'em*, which is why the word is pronounced as two syllables, *r'em*, and not *rem*. Furthermore, Hebrew was originally written in a primarily consonantal script, and the vowels that mark the word as *r'em* and not, say, *r'am*, were added many centuries after the Septuagint was created.

The Hebrew for *r'em* is, in fact, just three letters: Resh (R), Aleph (silent), and Mem (M). This could spell *r'em*, *r'am*, etcetera, but also, if the Aleph were truly silent, *ram*.

And it just so happens that the Hebrew word *ram* means "exalted."

What we see, in other words, is two traditions. In one, based on the Hebrew, we have the word *r'em*, which is a horned animal. In the other, based on the Greek in the Septuagint, we have what looks like a translation of the word *ram* instead of *r'em*.

Which one is right? Did the Hebrew originally say *r'em* or *ram*?

Though the details of Isaiah 34:7, where this word appears, may not seem all that important, the explanation behind the different textual traditions helps us better understand the text of the Bible, because Isaiah 34:7 is not the only place where the text of the Septuagint differs from the Hebrew text of the Bible. There are many such instances. So we turn to a little more background about where the Hebrew and Greek texts come from since, more specifically, the current text of the Septuagint differs from the current text of the Hebrew.

The Hebrew as we know it now is called the Masoretic text (MT), because it was standardized for the most part about 1,100 years ago by a group of people known as the Masoretes and living in Tibereas. (Their name, which comes from the Hebrew *masora*, roughly means "tradition-people.")

As we just saw, the original Hebrew by and large contained only consonants. But after the Jewish exile in A.D. 70, the Jews gradually stopped speaking Hebrew natively, and it became increasingly difficult for them to read the Hebrew consonantal script. By the end of the first millennium A.D., most Jews needed help. So the Masoretes added vocalic reading aides and, when necessary, decided between alternative consonantal traditions.

This Masoretic text, then, is a ninth- and tenth-century understanding of a text that was copied and recopied over the course of more than a thousand years. There's no reason to think that these Masoretes did a perfect job, just as there's no reason to think that the hundreds of years of copying were completely error free. (We'll see one clear case of a Hebrew copying error below.) But we know from manuscript evidence that the Hebrew has been almost perfectly preserved for the past thousand years.

So the Masoretic text is one way of understanding the ancient text of the Hebrew Bible.

The Greek text of the Septuagint, too, is compiled from various copies of copies, among them manuscripts in book (or "codex") form. Three of these are particularly important: the Sinai, Vatican, and Alexandria codices, more commonly known by their Latin names: Codex Sinaiticus, Codex Vaticanus, and Codex Alexandrius. All three of these contain the Greek of the Septuagint and the Greek New Testament. In other words, they are Greek Bibles with both the Old and New Testaments.

Codex Sinaiticus is one of the oldest surviving manuscripts of the Bible in any form, dating from sometime during the fourth century A.D. Of course, the fourth century is about six hundred years after the first parts of the Septuagint were composed. Normally a handwritten copy of something six hundred years after it was written would be suspect, and we would be reluctant to rely on it too heavily. But in this case, Codex Sinaiticus, along with Codex Vaticanus, is just about the best we have.

The "Sinai" part of the name comes from the Monastery of Saint Catherine in the Sinai Peninsula, where the manuscript was found in 1844. (The locals claim that the monastery is built next to the site of the burning bush of Exodus.) The manuscript was probably in the monastery in 1761, too, because it matches the description of what an Italian named Vitaliano Donati described when he visited the holy site. And because the monastery dates back almost to the fourth century, there's no reason to think that the manuscript hasn't been in the Monastery of Saint Catherine for some time longer.

For complicated reasons ultimately traceable in no small part to imperial colonialism, the manuscript is currently kept in various pieces in four different institutions, with the largest section residing in the British Museum, where it ended up via Russia. Smaller pieces are kept in the University of Leipzig library in Germany, the National Library of Russia in Saint Petersburg, and the monastery at which the manuscript was found, which officially classifies the other pieces as "stolen." A high-quality reproduction is also available online.

The manuscript has worn away in places, so it's no longer complete, but it's in remarkably good shape. Some of the Septuagint and most of the New Testament that it originally contained are still visible.

So one copy of the Septuagint is the one discovered in the nineteenth century, probably observed in the eighteenth century, and probably dating to the fourth century.

About as old is Codex Vaticanus, which, not surprisingly, is kept in the Vatican. While some of it, too, has worn away, the Septuagint part is more complete than in Codex Sinaiticus, though at times the text of the Septuagint in Codex Vaticanus seems to have been emended long after it was originally written. Codex Vaticanus is our second bit of evidence as to what the Septuagint originally looked like.

Around the beginning of the seventeenth century, the patriarch of Constantinople and former patriarch of Alexandria, Cyril Lucar, sent a gift to King James I of England (the same King James who commissioned the King James Version translation of the Bible). It didn't reach England until after James died, so in 1627 it was accepted by King Charles I. The gift was a manuscript of the Septuagint and New Testament dating to, it would seem, the fifth century, not long after Codex Vaticanus and Codex Sinaiticus were written. Because Lucar was from Alexandria and, we assume, took the manuscript with him when he left for Constantinople, the manuscript is known as Codex Alexandrius. With Sinaiticus and Vaticanus, it forms the third of the three major known copies of the Septuagint. It is mostly complete.

Together, these three manuscripts give us a pretty good idea of what the Septuagint was like in the fourth and fifth centuries. But we also know, from earlier evidence, that the Greek underwent considerable changes before those three major manuscripts were created. In the third century A.D., a theologian in Alexandria named Origen created a massive work comparing four different Greek translations of the Old Testament, including the Septuagint. His work, which also recorded the Hebrew text and a transliteration of the Hebrew text, is known as the Hexapla, because of the six-columned format that he chose. But Jerome, a scholar who lived in the fourth century A.D., writes that Origen also changed the Septuagint as he created his Hexapla so that, Jerome says, there is hardly any existing copy of the Septuagint uncorrupted by Origen's changes.

All of this evidence, and more, points in the direction of a Greek translation of the Five Books of Moses that grew over time, gradually encompassing the rest of the Hebrew Bible and also gradually changing.

Unfortunately, the term "Septuagint" (or "LXX") is generally applied indiscriminately to all of these various translations, from the original third century B.C. Greek version of the Five Books of Moses (though we don't have any actual copies of it) to the fourth-century A.D. Codex Vaticanus, which contains, probably, Origen's modifications to the original text, as well as numerous subsequent translations of the other books of the Old Testament.

So when we talk about "what the Septuagint says," we are not usually talking about what was written in the third century B.C. but rather an ongoing translation that began back then and ended hundreds of years later.

Similarly, as we saw, even when we talk about "what the Hebrew says," we usually mean one interpretation of that Hebrew, though the Hebrew has generally been better preserved.

This is why we have a puzzle to be solved every time we see a difference between the Septuagint and the Hebrew. Why are the two versions different? Did the translators get the Greek translation wrong in the third century B.C.? Was correct Greek miscopied at some point?

Was the Hebrew miscopied at some point, so that the Greek shows us the original text? And what does all of this teach us about the Bible as it existed in antiquity?

We've already seen one such puzzle, in the form of the Hebrew *r'em* (an oxlike animal) that variously became a unicorn and even the completely different "exalted one" in the Septuagint. Proverbs 18:10 demonstrates another kind of puzzle. In Hebrew we have "the name of the Lord is a tower of might," while the Septuagint runs along the lines of "the name of the Lord is of great might." In other words, the Masoretic text has a tower that the Septuagint doesn't. Why?

In this case, a bit of Hebrew grammar explains what happened. (Readers who know Hebrew may wish to try to solve this themselves: how could "is a tower of might" become "is of great might"?)

The Hebrew word for "tower" is spelled M-G-D-L, and, at least according to the tenth-century Masoretes, pronounced *migdal*. The word has two parts, a root G.D.L and a prefix *m*-. The root has to do with greatness and, in particular, size. The prefix *m*- is one way of creating a noun. Together they indicate a specific big thing (or perhaps mighty thing), namely, a tower.

As it happens, there's another prefix *m*-, spelled the same way but with a different meaning: "from" or "of." It seems as though the Septuagint translators saw M-G-D-L and read it differently. Instead of seeing a noun, *migdal* ("tower"), they saw the other prefix and read the word as "of G-D-L." The letters G-D-L also make up a noun (pronounced *godel*, according to the Masoretes) that means "greatness." This led the translators to render the text as "of greatness of might" in Greek instead of "a tower of might," as the Hebrew has it.

Which one is right, the Masoretic Hebrew or the Septuagint? Both make sense, particularly in the poetry of Proverbs. And both are possible based on the original consonantal text.

In this case, we have strong evidence that the Septuagint got it wrong, for two reasons. First, the second half of Proverbs 18:10 notes that the righteous can run into it (the thing from the first part of the verse) to find refuge. Running into a "tower" makes more sense than running into "great might." Furthermore, Proverbs 18:11 talks about a "city of might." So if the Masoretic text is correct, verses 10–11 form a pair, the first about a "tower of might" and the second about a "city of might," while if the Septuagint is right, there's no poetic connection between the two verses.

One wonders, though, how this error crept in. If we as modern readers can easily see that the second part of the verse points in the direction of "tower" and not "greatness," why couldn't the Septuagint translators? The answer is that they seem to have been looking only at the single word, MGDL, and not at the context. And this is not the only case where the Septuagint translators seem to have ignored the context of the words they were translating. It's a recurring deficiency of the translation.

Another puzzle comes from Proverbs 31, the text extolling the virtues of women, so central that Jewish men traditionally sing it to their wives on the eve of the Sabbath. (This religious song is usually referred to by its first two words: *eshet chayil,* that is, "woman of valor." The original Hebrew word *chayil* combined valor in general with the prowess of a warrior. Modern Hebrew retains the word but focuses more narrowly on its military overtones. This is why *eshet chayil* was an apt and even literary translation of the title of the television series *Wonder Woman* when it first aired in Israel. Unfortunately, because of the title and its religious familiarity, thousands of ultra-Orthodox men tuned in and were then shocked to find a woman in her underwear.)

The Hebrew of verse 21 reads, "She need not worry about snow in her household, because her entire household is clothed in crimson." Though not entirely clear, the point of the line is probably to juxtapose the whiteness of the snow with bright red clothing. But the

Septuagint has a completely different reading, "The husband is not concerned about the household when he tarries anywhere . . . ," as if to say, he trusts his wife even when he's out of town.

At first glance, the Septuagint and Masoretic text seem completely different. The Hebrew is about snow, while the Greek is about dawdling and potential hanky-panky. How could one mix them up? Here the answer comes not from a closer look at Hebrew but rather at Greek. (And Greek speakers may now wish to try to solve this puzzle themselves before reading on.)

In Greek, "snow" comes from the root *xion* while "tarry" comes from the root *xron*. They're almost the same. The most likely explanation here is that somewhere in one of the various copies, the Greek *i* was accidentally changed to an *r*. Then the rest of the Greek was changed to make sense of a word with the new root.

On the one hand, this is probably just a mistake in copying, not a mistake in translating. But it also shows us something else about the Septuagint. When something didn't make sense, the translators—or, more likely, later copyists—sometimes reworked things. What could have been simply a misspelled word ("snow" in Greek with an *r* instead of an *i*) ended up instead as a correctly spelled word in a newly invented sentence. This troubling tendency to revise things makes it harder to recover the original text of the translation.

A really difficult puzzle comes from Proverbs 29:1. The Hebrew there says of a reprover who is stiff-necked, "He will suddenly be broken, and there will be no healing." But the Greek has a different fate for the reprover, "He will suddenly be set on fire (!) and there will be no healing." What's going on? Where is the fire coming from?

The first Hebrew word of the verse is *ish* ("man"), spelled Aleph-Yud-Shin. If the Yud is removed, we end up with *esh*, "fire." But the Greek translates *ish* as *aner* ("man") here, so it seems that the translators correctly understood that word. And, in any event, it's in the wrong part of the sentence. So there seems to be nothing in Proverbs 29:1 that has anything to do with fire.

A potential answer comes from Proverbs 6:15, which, in Hebrew, also ends with, "He will suddenly be broken and there will be no healing." There, though, the sudden break and lack of healing is the second of two phrases that describe someone's fate. The first phrase, with the same general meaning, is "his calamity will come suddenly." The Hebrew for "his calamity" is *eido,* spelled Aleph-Yud-Daled-Vav. The final Vav means "his," and we can ignore it for now. It's the Aleph-Yud-Daled that spell "calamity" that we care about.

In antiquity, the Hebrew letters Yud and Vav were written almost identically (they still are), so it would have been easy to mix them up. Therefore, it wouldn't have been hard to read Aleph-Yud-Daled as Aleph-Vav-Daled, and that just happens to spell *oud,* which means "firebrand." And that's where the fire may come from.

It looks as though there was some confusion between Proverbs 29:1 and Proverbs 6:15, and the Septuagint put a misunderstanding of Proverbs 6:15 into the very similar Proverbs 29:1.

These are just a few of the puzzles that are presented by the different Hebrew and Greek traditions.

When the Masoretic text and the Septuagint disagree, most people assume that the Septuagint has it wrong, as in the examples we've seen so far. The Masoretic text seems to have been copied much more faithfully and with considerably greater precision, because the text was deemed holy. The Septuagint, on the other hand, as a translation, might have been wrong from its inception, and, furthermore, it was changed more frequently and copied less accurately, because the stakes were lower.

This is why, when scholars noticed that the text of Deuteronomy 31:1 in the Septuagint says something different from the text of the

Masoretic text, they assumed that the Septuagint had it wrong. The Hebrew of the Torah, after all, had been copied most carefully of all.

The Hebrew text of Deuteronomy 31:1 reads, "Moses went and spoke these words to all of Israel." But it's an odd way to begin chapter 31, because chapter 30 ends with Moses speaking to the same people of Israel. Where did Moses go if he kept talking to the same group?

Various attempts to understand this apparent anomaly have been suggested, including the possibility that this was an expression of sorts, along the lines of, "Why did he have to go and do that?" But it doesn't seem likely.

The Septuagint, by contrast, starts chapter 31 differently. It reads, "Moses finished speaking all of these words to all of the children of Israel." On the one hand, the Septuagint makes more sense. On the other hand, the generally inaccurate nature of the Septuagint led scholars for many years to think that this was simply a mistake in the Septuagint, just one of many.

But then along came the Dead Sea Scrolls. And while most of the time the scrolls agree with the Masoretic text, in this case their text differs by two letters, which appear in reverse order. The Hebrew in the Masoretic text has v-y-l-k. The first two letters are part of the complicated tense system in Hebrew and combine to indicate the third person singular ("he") in the past tense ("did"). The last two letters are the verb "go": so, "he did go" or "he went."

But where the Masoretic text has l-k at the end, the Dead Sea Scrolls have a different verb, k-l. And that verb means "finish." So the scrolls, like the Septuagint, have "Moses finished speaking," which is the same as "Moses went" in Hebrew except for the order of two letters in the verb.

Based on the evidence in the Dead Sea Scrolls, most scholars now think that this is a rare case of the Septuagint getting it right, and not the Masoretic text. Chapter 31 probably once began with the information that Moses finished his first speech and then began his second.

So here the Septuagint almost certainly shows us the original text from over two thousand years ago, while the accepted Hebrew is the result of a scribal error.

In addition to mistakes that make the Septuagint and Masoretic text differ, sometimes the translators of the Septuagint purposely updated the text to make it more relevant.

For example, Deuteronomy 23:18 (also numbered 23:17) reads, "None of the daughters of Israel shall be a temple prostitute; none of the sons of Israel shall be a temple prostitute." The verse is obviously about avoiding the temptations of the cult prostitutes (prostitutes who worked in and around sacred sites) in the time of the Temple.

The Septuagint has a longer version. The first part is close, though different, warning against female and male prostitutes more generally. Then the Septuagint adds a whole second phrase that doesn't translate anything in the Hebrew but, rather, mentions more current cultural icons of the day, probably having to do with a non-Jewish Egyptian Mystery cult. In this sense, the Septuagint is both a translation of the Hebrew and a commentary on it, like a modern American translation adding a line to Deuteronomy 23:18 warning Israelite women and men not to be Wiccans.

We see the same kind of updating in Isaiah 3:18–24, a particularly difficult passage to translate because it deals with various fashion accessories. For example, the NRSV translation of Isaiah 3:21, trying to understand the Hebrew, refers to "the signet rings and the nose rings." By contrast, the Septuagint substitutes two Egyptian dress items. The next verse mentions the Hebrew *charit*. The KJV calls this a "crisping pin," while the NRSV understands it differently and calls it a "handbag." But the Septuagint refers specifically to a Laconian (Spartan) transparent garment. It's possible that the reference to Laconia (the capital of which was Sparta) had lost its geographic sense by the time it was used (just like Danish pastries, which don't have to come from Denmark), but it's more likely that this was a contemporary cultural reference, like the Egyptian Mystery cult.

Again, the Septuagint took a verse in the Old Testament and offered an updated version.

Throughout the Septuagint we find this sort of variation, usually with only small changes, additions, or emendations, but sometimes the differences are much bigger. In the Book of Esther, we have an entire story that is reframed and revised, starting right at the beginning. The Book of Esther, set in the ancient Persian city of Susa ("Shushan" in the Masoretic text, "Shush" now), describes how the Jewish Mordecai and Esther rise up against religious Persian tyranny, or, depending on your point of view, how a people called the Jews refuse to get on board with the Persian Empire.

Everything about the story suggests an historical allegory—that is, a fictional story set in real history with real historical themes. Shushan, or Susa, is a real historical place in Persia, located about 150 miles east of the Tigris River, between two smaller rivers called the Dez and Karkheh. Persia and Media, also real places, are mentioned in the text, too.

The reigning king in the story is called Ahashverosh in Hebrew. The Hebrew word *rosh* means "head," so the name Ahashverosh may be Ahashve-rosh, that is, Ahashve "the Great." Or the name may be derived directly from the Persian form that gives us the Greek and English Xerxes. Either way, Ahashverosh in the Book of Esther would correspond to Xerxes the Great, who ruled Persia from 485–465 B.C. In the Septuagint, the king is called Artaxerxes, whose rule was several decades later, from 404–358 B.C.

The Jewish heroes of the story are called Mordecai and Esther, names that suggest the pagan gods Marduk and Isthar, both known to the Persians and to the Babylonians. The heroes are thus the perfect symbols of Jews who have assimilated, the way modern-day Jews named Jesus or Christina might be. The Septuagint hellenizes Mordecai's name into Mardochaeus, but leaves Esther the way it is. In the Hebrew, but not the Septuagint, Esther also has a Hebrew name, Hadassah. Again, this makes her remarkably like many modern American Jews, who have both an American name and a Hebrew one. In the text, Mordecai is identified as the great-grandson of Kish, who had left Jerusalem with the Babylonian exile, which took place about a hundred years earlier than the events in the story (if the king is Xerxes, as the Masoretic text has it) or about two hundred years earlier (in the case of Artaxerxes of the Septuagint). While the first scenario is within the realm of biological plausibility, the second is not. But either way, most scholars agree that the story comes under the category of historical fiction and was probably meant as such when it was written.

In Hebrew, the story jumps right in with the setting and the plot, "In the days of Ahashverosh . . . in the third year of his reign, he gave a banquet." The Septuagint similarly opens with the setting ("In the second year of the reign of Artaxerxes"). But before introducing the plot, the Septuagint describes a vision.

Mordecai sees two serpents "ready for battle" come forward amid thunder and earthquakes on a day of darkness and doom across the entire earth. Through their voice (or roar, or whatever serpents do), every nation prepares for war to battle the "righteous nation," which in response calls out to God. Then, "like a great river from a small spring" comes light with the sunrise, and the "lowly are exalted." Mordecai, the Septuagint tells us, understands God's plan from the dream. Then the Septuagint picks up the plot, as in the Hebrew version of Esther.

The Greek word for "serpent" here is *drakon,* and to understand the full imagery of the intriguing dream we have to take a brief detour through that Greek word and the English "dragon" that is derived from it. Because of the similarity between the English and Greek words, some translations wrongly assume that the ancient Greek *drakon* was a modern dragon, but it wasn't. Rather, the *drakon* was a water-dwelling creature along the lines of a serpent. For example, when Moses throws down his staff to turn it into a snake in Exodus 7, it becomes a *drakon* in the Greek of the Septuagint. Psalms 103:26 (also numbered 104:26) connects the *drakon* to ships, and Job 7:12 connects the *drakon* to the sea. The only way the animals in Mordecai's dream could have been dragons is if they were like the magic Puff who lived by the sea. The point is, rather, that they were creatures that would naturally dwell in the water of the dream.

The dream thus presents the reader with two images: ordinary creatures in their usual habitat are set for battle, and the whole earth will go to war. These combine to suggest an epic and universal event, perhaps even the apocalypse (which, as we saw in the last chapter, was a common concern toward the end of the first millennium B.C.). Furthermore, the exaltation of the lowly ("the lowly are exalted") tells the reader that this is a story with an underdog who will eventually triumph. This second aspect becomes clear to anyone who reads the story, because in the end the Jewish minority successfully defeats a prince in the king's court.

But the first message of the dream—the fact that the story is universally important—is much less prominent in the Hebrew.

The details of the dream are explained in another Septuagint addition later in the story. Mordecai comes to understand that the river is Esther and that the two serpents are Haman (the Persian prince in the story who wants to destroy the Jews) and himself. This second addition doesn't quite seem to match up with the dream, because in the dream the serpents appear to be jointly aligned against Israel, while in the explanation one of the serpents is Mordecai himself, who sides with Israel rather than against it. Some people therefore suspect that the dream was independently known and retrofitted into the story. (A more daring explanation might suggest that both Mordecai and Haman, by refusing to work things out, were both responsible for the carnage.)

The additional text in the Septuagint also adds two other significant bits of information. First, it expands on the central theme of Jewish salvation by comparing it to two lots that God created, one for the people of God and one for the nations. As in English, the Greek and Hebrew words for "lot" have two meanings. The first is a way of making a random choice, such as by "drawing lots" in English, or the related word "lottery." The second meaning is that which is obtained by such a random drawing and, in particular, what will happen in the future. This is reflected in the English "my lot in life."

The theme of lots is central to the story in the Book of Esther, even being reflected in the word *purim,* which is the name of the holiday that celebrates the salvation of the Jews here and, according to the text, means "lots" (though as it happens, there is in fact no Hebrew or Persian word *purim* that means "lots"). According to the Hebrew, the connection is that lots were thrown to determine when to kill the Jews. The Septuagint adds a second interpretation along with the first— namely, the two lots that represent God's people and the other people.

This notion of God's people versus other people, and, in particular, a "lot" for each one, is a common theme in the Dead Sea Scrolls. Its inclusion here, too, suggests that the Dead Sea Sect and whoever wrote this bit of text for the Septuagint may have been thinking along similar lines.

Second, the Septuagint adds a note (technically a "colophon") indicating when and where the book, called a "letter" by the note itself, was written. The Septuagint puts the creation of the letter in the "fourth year of the reign of Ptolemy and Cleopatra." Unfortunately, there were so many people named Ptolemy and Cleopatra that this only narrows things down to approximately several hundred years after the setting of the story, which is appropriate, but we have no reason to believe that the colophon was written at the same time as the rest of the text. The colophon is, therefore, primarily of interest to scholars who want to understand the evolution of the text.

One final detail is worthy of note. The text of the Masoretic text repeatedly calls Haman (the antagonist) an "Agagite," a people about which not much is known, though from 1 Samuel 15:8, we do know that Agag was king of the Amalekites. The Septuagint, on the other hand, uses either "Bougean" or "Macedonian," where the Masoretic text has "Agagite." There are no known people called the Bougeans, but the Macedonians were the people in charge of Ptolemaic Egypt and the people who, from time to time, were in charge of Persia, too, as well as Jerusalem. But the Jews by and large liked the Macedonians, at least until the campaign of Antiochus IV ("the Mad") in the second century B.C. led to the Maccabean revolt.

In short, the Greek and Hebrew texts have different villains.

The dream, as the first major segment of text that appears in the Septuagint but not the Masoretic text, is commonly known as Addition A, while its explanation, the sixth additional segment, is Addition F. In between are, of course, four more additions. Two of them (Addition B and Addition E) are expanded texts of royal decrees, and a third (Addition D) describes Esther as she enters the king's chamber.

We've looked at Addition A and the universality it introduces to the story through Mordecai's dream. And we've seen that Addition F expands on the notion of lots.

It's Addition C, though, that, along with Additions A and F, changes the entire nature of the story. Addition C contains the text of two prayers to God, one by Mordecai and one by Esther. The Hebrew text of the Book of Esther doesn't contain God's name, making it the only book of the Bible not to mention God explicitly. Obviously, this is no small matter, and God's apparent absence has given rise to discussion about where God was, whether the story may allegorically allude to a godless exile, how God works behind the scenes, and so forth. But the dream in Addition A and its explanation in Addition F refer to God's plan, and Addition C is an actual acknowledgment of God. The whole discussion of why God seems to be missing from the Book of Esther only applies to the Hebrew version, not the Septuagint.

These additions and nuances raise questions about the very nature of the story. Is it about God's plan, or a godless exile? Who is the real villain in the story? Why is the notion of lots so important? What is the connection between the Greek text and the Hebrew? All in all, we are left wondering if we have perhaps misunderstood what the story is really about.

We are also left wondering why this is both the one book of the Old Testament that's missing from Qumran and the one book that the Septuagint completely revises. It would be a surprising coincidence, but so far no convincing reason has been put forth to explain the connection.

Was the Book of Esther so radical that the Dead Sea Sect had to reject it and the authors of the Septuagint had to change it? Does it reflect a deep division in Judaism toward the end of the first millennium B.C.? Something else completely? We just don't know.

In addition to the cases we've seen so far, in which the Septuagint gives us new insight into what the text may have originally meant, the Septuagint is an invaluable guide to how Hebrew may have sounded in antiquity.

Our current tradition of pronouncing Hebrew stems from the Masoretes, who lived in Tiberias about 1,100 years ago. But as we've seen, they lived long after Hebrew had ceased to be spoken natively.

We now refer to the Masoretes' system of dots and dashes that record the sounds of Hebrew as "the vowels," because the original way of writing Hebrew by and large only indicates the consonants. So a name like Rebecca, in the ancient Hebrew system, was recorded as R-B-K-H. The H at the end indicated the vowel /a/. But beyond that, the spelling doesn't tell us if the name was pronounced as Rabaka, Ribika, Rubeka, etcetera. And, furthermore—at least if we are to believe the Masoretes—some letters, such as the Bet (*B* or *V*), had more than one pronunciation, so R-B-K-H might also have been Revuka, Ruvika, and so forth.

Anyone who spoke Hebrew would know the words and therefore know how to pronounce them, just as English speakers can read "a long, windy road" and "a really windy day" and know to pronounce "windy" differently in each case. But by the time the Masoretes lived, most people didn't speak Hebrew anymore, and the old system of writing was insufficient to tell these non-Hebrew speakers how to pronounce the words. The Masoretes sought to correct this apparent deficiency in Hebrew writing, and their solution was a system of diacritics over, under, and in the letters to indicate their exact pronunciation.

Unfortunately, we have no reason to believe that the Masoretes knew how Hebrew had been pronounced in the days of the Bible. They lived too long after the language had ceased to be spoken natively, and in addition we find considerable disagreement among the Masoretes themselves. Our current pronunciation comes from the Tiberian Masoretes, but other groups understood Hebrew differently, and we even find discord among the Tiberians. This disparity is hardly surprising. Their task was similar to asking modern Americans how they think Chaucer pronounced his words. (As it happens, we have a reasonably good sense of what Chaucer's English sounded like, but not from asking speakers of modern English. Our information comes from the kind of science that wasn't available to the Masoretes a thousand years ago.)

But at least the earliest parts of the Septuagint date to a time when Hebrew was still spoken widely. And we can get a sense of what that Hebrew sounded like by looking at how Hebrew names are spelled in Greek.

Returning to Rebecca's name, R-B-K-H, we find the form "Rivka" from the Tiberian Masoretes, but in Greek we have "Rebekka," an understanding that differs greatly from the Masoretic pronunciation. The vowels are different, *e* in Greek versus *i* in Hebrew. And the Septuagint records a trisyllabic word where the Masoretic name has only two syllables. Because the Greek writing system includes more pronunciation information than the original Hebrew, we tend to trust the Greek more than the Tiberian understanding of the Hebrew from a thousand years afterward. In this case, the Tiberian Masoretes correctly conveyed the general nature of the name Rebecca, but not the details.

In general, this is the pattern we find. The Masoretes tended to get the pronunciation of consonants right, it seems, but not the vowels. Most of our English names in the Bible come from the Greek, not the Hebrew, which is why the English names so often differ from their Hebrew counterparts. In addition to "Rebecca" for "Rivka," the Hebrew "moshe" is "Moses" in English, for example, the Hebrew "yerushalayim" is "Jerusalem" (originally, "Yerushalem"), and so forth. These all reflect the Greek in the Septuagint, which in each case is nearly identical to our English.

The fact that we get our English names from the Greek alludes to the cultural importance of the Septuagint. One might expect that the original Hebrew would take precedence over the Greek translation, and it normally would, except that Greek ended up as the official language of the nascent Christianity in the first few centuries A.D. So among Christians, the Greek translation in the Septuagint became

the primary text of the Old Testament, and it was the Greek translation that formed the connection between the New Testament and
scriptural tradition.

By and large, this nuance only affects names (for example, "Moses"
instead of "Moshe" when he appears in the New Testament) and a few
other details, as we've seen. But every so often, the New Testament
quotes a section of the Bible in which the Greek and the Hebrew differ
dramatically, so the New Testament quotation of the Old Testament
doesn't actually appear in the Hebrew of the Old Testament.

One such case lies at the center of an ongoing bitter controversy.

The Gospel of Matthew in verse 1:23 connects the virgin birth of
Jesus with Isaiah 7:14, quoting the prophet, in Greek, as saying,
"look, the virgin is pregnant and will bear a son, who will be named
Emmanuel." The Hebrew name Emmanuel looks like a combination
of *emmanu* (or *immanu*), which means "with us" and *el* ("God"), so,
as the Greek of the New Testament explains, the name Emmanuel
means "God is with us," further cementing the connection between
Isaiah 7:14 and the birth of Jesus.

The Greek word in Matthew for "virgin" is *parthenos,* and it does
mean virgin. The same Greek word, *parthenos,* appears in the text of
the Septuagint translation of the prophet Isaiah. This is why Matthew
can make the connection between the two passages. They both contain the word *parthenos.* However, the original Hebrew for Isaiah
7:14 refers not to a virgin but rather more generally to a young woman
(*alma,* in Hebrew). In other words, Matthew's citation of Isaiah relies
on the Greek mistranslation.

We have already seen two aspects of the Septuagint that help explain how the translators could have made such a mistake. They
tended to look at each word individually, so the fact that this young
woman was pregnant may not have influenced their translation decision. And they tended to translate loosely.

A third bit of information about antiquity is helpful here. Most young women were virgins, and most virgins were young women. The situation is similar to teenagers and high school students in America. By and large, teenagers today are in high school, and high schoolers are in their teens, though the fact that college usually begins around age eighteen makes the comparison imperfect. Still, it wouldn't be a terrible translation mistake to change, "he saw a group of ten teenagers" into "he saw a group of ten high school students."

Similarly, it wasn't usually a terrible gaffe to use "virgin" for "young woman," and Isaiah 7:14 isn't the only place we find this error in the Septuagint. For example, in Genesis 24:16, Rebecca is described in Hebrew as a "young woman who was a virgin." In Greek, she is described twice as a *parthenos,* yielding the somewhat odd, "a virgin who was a virgin."

Usually, this kind of translation looseness didn't make much difference. Literary style aside, the meaning of Genesis 24:16 remains pretty much the same whether Rebecca is a young woman who is a virgin or a virgin who is a virgin. But, of course, there is one case in which the difference between virgin and young woman is huge, and that is when she is pregnant.

Unfortunately, the loose character of the translation in the Septuagint (which allowed "virgin" in Greek for what was "young woman" in Hebrew) was made even worse by the translators' inattention to context (so they didn't take into account the woman's pregnancy when they translated the word describing her). And the Greek ended up, inadvertently, making a virgin pregnant in Isaiah 7:14.

Then the New Testament quoted the line—in Greek, of course—ensuring the continued centrality of a translation mistake.

Other ancient Greek translations use the more accurate Greek word *neanis* ("young woman") in Isaiah 7:14, but we don't know if their authors did so trying to be more accurate or advancing an agenda to downplay the virgin birth. Similarly, it's possible that the Septuagint was emended in light of Matthew's text. As we've seen, we don't have any Septuagint manuscripts going back to the formation of Christianity, so we don't know for sure what the original translation was.

The mistake doesn't affect the Gospel of Matthew or the virgin birth itself. The virgin birth is clearly and amply described elsewhere in the Gospel of Matthew and other books of the New Testament. And Matthew knew that the details of his story didn't match Isaiah 7:14 perfectly. (For one thing, the child Matthew is describing was called Jesus, while the child in Isaiah is called Emmanuel.) And for that matter, a young woman can be a virgin. But we do see how a project originally designed simply to bring the Five Books of Moses to Greek-speaking Jews in Egypt ended up both changing the Bible itself and preserving alternative traditions of what should be in it.

Like the Dead Sea Scrolls, which encapsulated one version of pre-Christian Judaism and kept it sealed in a virtual desert vault, the Septuagint records what various groups of people thought the Bible said. Some of these people, perhaps through historical accident, would become the minority. In at least one case (where two letters were switched in Hebrew), we are almost sure that this "minority" opinion used to be the majority, until a copying mistake became mainstream. In another case (the young woman becoming a virgin), we are equally confident that it was the Septuagint that introduced the mistake, even though that error, too, became mainstream. In many other cases, though, the differences don't reflect right and wrong but rather varied legitimate points of view. The additions and changes in the Book of Esther, for example, suggest a particularly vehement disagreement, although we are left with the uncomfortable feeling that we haven't quite understood its essence. Even the different pronunciation traditions evidence divisions that were later smoothed over.

All of these might have been lost to history were it not for the seventy-two men from the Twelve Tribes of Israel who took seventy-two days to translate the Bible—even though the men probably weren't from the Twelve Tribes, probably didn't take seventy-two days for their translation, and probably didn't even number seventy-two.

4

JOSEPHUS: THE ONLY MAN
TO BE A FLY ON EVERY WALL

History is truly the witness of the times, the light of truth.
—CICERO

The year was A.D. 37. Just a few years earlier, Jesus had been crucified, an event that would be commemorated by Christians around the world for at least the next two thousand years. Thirty-three years later, the Jews would be exiled from Jerusalem, an event that would be commemorated by Jews around the world for at least the next two thousand years.

Even if nothing else had happened in the first century A.D.—if the inhabitants of the world had slept for a hundred years, waking only twice to witness the dawning Christianity and the demolition of the millennium-old Jewish capital—those hundred years in and around Jerusalem would have shaped Western life.

But, obviously, much more happened in that tumultuous century. The Romans expanded, not just annexing Jerusalem in the east but also Britain in the west (where they created a city called London). Rome's first emperor, Augustus, died, as did Ovid, the famous Roman poet. The Gospels were written. A group of Jews fled to a Herodian fortress in the Judean Desert and, after unsuccessfully defending themselves against a Roman onslaught, committed mass suicide. A community in Qumran, also in the desert, came to an end after nearly three centuries, leaving behind scrolls that would remain hidden for almost two millennia. The Rabbis, who would give the world Judaism as it is known today, rose to power. And so on.

Our single biggest source of information about most of these events are the writings of a Jew born in Jerusalem in A.D. 37 with the name Yosef ben Mattityahu in Hebrew. Joseph, son of Mattathias. In Aramaic, another language commonly spoken in Jerusalem, he was Yosef bar Mattatyahu. And in Greek, the third major language of Jerusalem, his name was Josepos. But it is in Latin, a language despised by the denizens of Jerusalem, that he is best known: Flavius Josephus.

In addition to what he tells us about history, Josephus provides historical and other background information that's missing from the New Testament (like why Herod was so important, and the real relationship between Jesus and John the Baptist). And in a work variously called *Jewish Antiquities, Antiquities of the Jews,* or for convenience just *Antiquities,* he summarizes the Old Testament, providing pivotal details (like the purpose of the Tower of Babel) that were cut from the text that we now have.

Any one of these three achievements—a comprehensive history, explanations of the New Testament, and explanations of the Old Testament—would have been enough to ensure the centrality of Josephus. Taken together, they explain why he is unmatched.

Josephus was born to no ordinary family, descended from priestly Hasmonean kings on his mother's side and from nobility on his father's side as well. He was a prodigy, with a keen intellect, superb memory, and great insight, which is why even when he was a child, high priests and other notables frequently came to ask his opinion about some facet of the law. In short, he was a child wonder. We know because he tells us so himself.

It was this same love of learning, he says, that drove him at age sixteen to try to understand the three sects of Judaism of his day: the Pharisees, the Sadducees, and the Essenes. He also spent time in the desert with a chaste hermit named Bannus.

As a young man of twenty-six, Josephus set sail for Rome to try to free some Jews kept captive there. His mission was successful despite a shipwreck that would prove to be just the first of many harrowing experiences in his life (or the second, if you count living in the desert with an ascetic hermit). Josephus even managed to ingratiate himself with Emperor Nero's mistress.

Tensions between Rome and Jerusalem had long been simmering, and it was becoming increasingly clear that armed conflict was not far off. Some decades earlier, in A.D. 6, Augustus had removed Herod the Great's children from power, turning Jerusalem and the surrounding areas into the Roman province of Iudaea. Though few Romans lived in the area, there were still plenty of Hellenistic Greeks around, and initial tension between those Greeks and the Jews proved to be the fuse that would spark outright rebellion.

Josephus, having seen Rome's great might, tried and failed to convince the local Jews in Jerusalem not to rebel. They had no chance of success, he explained. But Josephus was unable to forestall the ill-fated revolt, indirectly setting the stage for a long career of switching sides that would variously earn him admiration as a survivor and condemnation as a traitor.

As tensions rose, he ended up in command of the Jewish troops north of Jerusalem in the Galilee, where he tried to dissuade hawkish local commanders from going to war. When his pleas went unheeded, he reorganized the northern forces, stocked up on food and provisions, and trained the troops.

As chance would have it, the Roman military commander Vespasian (later to take over the job of emperor in the aftermath of Nero's suicide in the year 68) chose to approach Jerusalem from the north. Josephus was thus in command of the army of his Jewish kinsfolk who would defend Jerusalem against the Roman army he so admired.

But the local Jews deserted, leaving Josephus nearly alone. He holed up in a fortress at Yodfat (also called Jotapata), where he endured a bitter siege at the hands of the Roman legions. As his own defeat drew near, he and some forty others hid in a cave, so he was out of harm's way when the Romans finally breached his protective walls. But though he was temporarily safe, Josephus and his gang had no hope of successfully fighting back.

The people with Josephus preferred suicide over certain death at the hands of the Romans. But Josephus, the only one who had not lost his senses under pressure, objected. Nonetheless, the others convinced him, under threat of death, to help with their own destruction. Left with no choice, Josephus agreed to help the group draw lots to determine an order in which they would die. After each person drew the losing lot, one of the others would kill him, so the group dwindled in numbers one by one.

Fortunately—whether through luck or divine intervention—Josephus was one of the two men who were last to die, and, rather than kill the last man, Josephus convinced his fellow fighter to surrender. So Josephus lived long enough to be brought before Vespasian as a captive rather than a corpse. He next employed a bit of cunning to earn the trust of the Roman fighter: Josephus predicted that Vespasian and then his son Titus would become caesar ("supreme ruler") and emperor. Vespasian, though skeptical, was flattered enough that he decided to keep Josephus alive.

Within months, Nero committed suicide; three new caesars took the throne, only to be deposed and killed; and then Vespasian assumed the mantle of Roman leadership. Josephus was acclaimed a true prophet, freed from captivity, and treated as a dear friend.

Because no one was able to convey any of this to the inhabitants of Jerusalem, rumors flew about what had happened in Yodfat, and before long Jerusalemites were mourning the death of their beloved Josephus.

But as it became known that Josephus was actually alive and living a privileged life among the Romans, love turned to hatred, and the same Jews who had been mourning Josephus's death now cursed his life, variously accusing him of cowardice, desertion, and treason.

With his new access to the Roman power structure, Josephus returned to Jerusalem to intercede between the two opposing forces, a task that proved futile. Josephus pleaded with the leaders of Jerusalem to surrender instead of risking the destruction of the holy city. But, not surprisingly in light of all that had happened, his calls went unheeded. In the year 70, Rome destroyed Jerusalem and exiled its inhabitants.

With Jerusalem's destruction, Rome rewarded Josephus by giving him some land near the former (and, though they did not know it, future) Jewish capital and by releasing his friends and family from captivity. But Josephus preferred to live in Rome. He returned to the Roman capital, where he became a Roman citizen, moved into a Roman apartment, received a pension from Roman taxes (which he used to support his writing), and adopted the Roman name Flavius Josephus. It is no surprise that the Jews of Jerusalem hated him.

This gripping narrative comes directly from his own autobiography.

Unfortunately, as with so much of his work, some of what he says is patently ridiculous.

We might doubt his self-proclaimed childhood prowess and suspect his self-reported accounts of uncanny survival, but unlikely things do sometimes happen. Who's to say? In other cases, though, we know that we cannot believe Josephus.

For example, in one of his main works (*The War of the Jews*), he reports that the burning of the Temple was foreshadowed by signs and portents, among them a cow giving birth to a lamb in the Temple, the eastern gate of the Temple opening of its own accord, and a star shining in the shape of a sword.

In that same work, he puts the height of Mount Tabor at "30 furlongs." A Roman furlong is 125 Roman steps, and a Roman step is five Roman feet. Though the Roman foot was slightly smaller than our modern foot, Josephus still gives us a height for Mount Tabor of well over eighteen thousand feet, while the mountain is actually less than two thousand feet. (Even Mont Blanc in the Alps only rises to about sixteen thousand feet.)

In addition to such obvious inventions, exaggerations, and errors, Josephus reports things he could not possibly have known, including verbatim accounts of conversations he did not hear. The account of what King Hyrcanus told Pompey in Damascus in chapter 1, for example, comes directly from Josephus. But as we noted at the time, there is simply no way Josephus could have known what was said. These were private meetings at which no minutes were kept, and none of the parties involved lived long enough to speak to Josephus.

And this is far from the only unheard conversation Josephus records. In one particularly telling case, Josephus gives us the full speech that Eleaser gave on Masada before the famous mass suicide there. But, of course, that is precisely the problem. Josephus could not possibly have known the words that were said minutes before everyone who heard them died. (In fact, even though the popular myth has everyone on Masada dying, some people may have survived. But Josephus could not have spoken to the survivors. And, in any event, those traumatized few could not have provided a verbatim report of the speech, something any historian would recognize immediately.)

So why do we bother reading Josephus at all? Why don't we discount his reports completely?

For one thing, embellishing historical accounts with conversations and other direct quotation seems to have been a popular style in antiquity. The famous historian Herodotus (fifth century B.C.) invented quotations, and the historian Thucydides (also fifth century) specifically advises the reader that he cannot "remember exactly" what specific people said and that he does not know if he actually heard their words or only reports of their words, but he includes the text anyway. Perhaps both readers and historians back then knew which parts of a work were supposed to be history and which parts were simply provided to make for a better reading experience.

By comparison, we might imagine a modern history book with a painting on the cover. Readers know that the artwork might not be as accurate as the textual accounts inside the book. And it's hard to imagine condemning a modern history book because of its creative cover.

For that matter, modern historians frequently include conjecture along with fact, telling the reader which parts of their account are tenuous with phrases like "might have" or "for all we know." Josephus may have used other literary devices for this purpose.

Josephus seems to have been writing in the then-accepted style of reporting history, and we assume that these firsthand reports of conversations were the usual way to convey the substance of what had happened. So they are not, by themselves, enough to cause us to reject Josephus completely.

The lamb born to a cow is a bigger problem. Here we must assume that Josephus was reporting what he had heard, not what he had seen. We might be surprised that so many people, including Josephus, believed such a thing was possible, but in this regard it's helpful to remember that the ancient worldview didn't yet have a scientific outlook. All sorts of things were possible. Herodotus listed the phoenix along with the crocodile as animals that one might see in Egypt, not differentiating between what we would now call myth and science.

For that matter, as late as the seventeenth century A.D., scholars in Europe argued that griffins were real, and the only reason we didn't see them was that, quite naturally, these magnificent creatures tended to stay away from people who would steal their gold. Similarly, as we saw last chapter, the authors of the Septuagint and even the King James Version (seventeenth century) accepted unicorns alongside what we would now call real animals. So it is hardly surprising that Josephus, in the first century A.D., might believe that a cow could produce a lamb under the right circumstances. Even so, we have to assume that he didn't actually see this. It's unfortunate that he apparently combined rumors he had heard with facts he had verified.

And what about Josephus's boasts about his own prowess? Was he really a child prodigy? Did high priests seek his advice about the law? Again, we find in Josephus's style a common way of writing autobiographies, and he is far from the only figure to overrepresent his own abilities.

On the other hand, it is of little comfort that other historians embellished and exaggerated if we still cannot rely on Josephus, an issue we will return to below.

The dubious reliability of some of what Josephus wrote isn't the only problem. Most of his original manuscripts have been lost, either destroyed or, at best, buried somewhere and not yet rediscovered. All we have are copies of copies. And with one exception, the earliest of these date to about a thousand years after Josephus died. The surviving copies sometimes say different things, making it hard to know exactly what Josephus wrote.

At the end of the nineteenth century, the German scholar Benedict Niese tried to make order out of these various and contradictory manuscripts, creating the most well-known collection of Josephus's works. Most people, when they talk about "what Josephus wrote," mean "what Josephus wrote according to the scholarly compilation of Niese."

A cursory look at Niese's collection shows a range of disagreement among the various manuscripts that were available to him. This disparity is hardly surprising. Even the texts of the Old Testament, afforded the status of Word of God and scrupulously copied by the most expert of hands, have been miscopied from time from time (as we saw in the last two chapters). We would expect that the secular writings of a historian would naturally suffer from significantly more inadvertent variation at the hands of copyists.

In addition to the thousand-year-old copies, we have one tiny fragment that dates back much further, to the third century. It contains 112 words from Josephus's *War of the Jews*. And this is both good news and bad.

The good news is that the fragment helps confirm the antiquity of Josephus's writing and, along with considerable other evidence, helps rule out the possibility that Josephus's works were forged en masse.

But the good news is outweighed by the bad. In nine places, the fragment disagrees not just with one of Niese's manuscripts but in fact with all of them. This is devastating evidence about the reliability of Niese's collection in general. It suggests that Niese may merely have given us a careful analysis of mistaken manuscripts, with the original text completely lost.

Furthermore, sometimes the older fragment agrees with one set of Niese's manuscripts, sometimes with another. We would like to think that even though Niese's manuscripts disagree with each other, at least some are reliable even if others aren't, so that, perhaps, more study might help us figure out which set of manuscripts we should rely on. But the evidence from the third-century fragment is that all of Niese's manuscripts are unreliable. And this is evidence about the

War of the Jews, generally considered better preserved than Josephus's other important writings.

Still, we don't want to put too much faith in just one tiny fragment. Perhaps the fragment was a bit of creative writing merely based on Josephus, or maybe the scribe was in the early stages of dementia. But these same kinds of possibilities plague the later manuscripts that we have, too. So our best guess, even if we can't prove it, is that the fragment shows that our manuscripts are inaccurate.

In addition to the copies of copies, though in roughly the same category, we have various translations of Josephus's work. These, of course, suffer from even more variation, because of the nature of translation.

So our knowledge of what Josephus wrote is entirely indirect, coming from copies of copies and from translations. Frequently the people doing the copying or translating were funded by sources that could have benefited politically or religiously by revising history, so the copyists and translators would have been tempted or directly pressured to alter their work to please their funders. Did they? We have no solid way to know.

Fortunately, we do have some positive news about the works of Josephus. A few other historians from his day mention him, and some of the details of what he writes can be verified in other sources. These confirmations, naturally, are subject to the same kinds of objections as we saw regarding Josephus's works. But they still tend to support the veracity of much of what Josephus wrote.

We also have archaeological evidence to support the main events that Josephus describes.

So despite all the impediments—both the lack of entirely reliable manuscripts and the obvious errors of fact in what we do have—it seems that Josephus gives us a pretty good idea of what happened, at least in broad strokes. We may doubt his early academic prowess, the details of a conversation between two world leaders, or the height of a mountain, but we can be more confident in the general picture he paints.

For example, we have unearthed ancient coins from Jerusalem that verify the rulers that Josephus mentions, among them Hyrcanus I and Alexander Jannaeus. While we don't know if every detail that Josephus presents is accurate, we do know that men by those names lived because we have coins that bear their names. Alexander Jannaeus, for example, ruled (viciously) more than a century before Josephus wrote, but Josephus nonetheless seems to have an accurate picture of his reign. This suggests that a skilled historian was at work.

Josephus's account of what happened at Masada is particularly telling, because we have so much independent archaeological evidence. For example, Josephus writes that the Jews took everything that they had, put it in a single heap, and set it on fire. Archaeological evidence suggests more than one heap was set ablaze. We might take this as evidence that Josephus invented the story, because we know that there wasn't just one heap. But we can equally note what Josephus got right: There were Jews on Masada. Rome advanced on the heavily protected desert fortress, finally taking it. The Jews died. And their possessions were burned.

This is probably typical of the degree of accuracy we find in Josephus: He described real people and real events, conveying the flavor of the political and military tensions that surrounded them. But he did so with imprecise and sometimes invented details. So, fortunately, we know the broad strokes of history from the fascinating and influential period around the start of the first millennium A.D.

We also suspect that the broad details of Josephus's life, as he himself presents them, are mostly accurate. One thing of which we are fairly certain is that somehow this Jew from Jerusalem ended up a Roman citizen. At the time, Rome was the mightiest political and military power the earth had seen, and allying himself with the super-power probably seemed like a good way to ensure longevity for himself and his works.

He had no way of knowing, of course, that the defeated Jews would outlast the victorious Romans and that those same Jews would prove uncannily successful in preserving the writings that were important to them. Ironically, in siding with the victor, Josephus distanced himself from the people who could have best helped his works survive.

But they did survive, at least in part, and they offer an invaluable window into what was left out of the Bible, as well as into the people, places, and events that gave us the Bible we have.

With one exception, as we move forward we're going to ignore the fact that we're discussing possibly corrupted copies of what Josephus originally wrote since scholars have enough faith in the general accuracy of the manuscripts.

Josephus composed four works that we know of: two multibook histories, called *The War of the Jews* and *Jewish Antiquities*; an autobiography called *The Life of Flavius Josephus*; and *Against Apion,* which Josephus uses in part to defend himself against charges of anti-Semitism.

His book *Jewish Antiquities* claims to be an accurate history of the Jews based on the accounts in Scripture. It is therefore particularly helpful in figuring out what Josephus thought was in the Bible in the first century A.D.

The Community Rule found at Qumran purports to be a way of walking in God's ways and seems like a primarily religious document for a primarily religious community. Josephus takes a different approach, hoping—he says—to explain the contents of the Bible to the non-Jews of his day and "for posterity." His task seems less religious and more objective. He even promises not to add anything or subtract anything from what is contained in Scripture but, rather, simply to describe the contents accurately.

He opens with a bit of philosophy, noting that he is presenting his own opinion before he starts the real history. He explains two facets of Moses "the lawgiver" (or "legislator") that he thinks are important, and one bit of methodology that is even more important for us now.

First, Moses began differently than all other lawgivers, says Josephus. Lawgivers generally start with the law: contracts, rights, and so forth. Moses, on the other hand, started by directing people's attention upward to God. Once people had submitted to Judaism, they readily accepted Moses's laws.

Second, Josephus writes, other lawgivers ascribe human vices to their gods, thereby giving wicked people "plausible excuses" for their crimes. Moses, on the other hand, first demonstrated that God was perfect, and then he convinced people that they should strive to be like God.

This is no small bit of theology. After all, Genesis (3:5) ascribes the downfall of humanity to people who strive to "be like the gods" who know good from evil. The words are the snake's, who convinces Eve to disobey God; she then convinces Adam. The result is expulsion from Eden. The God of Genesis doesn't want people to strive to be divine.

On the other hand, Moses starts his great "holiness" exhortation in Leviticus 19 by quoting God, "You [the people] shall be holy because I the Lord your God am holy." So there is at least some sense in which people are supposed to be like God. But Josephus applies that thinking much more generally.

In terms of methodology, Josephus tells the reader that some parts of scripture are presented "plainly and expressly," other parts "allegorically." This division between plain meaning and allegorical meaning lies at the heart of how Scripture came to be interpreted. In particular, allegory forms a central part of the Dead Sea Sect (as recorded in the Dead Sea Scrolls), early Christianity (in the New Testament), rabbinic Judaism (particularly in the Midrash), and other streams of pre-Christian Judaism.

Josephus suggests that this inclusion of allegory is a "very curious philosophical theory." And it is, so much so that it still presents a primary point of contention in today's modern, Western society, with atheists often vehemently objecting to what they see as purposeful misreading of the Bible, while religious leaders are often so used to this kind of reading that they don't even realize how odd it seems to some people.

It is noteworthy not only that Josephus calls the reader's attention to the allegorical method of interpretation but also that he understands how some people may view it. Earlier writers didn't use this kind of allegory, and later writers often assumed that it was a valid method of inquiry. Josephus shows us here that he lived at a time when this kind of endeavor was at least relatively new.

Even more, Josephus shows us the degree to which he was self-aware and self-critical. He paid attention to what he was doing and to how his books might be read. And not just here but throughout his work. For example, regarding the advanced ages of people before Noah—generally many hundreds of years—Josephus writes that no one should compare (then-) modern life spans to the ancient ones and conclude that the account is false. After all, he explains, the ancients were beloved of God, and their food was of better quality, and, he adds, God gave them longer lives on account of their virtue and on account of the good use they made of it as they pursued astronomy and geometry. Belaboring the point, Josephus adds that he is not alone in reporting the advanced ages of early humans. Both Greeks (including Hellenistic Romans) and non-Greeks agree, and Josephus lists a dozen other historians to prove his point. But then Josephus concludes with the observation that his readers will judge these matters as they see fit. He all but acknowledges that there is no reason to believe that people used to live for many centuries.

Precisely because he comments on some parts of what he writes, we can assume that when he doesn't comment, he was probably simply reporting what he believed to be in the Bible.

And this is where things get particularly interesting, because his Bible seems to have been different from ours.

Josephus begins his main narrative with Genesis, starting with God creating light and dark and ending with the creation of humankind.

In fact, the Bible contains two accounts of how God created people. First, in Genesis 1:27 (during the six days of creation), God creates "humankind in his image . . . male and female." That's the first account. According to the second account, in Genesis 2:7–8 (after the Sabbath following the six days of creation), God creates man from the ground, waiting until Genesis 2:22 to create woman from the man's rib.

Why are there two seemingly contradictory stories in the Bible? And how does Josephus address them?

The standard scholarly answer to the first question is that there were multiple versions floating around when the text of Genesis was finalized, and both creation stories—woman being created with man and woman being created after man—were included in the final text. That answer applies not just here but to the many places where disparate accounts appear side by side and also to the places where a story seems to appear more than once.

For example, in 1 Samuel 17:50, David kills the Philistine Goliath with a "sling and stone," but then, in a less widely known account, the very next verse (1 Samuel 17:51) has David killing him with a sword. Curiously, 1 Samuel 17:50 expressly says that David didn't have a sword in his hand. It's a jarring switch, and 1 Samuel 17:51 therefore has to explain that David took Goliath's sword.

The text reads like two people bickering, with some of the dialogue missing: (1) "David killed Goliath with a sling and a stone." (2) "No, he killed him with a sword." (3) "David didn't have a sword." (4) "I'm telling you, he killed Goliath with a sword." (5) "Where'd he get the sword?" (6) "He took Goliath's sword." Our Hebrew text contains 1, 3, 4, and 6. The Greek from the Septuagint has 4 and 6. Josephus reconciles the texts differently, explaining that David stunned Goliath with a stone and killed him with Goliath's own sword. (An even more severe disparity comes from 2 Samuel 21:19, according to which it wasn't David at all who killed Goliath but rather a man named Elhanan.)

Similarly, Abraham twice presents his wife as though she were his sister, once in Genesis 12 and again in Genesis 20. (In Genesis 12 Abraham is still called "Abram," as he has yet to change his name to the longer version.) Scholars often assume that there was originally only one story but that it was accidentally inserted into the Bible twice.

The most common version of this scholarly theory posits four main authors of the Five Books of Moses: an Elohist (E), who uses the Hebrew word *elohim* for God; a Yahwist (J—because in German *j* makes the sound "y"), who uses the word *yahweh* for God; a Deuteronomist (D), who wrote most of Deuteronomy; and the priests (P). The theory also relies on there being one or more redactors (like editors)who took the disparate stories and unified them.

But the theory falls short, primarily in that it assumes that the redactors were smart, prominent leaders with a sound knowledge of all of the sources and enough backing among the populace that their redacted version of the holy text would be widely accepted. Alas, the theory also assumes that the redactors were idiots who didn't notice the obvious contradictions in the work they produced.

The theory also falls short in the timing that it demands. We suspect that the Five Books of Moses were a unified text, at least in some sense, by the third century B.C. because, as we saw in the last chapter, King Ptolemy II (or someone) wanted the work translated into Greek. For this reason, Ezra, who lived just after the end of the Babylonian exile, is a good candidate for the anonymous redactor.

But multiple versions of many of the stories continue to exist for many hundreds of years later. We saw some of these in the Dead Sea Scrolls and the Septuagint, and we'll see more in Josephus and more yet in the following chapters. Or, to look at things the other way around, if the text of the Bible was finalized by the third century B.C., why didn't Josephus write about the same version that we have now?

More likely, then, there were lots of religious texts floating around, and the inclusion or exclusion of some of them involved more chance than some people today would like to believe. This is, in fact, precisely why we speak of the Bible's cutting room floor.

The Dead Sea Scrolls gave us a look at some material that could have been included. But the Dead Sea Sect could be considered as an unauthoritative source because its members were, after all, living in a separatist community.

The Septuagint was more mainstream but, nonetheless, also written for a separatist group in some sense—the Jews in Egypt who no longer spoke Hebrew. And, in addition, it was in the end a poor-quality translation.

But Josephus was as mainstream as an author could be. He lived in Jerusalem (before moving to Rome). He was part of high society. And he was a scholar. When we see that Josephus's version of the Bible doesn't agree completely with our standard version, we see more evidence that our Bible has changed over time and is incomplete in places.

(Alongside scientific answers to why there are contradictions and redundancies in the Bible, we have the classical religious response, which denies their existence. If we think we see a conflict, it's because we haven't understood the text.)

Here, relating Genesis, Josephus includes both creation stories. He summarizes the first one, explaining that God created humankind on the sixth day. Unfortunately, the standard English translation of Josephus (by William Whiston) inadvertently distorts what Josephus meant by using the English word "man" here, "On the same [sixth] day he [God] also formed man." The Greek—at least, our best guess of the original Greek—is the more clearly inclusive *anthropos*: "human."

Then Josephus has to deal with the second creation story. He explains, "Moreover, Moses, after the seventh day was over, begins to talk philosophically; and concerning the formation of man, says . . ." In other words, Josephus reconciles the two accounts. The first is when the Creation took place. The second is when Moses talked more about it.

Here we see evidence that Josephus was looking at the same version of the Bible as we have now. Elsewhere, as we'll see below, Josephus includes stories that were cut from the Bible completely.

Before we turn to those stories, though, another element of what Josephus writes deserves our attention. Josephus describes the sequence of events that led to Adam and Eve's expulsion from the Garden of Eden (and to what Christians call the Fall): Adam and Eve ate from the tree, then they noticed that they were naked, and then they produced clothing to hide their nakedness. So far the account matches Genesis. But Josephus also tells us how Adam and Eve felt after they put on clothes, "They thought they were happier than they were before, as they had discovered what they were in want of."

This is a remarkably modern observation.

We'll leave the complex issue of the difference between "they were happy" and "they thought they were happy" for another volume, noting only the advanced understanding of human nature required to suggest that people can wrongly think they are happy.

Even more interesting is the way Josephus introduces a condemnation of materialism. Adam and Eve thought they were happy because they suddenly had a need (clothing) and then found what they needed (clothes). But when Josephus writes that they only thought they were happy, he suggests that this materialistic approach to happiness—creating a need and then finding a solution—doesn't work. Josephus alludes to the same issue when he equates Cain's wickedness with his desire to acquire things: "Cain was not only very wicked in other respects, but was wholly intent on getting things."

While Josephus perhaps dwells on this issue for personal reasons, he probably didn't make up the connection between Cain and possessions. Rather, the source for the connection is in the Hebrew text: the Hebrew word "Cain" sounds like the Hebrew word for "acquire."

This kind of loose linguistic reasoning based on similar-sounding words permeates the Old Testament and the considerable body of literature that never made it into the Bible. In Genesis (4:1) we read that Eve remarked about her new son that she "acquired a man with the Lord." The connection between Cain and "acquiring" was obviously widespread, and here we have two different ways of looking at the details.

It is, in fact, not uncommon to see more than one linguistic connection side by side. In Genesis 21:28, during a spat over wells and well water, Abraham makes a gift of sheep and oxen to a king named Abimelech as part of a covenant between the two leaders. Then Abraham makes a show of separating out seven ewes. Abimelech asks about the meaning of those seven ewes, to which Abraham responds that he is offering the seven ewes so that Abimelech will be a witness that Abraham dug the wells. "That is why the place is named Beersheba."

"Beer" (pronounced as two syllables in Hebrew, *b'er*) means "well," and "sheba" (*sheva*) means "seven." Beersheba is the "well of seven." That's the connection between the seven ewes and the name of the place.

But then the text adds that the place is so called, ". . . because both [men] swore an oath there." By chance, the Hebrew words for "swear" and for "oath" come from the same root as "seven."

In other words, the text of Genesis seems to have remnants of two explanations for the name "Beersheba." According to one, the name reflects a "well of seven," and according to the other, a "well of an oath." As it happens, the Septuagint calls Beersheba "the well of the oath" throughout the Five Books of Moses, though there's also a Greek version of the actual name later on in the Bible. (Josephus writes that Beersheba was still called Beersheba in his day. And the place still exists in modern Israel, lying at the top of the Negev desert and housing a major university.)

So in Genesis 21, we see evidence of two side-by-side explanations for the name Beersheba, with one given ever-so-slightly more prominence. In the case of Cain, we see one explanation in the Bible and another that might have been lost were it not for Josephus.

Josephus adds other details that do not quite accord with the standard account in Genesis. For example, Josephus explains that all the animals in the Garden of Eden were able to speak, but the snake was deprived of that skill after it abused its power. Another bit of information from Josephus is that Adam and Eve's punishment includes a change in the state of the earth; while it used to produce food of its own accord, now it will do so only when "harassed by [human] labor," and even then it will yield some kinds of food but not others. (We will see this theme of having to work the land again in chapter 5.)

Particularly interesting—and, again, remarkably modern—is another note Josephus give us about Cain. We have already seen that

Cain represents wickedness and, because of his name, material acqui-sition. Josephus adds that Cain is the "author of measures and weights," the introduction of which destroyed the previously simple way of living, turning it into a world of craftiness, according to Jose-phus. Cain was also the guy who introduced borders around lands.

By associating the older, simpler days of yore with the pre-evil days before Cain ruined things, Josephus makes a value judgment about his own culture, and not for the better. Apparently, nostalgia for the past is not only a modern phenomenon. Nor was it universal. The quotation from Ovid at the start of chapter 1 now takes on the flavor of one side of a debate. When Ovid wrote that he was glad to live in what he thought of as modernity and that he would "let others praise ancient times," Josephus was in fact praising ancient times.

Josephus turns next to one of Cain's children, Enoch, mirroring the Bible's account. This is not "the" Enoch (of our chapter 7, de-scended from Seth, another of Adam's sons) but another Enoch. It's hard to know what to make of the two Enochs, both important peo-ple, it would seem, and both descended from one of Adam's children. This Enoch continues his father Cain's wickedness, and even has a city named after him.

Josephus returns to Adam, noting that the first man had another son because he desired posterity and "had a vehement desire of chil-dren," being 230 years old. In another passage that might strike many readers as more twenty-first century in flavor than first century, Jose-phus says that Adam fathered Seth "and others" but that it would be "tedious" to list everyone, so he doesn't. It seems that modern readers are not alone in finding some of the Bible's long lists of names tiresome.

Yet just a few paragraphs later Josephus will indulge in an equally tedious description of the genealogy of Seth. Josephus singles out Seth and his family, ignoring the others, because it was the line of Seth that would give us "the" Enoch and Noah.

Seth, we learn, was a good person, as were his children. According to Josephus, Seth's descendants invented astronomy and, further, recorded their inventions on two pillars, one of brick, the other of stone. The stone pillar was a backup pillar, intended to outlast the flood even if the one of brick did not. The pillars, Josephus writes, survive in the land of Siriad.

Unfortunately, we don't know where Siriad is, though many people suspect it might be Egypt. And we don't know what to make of these pillars, which do not appear in the Bible but seem important to Josephus. Were they in Josephus's Bible?

The translator William Whiston (whose translation of Josephus's works into English is by far the most widespread, and the one that most people read) thinks that Josephus confused Seth here with an Egyptian ruler named Sesostris, who appears in the writings of the historian Herodotus. We don't know who Sesostris is, either (because Herodotus doesn't tell us), but some people think that Sesostris may have been invented, perhaps accidentally, as a combination of more than one pharaoh. And in part because the pharaoh Seti I erected a pillar in Beth She'an (in Modern Israel), some people think that Sesostris here may refer to Seti I. The names Seti and Seth are written similarly in Greek, which might explain how Josephus mixed them up, though we might still wonder why Josephus thought the pillars in Beth She'an were in "Siriad."

But even if Josephus confused Seti and Seth, we still have a nagging question: Why did Josephus include this bit of information at all?

In general, Josephus seems to have been following the order of the Bible pretty closely. He included both creation stories, for example, in the order in which they appear in the Bible. He didn't want to enumerate Adam's second batch of children, other than Seth, but he nonetheless mentions them and even tells the reader that he's skipping them; he presumably does this because the Bible enumerates them.

So when we find this nonbiblical bit of information, one obvious possibility is that Seth's pillars in Siriad were actually in Josephus's Bible, or at least in a version of it. Josephus's Siriad might be related to the biblical Serad (one of Zebulun's children and, therefore, Jacob's grandchildren) or to Serada, part of the territory owned by Reuben. But we don't know.

Josephus tells us, in the same passage, that Adam predicted that the world was to be destroyed by water (that is, after all, how Seth's descendants knew to build two pillars to preserve knowledge of their discoveries). But Josephus's full account is that Adam predicted "that the world was to be destroyed by the force of fire, and at another time by . . . water." Where is this notion of fire coming from? There's a huge difference between a single destruction by water and a double destruction, once by water and once by fire. Again, we wonder if Josephus wasn't reporting an alternative tradition.

2 Peter 3:1–7 in the New Testament has a remarkably similar account. There, the apostle Peter explains that just as the world of old was deluged with water, "by the same word, the present heavens and earth have been reserved for fire." Still, Peter does not completely agree with Josephus. Peter is clear that the destruction by fire will come long after the destruction by water, while Josephus seems to indicate that the fire comes first. And Peter doesn't equate the fire with Noah, except, perhaps, obliquely through his phrase "by the same word."

Along similar lines, Jewish tradition posits a flood that combined cold water and hot water (in the Midrash and, later, in the fifteenth-century mystical collection from Spain called the Zohar, among other places).

Was there a single tradition of fire connected to Noah and complementing the flood that made its way into Josephus, Peter, and the rabbinical writings but not Genesis? Or were they separate traditions, invented independently of one another? After all, fire and water are common complements. Or was Josephus just editorializing? We don't know for sure, but Josephus's inclusion of fire at least suggests that there was some debate over whether the world would be, or had been, destroyed by fire.

Josephus then jumps seven generations forward, during which time, he says, Seth's descendants abandoned the virtuous practices of their ancestors: In place of the "degree of zeal they had formerly shown for virtue, they now showed, by their actions, a double degree of wickedness."

In this context, Josephus turns his attention to one of the most mysterious aspects of Genesis: the angels who mated with human women. These women bore people called in Hebrew *nephilim* ("fallen ones"), or, in Greek, "giants." They appear in the Hebrew and Greek texts of Genesis and pop up again from time to time in other books, but, though intriguing, they are minor characters in the Bible.

By contrast, they seem to have been central in antiquity: They feature prominently in the once-popular Book of Enoch (discussed in chapter 7). And Josephus mentions them here. But he hedges just a little. He writes that angels of God came to human women and fathered "unjust sons" who "despised all that was good." These men did what looked like "the acts of those whom the Greeks call 'giants.'" But then Josephus adds, "and that's the tradition," perhaps the way a modern author might write, "at least, that's what they say." It seems that Josephus didn't believe it and though not meaning to openly deny the biblical account, didn't want his readers to believe it, either.

Josephus apparently feels differently about Noah's ark and the flood. He tells the story of the great flood—the forty-day rainstorm, water covering the earth, the ark that saved Noah and the animals, etcetera—and then adds that in addition to his own reporting, lots of other writers can attest to the flood. Josephus quotes Berosus the Chaldean (fourth century B.C.) as saying, "It is said there is still some part of this ship in Armenia . . . and that some people carry off pieces of the bitumen [from which it was made according to the biblical account]." He adds that Hieronymus the Egyptian and Mnaseas and "a great many more" say similar things. Even Nicolaus of Damascus, Josephus says, writes about "a great mountain in Armenia . . . upon which it is reported that many who fled at the time of the flood were saved, and that one who was carried in an ark came on shore upon the top of it. . . . This might be the man described by the Jewish Moses, the lawgiver."

The contrast between Josephus's apparent dismissal of the *nephilim* and his emphatic insistence that "everyone knows there was a flood" is striking. (It is also surprisingly modern. While it is rare to find people today who believe seriously in the *nephilim,* a recent poll suggests that almost two-thirds of Americans believe that Noah's ark and the flood were historical events.)

The well-known Tower of Babel comes next in Josephus's account, and, except for an intervening genealogical list of Noah's descendants, it also comes next in the Bible. For all its fame, though, the story of the Tower of Babel occupies just nine verses in the Bible.

On the other hand, Noah's genealogy in the Bible takes up fully fifty-five verses, in two sections, one before Babel, one after. The length of this genealogy suggests that it was much more important than the story about Babel. Though Josephus divides the information slightly differently than the biblical text, he also emphasizes the importance of the list by devoting a lot of space to the names.

The reason the names were so important is that their purpose, probably, was to explain the political landscape. For example, Genesis

10:6 reads, "The descendants of Ham were Cush, Mitzraim, Put, and K'na'an." To most modern readers, this line, like many of the others, is relevant to nothing.

But Cush is probably Ethiopia. We find it first in Genesis 2:13 as the area through which the river Gihon flows, and again in Esther 1:1 as a terminus of King Ahasuerus's realm (which spanned "India to Ethiopia"). Amos scolds the people of Israel for their haughtiness, "Aren't you just like the Ethiopians ["Cushites"] to me?" (9:7).

Mitzraim, the next in the list, is clearly Egypt. Put is probably another region in Africa (based on, for example, Nahum 3:9, where the word appears in the list: Ethiopia, Egypt, Put, and Libya). And the last name in the list, K'na'an, is Canaan.

In other words, the line tells the reader that Ham is the father of the Ethiopians, the Egyptians, the Putites, and the Canaanites. This is not just a list of names. It's a lesson in history and international relations.

One of Ham's brothers was Shem, or, in Greek, Sem, a word that survives to this day in the words Semite, anti-Semitism, and so on. These would become the Hebrews and the Arabs, as indicated by Shem's children: Ashur, Arpachshad, Lud, and Aram. Ashur is Assyria. Arpachshad's grandson was Eber, or, in Greek, Heber, related to the "Heb(e)rews." The name Aram is the source of our English word Aramaic, which was the lingua franca of the Ancient Near East. (We don't know what Lud is.)

Here's the flavor of what Josephus wrote:

> Ashur lived at the city Nineve; and named his subjects Assyrians, who became the most fortunate nation. . . . Aram had the Aramites, which the Greeks called Syrians. . . . Of the four sons of Aram, Uz founded Trachonitis and Damascus: this country lies between Palestine and Celesyria.

For Josephus, and anyone else living in or around Jerusalem during the first century A.D., the biblical list itself would have been hugely exciting, not just because it was about their home, but because they were living in the very places mentioned in the Bible.

It was, therefore, easy for readers at the time to view their lives as the continuation of the biblical narrative: Doing business, perhaps, with someone from Syria, readers could learn that the Syrians were the same people that the Bible says descended from Aram, in turn descended from Shem, descended from Noah himself. Or, chatting with a Damascan, readers might know the person was descended from Uz, also descended from Aram, and cousins, therefore, of the Syrians. Or, visiting Amathe, near modern-day Homah in Syria, about thirty miles north of Hams, readers might consider another passage:

> The sons of Canaan were these: Sidonius, who also built a city of the same name; it is called by the Greeks Sidon Amathus inhabited in Amathine, which is even now called Amathe by the inhabitants, although the Macedonians named it Epiphania, from one of his posterity.

That passage taught them that the place was built by no less than Canaan's son.

Josephus's additional information—for example, other names of the places ("in Greek it's called") and factoids ("the most fortunate nation")—made the reading even compelling.

And yet despite this, it's the story about Babel that we now know best. In fact, we know one particular part of that story: the tower. Many people today don't even realize that the biblical story is about a city that has a tower, not merely about a tower.

And here we find a fascinating difference between the biblical account and Josephus's understanding. The Bible is silent as to why the tower was built. But Josephus tells us.

According to Josephus, the point of the tower was to be higher than any potential future flood, so the people would be impervious to future drowning at the hands of God. This is why, Josephus says, they used bitumen on the tower: to make it waterproof.

Bitumen is a kind of asphalt, called in Greek *asfaltos*. We don't know for sure how well it kept out water, but Noah used bitumen for his ark, and Moses's mother used the substance to fortify the basket in which she placed her son before sending him off on the waters of the Nile. So at the very least, bitumen had some connection to waterproofing.

Josephus's account makes perfect sense, while the biblical account leaves the reader wondering why bitumen is only used in three places: the ark, meant to float in water; Moses's basket, also meant to float; and the Tower of Babel. (The matter is slightly more complicated, because the Hebrew text uses a different word in its account of the ark—analogous to "bitumen" versus "pitch" or "asphalt" in English.)

The Bible even reads as though something is missing. According to Genesis 11:4, the people in Shinar want to build the City and Tower of Babel specifically so that they are not "scattered all over the earth." Then, in Genesis 11:8, we read that God "scattered them all over the earth." In other words, the scattering isn't the punishment for building the city and tower, it's what God was going to do unless the people managed to build Babel to protect themselves.

The tower was a way of warding off God's power. Josephus tells us how: The tower would have reduced the power of another flood.

Having given us his version of events, Josephus once again reinforces the veracity of what he writes by quoting others, starting with the Sibyl. The Sibyl was a prophetess, though accounts vary as to who she was, and even whether there was one or more than one of her.

Plato (fifth century B.C.) mentions her, and Heraclitus (a philosopher from a century earlier) probably does, too. We have a surviving set of Greek poems attributed to the Sibyl, but those poems, the Sibylline Oracles, were almost certainly written some centuries after the original Sibyl.

At any rate, Josephus quotes her as saying, "When all men were of one language, some of them built a high tower, as if they would thereby ascend up to heaven, but the gods sent storms of wind and overthrew the tower, and gave every one his peculiar language; and for this reason it was that the city was called Babylon."

It doesn't seem to bother Josephus that the Sibyl attributes the destruction of the tower to "the gods." For him, the Sibyl's mention of the tower helps prove its existence. And the genealogy connects the story to Noah.

Though Josephus doesn't mention it, the Book of Jubilees also devotes much more attention to the bitumen with which the tower was built than does our text of the Bible.

So the bitumen of the tower seems to have been a crucial element of the story. But without Josephus, we might never know why.

Noah's fame doesn't only stem from his connection to the flood and to Babel. As we've seen, Noah had three sons, among them Shem (Sem, in Greek), who would be the father of all of the Semites. Josephus's account of the successive generations, like the one in the Bible, can be hard to follow:

The son of Phaleg, whose father was Heber, was Ragau; whose son was Serug, to whom was born Nahor; his son was Terah, who was the father of Abraham, who accordingly was the tenth from Noah, and was born in the two hundred and ninety-second year after the deluge; for Terah begat Abram in his seventieth year.

The point of the genealogy, though, is to connect the father of monotheism to Noah. And, as we've seen, names were important, so it would be a mistake to ignore the details here.

Josephus claims that Abraham's descendants ("the Jews") are called Hebrews after his great-grandfather's great-grandfather, Heber. As we saw above, "Heber" is the Greek form of "Eber," which in Hebrew comes from the three-letter root Ayin.Bet.Resh. That root also signifies "across." Genesis 20:21 calls Shem the ancestor of "everyone who lived across," presumably, across the river. This accords with a common view that equates the "Hebrews" to the people who lived "across" from something. Josephus disagrees, connecting the name not to anyone across the river but rather to an ancestor.

Abraham himself, according to the Bible, was born with the name Abram. God added the middle H (in Genesis 17:5) as part of a covenant to make him the "father of many nations." The Hebrew for "father" is *ab,* and *ram* means "exalted." So "Abram" is the "exalted father," or, as we might say now, "tribal elder." Genesis 17:5, using a related meaning of *ram,* further connects Abram's name to "father of many" people.

The insertion of the H to form Abraham from Abram is hardly a coincidence. The Hebrews, around 1000 B.C., had augmented the Phoenician consonantal writing system by doubling up three consonants, using them also for vowels, starting with H for the vowel sound "ah." (These simple additions are different than the Masoretes' complex system of vowels that we discussed in the last chapter.) So whereas a simple word like *malka* ("queen") would have been spelled M-L-K by the Phoenicians, the Hebrews had the option of spelling it more clearly as M-L-K-H, using the final H to mark the vowel sound "a."

It was, in fact, this seemingly minor modification of the Phoenician writing system that paved the way for the alphabet, widespread writing, and, probably, Scripture itself.

The Hebrews seem to have recognized the importance of their new discovery by using it symbolically to change the "tribal elder" (*avram*) into the Jewish tribal elder: *avraham,* with an ʜ in the middle. Similarly, an ʜ turned Sarai into Sarah.

Even more strikingly, the common word *elim* ("gods") became, again with the insertion of an ʜ in the middle, *elohim*—the one and only Jewish God. In short, the patriarch, matriarch, and deity of the Hebrews all took their names from common words with the insertion of an ʜ—the very ʜ that made widespread writing possible, which in turn made Scripture possible. As we've seen, names were more important in ancient times than they are now, and even in that context, Abram's name change to Abraham was especially meaningful. The shift from Abram to Abraham is pivotal in the Old Testament.

Yet Josephus ignores it. While the backstory explanation about the Phoenician alphabet and the Hebrews' modification of it doesn't appear in the Bible, Genesis details the name change as part of God's covenant. Why didn't Josephus write about this?

Except for his chapter headings, Josephus's first mention of the Jewish patriarch is that Terah "was the father of Abraham." Then in the next sentence, Josephus writes that "Terah fathered Abram in his 70th year." Then Josephus uses "Abram" approximately until the point that the name is changed, and "Abraham" thereafter. The change—from Abraham once to Abram for a while and then back to Abraham—cries out for an explanation. But Josephus doesn't provide one.

We can only guess why the matter, so central to the original biblical authors (and referred to obliquely in Romans 4:17), didn't make it into Josephus's writings. Perhaps he didn't know the story, but, if so, why not? It's hard to imagine that he simply thought the story was irrelevant, because we've already seen how he warns the reader when he omits material that he thinks is tedious. So the other possibility is that he left it out on purpose.

Unfortunately, both possible explanations—that Josephus didn't know the story or that he purposely chose not to include it—seem unlikely. So we are left with a mystery about a seemingly central part of Genesis.

Of perhaps more theological importance is Josephus's account of how Abraham discovered monotheism. Surprisingly, the Bible doesn't tell us. As we'll see in chapter 6, the Apocalypse of Abraham gives us one detailed answer that seems to have been widely acknowledged in antiquity. Josephus gives us a different answer here.

Josephus sets the stage by describing Abram as a wise man with a talent for insight and persuasion; he therefore came to have higher notions of virtue than others. So he decided to "update" people's opinion of God, which is to say, he would take the old approach and turn it into a better new one.

As Josephus describes it, there are two parts to Abram's monotheism. The first is that there is only one God, the creator of the universe. The second is that any others, to the extent that they enhance people's lives at all, do so not by their own power but only according to what was given them. Abram came to this startling conclusion, Josephus says, when he saw that the sun and the moon and other bodies "do not preserve their own good order," that is, regular motions, and, therefore, must be subservient to God.

Josephus admired astronomy. We have already seen that Josephus ascribes the centuries-long life spans of early humans in part to their understanding of astronomy. And when Seth's descendants invented astronomy, the new information was so important that they recorded their knowledge on pillars, one of which was made flood-proof.

We are hardly surprised. The Greeks loved astronomy and were among the first to use celestial data not just for navigation and other practical purposes but to design experiments. In this way, the earth, moon, sun, planets, and stars formed the foundation of science.

Thales of Miletus (in the fifth century B.C.), for example, predicted eclipses, Aristarchus of Samos (third century) figured out that the sun was at the center of the solar system, and Eratosthenes of Cyrene (third century) used shadow lengths to compare local distances to the earth's circumference, coming up with a pretty good estimate of the size of the earth. (A possibly fictitious detail has Eratosthenes measuring one of the distances he needed for his work in units of how long it took a camel to travel from one point to another.)

It should come as no surprise, then, that Josephus, who lived in a world still flavored by the Greeks and their love of astronomy, projected admiration for astronomy into his account of the Bible, though we are perhaps disappointed that he either didn't know or didn't tell his readers that, in doing so, he was going beyond mere reporting.

As with other things that Josephus seems to believe, he buttresses his account here by introducing other writers. Berosus (fourth century B.C.) is quoted as describing a man from the tenth generation after the flood who was skilled in astronomy. Even though Berosus doesn't mention the man's name, Josephus thinks this is Abram (or Abraham). Hecatseus (in a work we now know was probably not actually written by him) mentions Abram, according to Josephus. So does Nicolaus of Damascus, who says that "Abram is still famous in . . . Damascus; and there is . . . a village named for him, the Habitation of Abram."

So for Josephus, Abram/Abraham was the man who was so well versed in astronomy that he was able to discern the universality of the one God and to reject polytheism.

As we've looked at how Josephus understood the first few chapters of the Bible—from creation to the first monotheist—a pattern has emerged. Josephus saw the basic structure in Scripture that we do now, and many of the details in his account match our text. But many do not. Some of these differences, like the emphasis on astronomy, were probably invented by Josephus. Others, like the connection between Cain and materialism and the connection between the flood and the Tower of Babel, were probably left out of our Bible as it was compiled. In some cases, as with the destruction of the earth by fire as well as by water, we don't know whether we're reading something that Josephus invented or that the Bible left out.

As we now turn to what Josephus tells us about the New Testament and Christianity, it's helpful to keep this pattern in mind: When we see something in Josephus that's not in the Bible, we first want to ask if Josephus is inventing something that was never there before we decide that he's reporting something that's missing.

We start with a little political background.

According to Matthew 2:1, Jesus was born "in the time of King Herod." For most modern readers, this phrase is but a barely relevant prelude to the real crux of Matthew 2:1, "Wise men [or "magi"] from the east came to Jerusalem." But "in the time of King Herod" was actually a crucial part of the story.

As we'll see soon, the New Testament tells us more about King Herod, but it leaves out the reason that King Herod was so important here.

This same King Herod (in Matthew 2:13) wants to "search for the child [Jesus] and destroy him," which is why Joseph, Mary, and Jesus flee to Egypt and stay there (according to Matthew 2:19) until Herod dies. But later, in Matthew 14:1, Herod, who apparently has already died, shows up to kill John the Baptist.

Luke 1:5 also mentions King Herod, who was reigning when the future birth of John the Baptist was predicted.

In Acts 12, Herod attacks some members of the nascent Church. He has John's brother James killed by the sword (Acts 12:2) and then arrests Peter (Acts 12:3). But for angelic intervention "from the hands of Herod" (Acts 12:11), Peter would have been killed.

How could Herod have died before Jesus began establishing the church yet also live long enough to kill some members of the church?

Josephus gives us enough background to sort things out.

It turns out that there were four generations of Herodian rulers. The man we now call King Herod reigned from 37 B.C. to 4 B.C., and, in particular, he ruled the Jerusalem into which Jesus was born. (Though B.C. stands for "before Christ" and A.D. stands for Latin meaning "the year of our Lord," Jesus was in fact probably born a few years before the year that we now call A.D. 1.) But in the New Testament, "Herod" refers not only to the man we call King Herod but also to his descendants.

When King Herod died, his kingdom was divided among his three children, one of whom, Antipas ("Herod" in the New Testament, as in "Herod [Jr.]"), killed John the Baptist. Unlike his father the king, Antipas earned only the lesser title "tetrarch"—technically, "ruler of one fourth of the land" and, more generally, "ruler of part of the land." This is why Herod in Matthew 2:1 is called "king," while in Matthew 14:1 he is called "tetrarch." They are different people. (Confusingly, Antipas is also the name of King Herod's grandfather.)

One of Herod's grandchildren, King "Herod" Agrippa I, is the one who had James executed. This is the King Herod of Acts 12.

But this is not the Agrippa that interviews Paul in Acts 25, finding the early Christian innocent. That Agrippa is his son Agrippa II.

So we have King Herod ("the Great"), followed by Tetrarch Antipas ("Herod"), followed by King Herod Agrippa I, followed by King Herod Agrippa II. (Another tetrarch, Antipas's brother Archelaus, briefly ruled Jerusalem after his father, King Herod, died. This is the Archelaus of Matthew 2:22.) So the historical details in the New Testament aren't inaccurate here, just incomplete. (Though we do find mistakes. For instance, Mark [6:14] connects "King Herod" to the death of John the Baptist when others, like Josephus as well as Matthew and Luke, agree that it was the tetrarch Herod, whom we now call Antipas.) In general, Josephus fills in the blanks, helping us piece together a more complete picture of the political and other figures in the New Testament.

Modernity highlights the religious figures in the New Testament more than the political ones, but modern readers who ignore the political figures often miss the point of key New Testament passages.

Perhaps the best example is the detailed story of how Paul appears before Agrippa.

Around the year A.D. 60, a man named Festus assumes the governorship of Jerusalem, the eighth man to have the role after Pontius Pilate less than twenty-five years earlier. Nero is on the throne in Rome. Wanting "to grant the Jews a favor" (Acts 24:27), the new governor, Festus, leaves Paul in prison, refusing to reverse the order of his predecessor, Felix. Paul appeals to the "emperor's tribunal." After conferring with his council, Festus grants Paul's wish to be heard.

As it happens, a few days later "King Agrippa and Bernice" arrive in the administrative center of Caesarea (northwest of Jerusalem, by the sea) to welcome Festus (Acts 25:13). Festus tells Agrippa and Bernice about this man Paul, still in prison from when Felix was in charge. Festus explains the circumstances surrounding Paul's imprisonment, including in particular "certain points of disagreement" between Paul and the Jews about "their own religion" (Acts 25:19). Governor Festus tells King Agrippa of Paul's request to be heard by the emperor, and Agrippa decides to investigate the matter for himself (Acts 25:22).

This is how Paul ends up before "Agrippa and Bernice," who had arrived with "great pomp" (Acts 25:23).

When Paul makes his case before the king, he publicly appeals to what he calls Agrippa's sound background in Judaism: "I count myself lucky that you are the one I'm appearing before, King Agrippa, as

I defend myself today against the accusations of the Jews, because you are especially familiar with all of the customs and controversies of the Jews" (Acts 26:2–3).

Though Paul addresses only the king, we have read three times that "Bernice" is with him. The obvious conclusion, when Agrippa and Bernice arrive together to welcome Festus, is that Bernice is Agrippa's wife, the queen. But she is not.

We learn from Josephus that she is his sister, with whom he is having an incestuous affair!

In this context, Paul's words take on a tone of supreme mockery. He publicly praises Agrippa for his knowledge of all things Jewish while inwardly ridiculing the man for his most heathenly, non-Jewish behavior. The trial is a farce.

More generally, we see a dynamic between Paul and the Roman Empire's representative. Paul gives lip service to the wisdom and authority of the Romans but holds them in contempt for how they behave.

This is not the only case where knowing more about the other characters helps us understand what Paul says. Immediately before Paul's mockery of Agrippa and his sister/mistress Bernice, Paul has the opportunity to address Festus's predecessor, Felix, who has arrived "with his wife, Drusilla, who was Jewish." In Acts 24:25, Paul chooses for his conversation with Felix the topics of "justice, self-control, and the coming judgment," which frighten Felix.

What's going on here? These are not Paul's usual themes. Why did he choose them? And why was Felix afraid?

Josephus tells us more about Felix and his wife, Drusilla. Drusilla had been married to a man named Azizus, but Felix contrived to steal her away. Drusilla thus (according to Josephus) "transgressed the laws of her ancestors" and married Felix. Felix is both an adulterer and a co-conspirator in sin. No wonder the topics of "justice, self-control, and the coming judgment" scare him.

Without the backstory from Josephus, we have no way to understand this otherwise obscure story or to appreciate the way Paul chose his words for their effect on his audience.

Returning to politics, we also learn more about King Herod the Great ("the" King Herod), though the information in nuanced, coming from two of Josephus's major works. In his *War of the Jews*—which in part seems to have been written to squash prevailing anti-Jewish sentiments—Josephus suggests that some people may not have liked Herod. But in his *Antiquities,* we find more detail and a considerably harsher condemnation.

In that second work—which appears more honest and less concerned with offending people—Herod is a man who is only technically Jewish by virtue of a recent forced conversion of his ancestors, has no legitimate claim to the throne, is universally despised in Jerusalem, and consistently sides with the Romans against the Jews.

The opening lines of the second chapter of Matthew, then, are laden with impact. The brief phrase "in the days of King Herod" succinctly conveys an image of a heathen monarch smothering the holy city of Jerusalem.

By comparison, today's reader might imagine a modern account of something that happened in "Stalinist Russia" or "under Mussolini." Far from being irrelevant background details, the mention of those leaders establishes a clear (and, for most, dismal) context.

Similarly, the text of Matthew 2:1 may as well read, "In those awful days when God's holy city was subject to Rome's oppression in the form of an illegitimate, irreligious, and cruel leader." Certainly the story of God's redeemer coming to earth takes on new importance in the context of that King Herod.

All of this background was so obvious to an ancient reader that the authors of the New Testament didn't bother to include it, any more than Woody Allen's character Clifford Stern, in *Crimes and Mis-*

demeanors, has to explain his comment about Lester, played by Alan Alda: "You'd think nobody was ever compared to Mussolini before," he says of his romantic rival. The audience is expected to know who Mussolini is and what he represents. So, too, the New Testament audience knew who Herod was and what he represented.

Herod is not the only political figure who plays an important role in the New Testament. Perhaps the most significant is Pontius Pilate. After all, in Matthew 27 Pilate tries to save Jesus from the bloodthirsty Jews. He knew that the Jews had handed over Jesus "out of jealousy" (verse 18), so he tried to save Jesus by offering the Jews the death of a known criminal, Barabbas, instead of Jesus. But, in an account repeated in Mark, Luke, and John, the Jews demanded the death of Jesus, even at the expense of letting the evil Barabbas go free.

The various reports include different details but point in a similar direction. In Matthew 27:24, "Pilate saw that he could do nothing" to save Jesus. In John 18:38, Pilate admits that he has no case against Jesus. In John 19:21–22, the Jews ask Pilate to write on Jesus' cross not that he was the king of the Jews but rather that he only claimed to be the king of the Jews; Pilate refuses. And so forth. The Pilate of the New Testament is a well-meaning, good-hearted man whose only crime, perhaps, was that he wasn't powerful enough to prevent Jesus' death.

But Josephus paints an entirely different picture of Pontius Pilate. According to Josephus, Pilate is the epitome of the well-known cruelty that increasingly defined the Roman rulers over Jerusalem. Pilate slaughters Samaritans apparently without justification. He taunts the Jews by bringing graven images into Jerusalem. He steals from the Temple treasury.

In fact, Philo of Alexandria, a contemporary of Josephus, laments Pilate's "corruption, insolence, cruelty," and so forth, in his work *Embassy to Gaius.*

It's worth noting that even in the Gospels we find some clues that something is amiss regarding Pilate. In John 18:31, the Jews tell him that they are not permitted to put anyone to death. The implication is that only Pilate has such authority. This reads like an answer to an unasked question: If Pontius Pilate played no part in Jesus' death, why is he so prominent is each account?

More significantly, the story of Barabbas the criminal, whom Pilate offers to kill instead of Jesus, is predicated on the supposed Jewish custom of releasing a prisoner at Passover. The Pontius Pilate of the New Testament hopes to release Jesus. The Jews demand Barabbas instead. But there was no such Jewish custom. In fact, it flies in the face of deeply held Jewish (and, for that matter, Roman) beliefs about justice.

So what are we to make of the two incompatible descriptions of Pontius Pilate? Who was this man, really?

Unfortunately, we have no easy answer to this simple question, because everyone writes with a bias. We can hardly be surprised that the Jewish Josephus (in accord with the Jewish Philo) assigns more blame to Pontius Pilate than to his own people. Nor can we be surprised that the Christian authors of the New Testament blame the already-despised Jews and not the representative of the establishment for the death of their leader.

But beyond that we see two enlightening facts that are missing from the New Testament: First, controversy surrounded Pontius Pilate even when he lived. Second, and even more important, we find overwhelming external evidence of a real man. The very fact that he was perceived by some to be cruel and by others to be compassionate speaks to his powerful presence in antiquity.

The contentious nature of Pontius Pilate combines with the conflicts we have already seen: the struggle between Rome and Jerusalem and the split between Christianity and Judaism. These all exploded in the waning days of Jerusalem's glory. But the New Testament only alludes to the drama. We need Josephus to really understand what happened.

So far, in addition to helping us understand the Old Testament, Josephus has given us insight into the text of the New Testament and some of the political figures in it. Josephus also offers commentary on three religious figures: Jesus' brother, James; John the Baptist; and Jesus himself.

The reader will recall that we agreed to distance our journey through Josephus's writings from the question of how accurate the current manuscripts are, but "with one exception." We have now come to that exception.

Though we expect to find copying mistakes and other variations in our current versions of Josephus's writings, we don't in general suspect that the message of his texts was purposely altered in any significant way, except concerning the pivotal Jesus, James, and John the Baptist. And here nearly every conceivable position has been proposed by scholars, including that Josephus didn't mention any of these people, but later Christians added text about them; that Josephus converted to Christianity, but his texts were changed to hide his belief in Jesus Christ; and that we have nearly perfect copies of what Josephus wrote.

We will not rehash the arguments in their entirety here. When so many well-informed and well-meaning scholars cannot agree, we must acknowledge that we do not have a conclusive answer. Without any new, compelling evidence, the authenticity of the passages referring to James, John, and Jesus will always be in question, and even the degree to which they are in question will be in question.

What we can do is work from the preponderance of the scholarly evidence. Fortunately, that points us in a relatively clear direction. The passages about James and John are mostly authentic. The passage about

Jesus is not, but it's based on an authentic passage that we can still learn from.

With that in mind, we start with John the Baptist.

Josephus offers us striking confirmation of the New Testament account of John's life. This is important, because some people, noting that the New Testament was written with a clear agenda, are reluctant to rely on it for anything historical. While Josephus, too, had an agenda, he could have accomplished his goals without any mention of early Christian leaders. So when we see John the Baptist in Josephus, we have confirmation of some of the reports in the New Testament.

And, interestingly, Josephus tells us much more about John the Baptist than he does about Jesus himself. Perhaps Josephus, at the time, really thought that John the Baptist was more influential than Jesus. (We'll see in a moment that John the Baptist had his own following, apparently independent of Jesus.) And if so, Josephus, describing the state of affairs of his day, may have been right to give John more space than Jesus. Or, writing from his Jewish context, Josephus may have been unaware of the power hierarchy among new Christians.

The Gospels portray John the Baptist as the man who baptized Jesus (Matthew 3:13–15, for example), as part of a broader campaign of baptism on his part. For instance, in Matthew 3:5, people from all around Jerusalem go to John the Baptist to be baptized in the Jordan River as they confess their sins.

This original dunking in water was different from modern baptism, precisely because it was original. Now, "baptism" is an established religious ritual. When John decided that people should be immersed in water, it was a new idea. (For this reason, it may be better to translate John's title as "the dunker" or "the immerser," so as to avoid the impression that John was doing the same thing that modern clergy do when they baptize people. But because "John the Baptist" is so well known, we'll stick with it here.)

We have already seen the contrast between fire and water. According to Josephus, Adam predicted that the world was to be destroyed both by fire and flood. Peter (2 Peter 3:1–7) compares the ancient flood to the future destruction of the earth by fire. In a similar vein, John may have been trying to use baptism in water as a way of staving off future judgment by fire.

Josephus introduces John the Baptist in the context of a military loss suffered by Herod, "Some of the Jews thought that the destruction of Herod's army came from God . . . as a punishment for what he did against John, who is called 'the Baptist.'"

Josephus next explains that John was "a good man, who commanded the Jews to exercise virtue . . . , righteousness towards one another, and piety towards God, and so come to baptism." And then Josephus gives us some of John's theology: "The baptism would be acceptable to [God] if they used it not to make up for sins, but for the purification of the body, which was already thoroughly purified by righteousness." (The terms "virtue," "righteousness," etc., are all approximate translations.) In other words, baptism isn't a "get out of jail" ceremony applied to sins but rather a way for people to mark their previous return from sinful ways. This contrasts with the way many people understand baptism now.

Furthermore, Josephus's John is more connected to Judaism than to Christianity! For Josephus, John the Baptist was so beloved among Jews that the Jews saw a connection between Herod's cruelty toward John and God's wrath.

Yet the Gospels present John the Baptist as the forerunner of Jesus, inextricably connected to the formation of Christianity. It was widely accepted in the first century A.D. that Elijah would announce the coming of the Messiah. So when Jesus was proclaimed Messiah, we read in Matthew 17, some disciples asked him how it was that Elijah hadn't reappeared yet. "Elijah has already come," Jesus replied, but he wasn't recognized (verse 12). According to Matthew 17:13, the disciples "understood that he was talking about John the Baptist."

What are we to make of these two traditions? Josephus writes that John the Baptist was Jewish, while in the New Testament he was the forerunner of Christianity. Which is it?

Both views are probably true.

John the Baptist seems to have had his own following, a fact reflected in at least two ways. In Luke 3:10–14, John the Baptist tells a crowd what he expects of them: sharing clothing and food, moderate taxation, equitable work practices, and the like. But John doesn't mention Jesus! Even more telling is Acts 19:1–5. Paul comes to a place called Ephesus, where he encounters people who had been "baptized into John's baptism," but they had never heard of the "holy spirit." These people, apparently, were followers of John the Baptist, not (yet) of Jesus. Paul had to rebaptize them, this time as followers of Jesus.

So John had his own following, later rejected by rabbinic Judaism and integrated into Christianity. But John himself was typical of the people of the first part of the first century A.D. He was Jewish, and—like the Rabbis, early Christians, and the leaders of the Dead Sea Sect—he was reacting to turbulent times by trying to revitalize his religion.

With Herod, then, Josephus gives us the cultural background that the Bible didn't bother to include. He also gives us information about John the Baptist that the Bible perhaps didn't want people to know about: John the Baptist was the leader of his own school of thought, and his notions of baptism originally had nothing to do with Jesus or Christianity. His role as precursor to Jesus came later.

We turn next to Jesus' brother, James.

The New Testament account of James is somewhat paradoxical. We know he is Jesus' brother from passages like Mark 6:3, where Jesus is "the son of Mary" as well as the "brother of James." Matthew

13:55 is similar. The problem is that John 7:5 is clear that Jesus' brothers, including James, "did not believe in him," while passages like Acts 15:13–22 and Acts 21:18 make James out to be an important church leader. Which is it? Was James a nonbeliever or a church leader?

This question did not escape the attention of later Christian leaders, who worked to explain his conversion, in accounts like the tantalizingly named *Secret Book of James* from, probably, not earlier than the fourth century A.D., or Eusebius of Caesarea's *Church History* from, again, the fourth century. These and other passages propose a miraculous conversion of some sort. Josephus helps a little. Though the details are complicated, Josephus asserts that James eventually rose to a position of power in the early church movement. This confirms the biblical account and is therefore of interest to people who try to reconcile the information from the New Testament. Again, we find confirmation of the accounts in the New Testament, which is helpful for verifying the New Testament in general.

Even more interesting is the way Josephus mentions James. Josephus is writing about a complex legal, religious, political battle, in which the high priest Ananus summons a man before what seems to be an arbitrary council. Whom does he summon? "The brother of Jesus whom they call Christ, whose name was James."

Josephus isn't telling us specifically about James. He's just using James as an example of some of what Ananus did. (And, in fact, he's using Ananus as part of his narrative about the ongoing conflict between the Romans and the Jews.) In this context, his statement about James isn't nearly so important as his presentation of the man as "the brother of Jesus."

This kind of narrative makes most sense if Josephus assumed that everyone would be interested in someone related to Jesus because Jesus was a well-known figure. Josephus's clarification that this is the

Jesus "whom they call the Christ" was probably intended to make it clear which man named Jesus he was talking about. Jesus was, after all, a common name.

The phrasing "who was called Christ," as opposed to "who is Christ" of course reflects Josephus's Jewish heritage. Josephus didn't think the man was the Christ, but, as a historian, he acknowledged that others did. (Some translations render the Greek here as "so-called Christ," a phrasing that imparts a skeptical tone to Josephus's words that we don't find in his Greek.)

We learn, then, that Josephus knew of a man named Jesus who was important enough that even a story about his brother would be worthy of mention. That is good news for readers of the New Testament who look for historical confirmation of Jesus' life.

But there's also bad news. According to Josephus, Jesus had a brother—an actual brother, not merely a brother in the general sense of colleague, friend, cobeliever, etcetera. This conflicts with the tradition that Jesus' mother, Mary, a virgin when she bore Jesus, remained a virgin.

In addition to this offhand reference to Jesus, Josephus has a passage actually devoted to Jesus, a text that has earned the title "Testimonium Flavianum," that is, the "Witness of Flavius [Josephus]."

We have already seen evidence that Josephus didn't believe that Jesus was the Messiah. That's why he wrote that Jesus "was called Christ." Similarly, the hugely influential Christian theologian Origen (second to third centuries) laments Josephus's lack of faith.

But in the text of the "Testimonium Flavianum" as we have it now, Josephus writes that Jesus was "a wise man, if it's proper to call him a man, for he was a doer of wonderful works. . . . He was the Christ. . . . And the tribe of Christians, so named from him, are not extinct at this day." This is the kind of language that transforms the text from a historical account into a witness to Jesus' divinity.

But we have no reason to think that Josephus actually wrote it. Josephus's works were well known almost as soon as he wrote them, and for this reason others frequently quoted or otherwise referred to him. But no one seems to have been aware of this particular passage until the fourth century.

Even the notion that there are "Christians" who were still around seems anachronistic. When Josephus was writing, the Christians were Jews who followed Jesus, hardly a separately named group, and certainly not a group about which Josephus might find it appropriate to remark, "They're still around." They were brand-new.

There are many other reasons to doubt the authenticity of this passage—ranging from style to other external references—and we won't rehash all of them here. Yet there are also reasons to suppose that our current text is at least based on something that Josephus wrote—an original comment on Jesus that, sadly, has been lost to history as generations of copyists have tried to insert their own words into Josephus's text.

So even though this "Testimonium Flavianum" is among the most widely cited passages from Josephus, it is ultimately of vexingly little value. And what little we do learn from it—that Josephus apparently knew about Jesus—we find confirmed with much more force from the passage about James.

Still, what we have is a lot.

The preeminent historian of his day knew about Jesus, knew that he was important, and knew that he was considered the Messiah. Josephus also knew about John the Baptist and, again, knew that John was important. And—though it may not be welcome news for everyone—Jesus had a brother James.

Equally, the picture Josephus paints of two camps—one led by Jesus, the other by John—seems to capture the flavor of the first century A.D. perfectly, particularly when combined with his description of Herod. In the context of unprecedented turmoil and upheaval, lots of groups—led by John, Jesus, people at Qumran, and, almost certainly, many others— were trying to make sense of rapidly changing times. This is the milieu that gave the world Christianity and rabbinic Judaism.

In addition, we learn from Josephus that the holy writings of those two groups, compiled as the Bible, are incomplete. Josephus gives us crucial background information that the original authors didn't bother to include and fascinating details that—by accident or design— were omitted.

Josephus thus joins the Dead Sea Scrolls and the Septuagint as an ancient source that fills in the blanks of the Bible, giving us better insight into the full spectrum of information from which the text was culled.

In addition to these missing bits as revealed in Josephus, the Dead Sea Scrolls, and the Septuagint, whole books were left out of the Bible, too, as we see next.

5

ADAM AND EVE: FALLING DOWN AND GETTING BACK UP

Judge a tree by its fruit, not its leaves.
—LATIN PROVERB

Perhaps surprisingly, their first question wasn't how to survive. It was why they had to survive. Or, more precisely, why no one was taking care of that for them.

Up until now, in their brief and sheltered experience, everything had automatically been attended to, requiring no effort on their part. Survival had been easy. But no more.

Their new reality was so shocking, in fact, that it would take them a whole week to realize that they were hungry.

So their first question was, Why? And not just why they suddenly had to take care of themselves. They wanted to know why things had changed.

The simple answer was that it was their own fault. They had known the rules and willingly broken them. And considering what the consequences could have been, their sentence had perhaps even been lenient.

But, though accurate, that answer seemed unsatisfactory. So even amid the demands of their new and surprising need to survive, they tried to make sense of things.

They are Adam and Eve, and the account of their life after Eden comes from a variety of documents in Greek, Latin, Georgian, Armenian, Slavonic, and even Old Irish. Most of them are translations, either of each other or of original documents that have long been lost. Some are obvious adaptations. The work is usually called the Life of Adam and Eve, though the Greek version is sometimes misleadingly titled the Apocalypse of Moses, because that text purports to show the life of Adam and Eve to Moses.

The various versions are not entirely consistent with each other, making it difficult to pin down exactly what the original text was, when it was written, and in which language. Still, by carefully combining the different versions, we can get a pretty good sense of the text. And we can date it with reasonable confidence to the days of Jesus. It was probably written in Hebrew or Aramaic.

In other words, the Life of Adam and Eve is the second half of the Bible's Adam and Eve story, and it dates to the days when the content of the Bible was still in flux. As it happens, the first part of the story features prominently in Genesis, while this second part was relegated to the obscurity of the cutting room floor, which is a shame, because in many ways it's the post-Eden part of the story that speaks most directly to the human condition.

The Genesis account of Adam and Eve in Eden spans less than a few dozen verses, yet the story continues to have almost unbelievable impact. It is hardly a coincidence that Adam and Eve are the focus of artistic expression from Michelangelo's *Adam* to Marc Chagall's *Creation,* in addition to works named *Adam and Eve* by such luminaries as Rubens, Raphael, and others, or that Milton based his *Paradise*

Lost on the story and Shakespeare used some of its themes—like the snake and the garden—in *Hamlet*.

Adam and Eve themselves—whether as historical or literary figures—represent all of humanity, a fact reflected in their names. The Hebrew *adam* means both "Adam" and "human," while Eve's name is connected to the Hebrew root that means "life." The story of Adam and Eve is the story of human life on earth.

The basic plot in the Bible is deceptively simple. God puts the first people in a paradise that provides for everything they need—including plants and trees for food. The only caveat is that, under alleged penalty of death, they're not allowed to eat from one particular tree, the Tree of Knowing Good and Evil. Then a snake or serpent comes along and convinces Eve to eat from the tree. She does and convinces her husband to do the same. As punishment, they are both exiled from Eden and punished in other ways, too.

Hidden in this simple plot of disobedience and punishment are tantalizing details and nuances.

Though the text is intertwined with the creation story—making it unclear where exactly this story begins—a reasonable starting point is Genesis 3:1, with the appearance of the snake. But the context from the previous verse in 2:25 sets the stage: "The man and his wife were both naked, but they were not ashamed." Near the end of the story, in 3:21, God makes clothing for Adam and Eve. Apparently, in addition to everything else, this is a story about nakedness, clothing, and shame.

The snake's first appearance is as "the snake," as if the reader should already know which snake the text intends. Though this particular snake actually walks upright on legs, its mobility is not its most surprising attribute. It can also talk, making it one of only two talking animals in the Bible—the other being a donkey in the book of Numbers.

But even its speech is not what the text highlights. Rather, the snake is described as "crafty."

In English, the word seems irrelevant and almost out of context. But the Hebrew word for "crafty" is spelled the same way as the word "naked." Once again, we find the themes of nakedness, clothing, and shame.

Furthermore, though demonized, the snake actually comes off as honest, where God is deceptive. God tells Adam that he will die if he eats from the tree, while the snake tells Eve that God is lying. After Adam and Eve do eat from the tree, the reader learns that God was in fact lying and that the snake was telling the truth. What, exactly, was the snake's crime here?

Yet the snake is the first to be punished. It—or, perhaps, "he"— loses its legs, and in addition snakes from then on have to suffer strife with women. (Rabbinic tradition asks why the snake would care and answers that the snake had hoped to marry Eve.)

In addition to their joint exile, the man and woman are punished individually. Women will endure pain in childbirth and suffer a love- hate relationship with their husbands, while men will have to toil in "cursed" ground, working hard to obtain food.

The themes of paradise and exile resonate deeply with most people. Nearly everyone finds themselves, in one way or another, longing for what was. Whether it's the innocence of childhood, a better place, the simpler days of yore, or even just youthful times when dreams seemed within reach, there's a sense in which we are all living in exile. We are all post-Eden.

And it's not just exile that mirrors our own lives. We are imperfect. Like Adam and Eve, we have done what we were told not to do. And, again like Adam and Eve, we have felt ashamed.

This state of imperfection often goes by the technical term "fall," and postexilic Adam is the "fallen Adam." For the great theologian Paul, whose contributions to the New Testament helped shape Christianity, we are all in a state of fallenness because we are all Adam, all imperfect, all sinners.

More generally, whether specifically in the framework of fallenness or more broadly in the context of living an imperfect life, the expulsion from the Garden of Eden serves as a metaphor for the reality of life, as contrasted with what life could be or once was. In this sense, the most important part of the story is not what happens in Eden but what happens afterward.

The text in Genesis asks the question, What is life like? The Life of Adam and Eve offers some answers. So we pick up the account with Adam and Eve as they are newly exiled and trying to understand their world.

Their first overt task was to build shelter. Adam fashioned a hut, which turned out to be a house of mourning. Their second overt act was to weep. For fully seven days they were consumed with regret, longing for the kingdom from which they had been expelled. Then hunger finally overtook sorrow, and they realized they had to eat. Eve told Adam to go find some food.

The search for food was an emotional compromise on their part. On the one hand, for seven days they had done almost nothing to further their own well-being, focusing their attention only backward, to the lost Eden. Now they were taking their first significant step forward. Still, they saw Adam's task as nothing more than a temporary measure, meant to last them only until God took them back into Eden. As is so often the case, they had started to come to terms with the tragedy, but not with its permanence.

At first it looked like even finding temporary sustenance would prove too difficult a task. Adam saw nothing he recognized as edible. So he was forced to return empty-handed to Eve and give her the news that they were going to die of starvation.

But rather than help her husband find food, Eve focused her

energy on a muddled mix of regret and pleading. "If I were dead, God would take you back into the Garden," she told her husband.

"I don't know whose fault this is," he replied. Like his wife, he was reliving the past, not dealing with the present.

"Kill me," she pleaded, "so God will no longer be angry with you and will let you back into the Garden."

"How could I make my own flesh suffer?" Adam asked. But he also responded, "Don't even say such a thing, for God might bring about more judgment if there's a killing." Was he really incapable of killing his wife? Or was he just afraid of the consequences?

"Then let's go look for food together," Eve said.

Even working in tandem, they found nothing like their food from the Garden—their angelic food, so much better than ordinary food, fit only for beasts.

Still refusing to confront their new reality, Eve hatched a plan by which they might purposely suffer in penance, convincing God to pity them and give them food so they wouldn't become like the animals.

"For how long?" Adam wanted to know. It was a matter of some importance to him.

He wanted to suffer longer than his wife, confessing that their current predicament was his fault. Like many people in the throes of anguish, he blamed himself, but only as part of a larger and less-organized reaction that cast blame on everything and everyone.

And also like many people who suffer, he was terrified that things would get even worse. That's the second reason he needed to know how long his wife planned to suffer. He wanted to make sure it was a reasonable plan. If she cut her suffering short, God might punish them for that, too.

And—yet again like people who suffer—he was focusing his attention in all the wrong places. His idea of "reasonable" was an appropriate amount of time to suffer to make God take them back in. A more objective reasonable approach might have been to go find food.

Their suffering would consist of wading neck-deep into a river, clothed only by the water. In the end, they decided on forty days for Adam, in the Jordan, and thirty-four days in the Tigris for Eve.

This is how it happened that Eve met the Devil.

The Devil first transformed his shape. Then, dressed in splendid attire that contrasted with Eve's tear-stained clothing, he approached the bank of the Tigris. Weeping false tears, he told Eve that her suffering had worked. God had seen what she and her husband had done. "We have also prayed on your behalf," he said, not making it entirely clear who "we" might be. "God sent me to you to give you the food you want."

Eve didn't respond.

"Come out of the water," the Devil continued.

Still no response from Eve.

"I just spoke with Adam. He told me to come get you and bring you back to him."

Eve relented and exited the Tigris, long before the thirty-four days that she had promised. Her skin wrinkled from the cold water, she found that her ordeal had robbed her of her beauty. And it had exhausted her. She spent two days lying on the shore before she had enough strength to move.

Then she finally followed the Devil back to Adam.

When Adam saw Eve escorted by the Devil, he wept with tears so bitter they burned his eyes, and through them he shouted at his wife, "Why didn't you do what I told you? How could you let yourself be deceived again by the one who made us refugees in the first place?"

But like children who don't understand the power of their words, Adam was surprised to see Eve's reaction to his condemnation of her. She, too, broke out in tears and fell to the ground.

It wasn't until he saw Eve lying motionless like a corpse that Adam turned his anger to the Devil. "What did we ever do to you?" he demanded.

"It's your fault that we were evicted from the Garden," Adam continued. "Are you angry with us because we caused you to be expelled from the Garden? Is it because of us that you lost your glory? Is it because of something we did? Or are we the only creature of God, so we have naturally become your only enemy?"

Adam may have meant his tirade of questions to be rhetorical, but the Devil insisted on telling his side of the story.

"My greed and anger are directed at you because you caused my downfall. I used to be a winged angel, but because of you I now walk on feet."

"What did I do to you?"

"You didn't do anything to me, but it's still your fault that I've fallen to earth."

The Devil explained that the problems began when God created humans, because humans were created in the image of God.

The angel Michael came and had the human bow down before God, because, even being in the image of God, they were not God.

Then Michael summoned all the angels and had them bow down before the newly created human, before the new image of God. But the Devil refused to bow down to a younger creature, claiming that it was improper for the old to serve the young. Other angels heard the Devil's words, and they, too, refused to bow down.

So God grew angry and ordered that the Devil and these other angels be cast down to earth as punishment, while he ordered that Adam be put in the Garden as a reward.

"When I realized that I had fallen because of you—that I was in distress while you rested—I started hunting you, to exile you from the Garden just as I had been exiled."

Adam had originally blamed Eve. Then he had refused to blame

Eve. Then he had blamed himself. When he first saw the Devil, Adam blamed him, too. Now, still confused and distraught, he cried out to God to send away the one who had caused Eve to be lost. Eve was still the instigator, but the Devil was at fault, too, and God was an enabler.

Just then, the Devil became invisible.

Eve similarly felt that she was primarily responsible. She had now let the Devil trick her twice, once in the Garden of Eden, leading to their exile, and now again, leading her to abandon the plan to get back to the Garden.

From the shores of the Jordan, with her husband still standing neck-high in water in order to gain God's pity, Eve cried out, "Save yourself." And, with that, she set off to die, walking westward and eating only the grass that feeds the animals. She knew it couldn't support her.

After three days of walking away from her husband, she, too, built a hut.

What she didn't know was that she was three months pregnant.

Adam was still in the water, hoping that God would provide him food. Instead, God sent the angel Michael with a packet of seeds, marked by the divine seal. Michael showed Adam how to sow the seeds and how to work a field so that Adam would be able to make his own food.

It wasn't the solution Adam had hoped for. He was still in exile. He was alone. And God wasn't giving him food. But at least he could eat.

Eve was alone, too. But when she finally went into labor, she cried out to God, asking for her husband, Adam, to console her in her pain. Knowing that he was too far off to hear, she even begged the stars to send word to her husband.

Though Adam was distant, he still heard Eve's cries and recognized them as the voice of his own rib. Thinking that perhaps the Devil was attacking her again, he ran off to find her.

He found her in enormous, almost unbearable pain. She was crying out for relief, either in the form of less pain or in the form of death—anything to make the suffering stop.

Adam, too, prayed on her behalf, and it was his prayer that was answered, in the form of angels who came to console Eve. "You will live through this," they told her, "because of your husband. Were it not for him, you would have conceived a child whose birth you would not have survived." Then the angels taught Eve about childbirth.

After Eve had given birth, to Cain, she heard a warning, "This child of yours is perverse, the kind of person who plucks up the fruit-bearing tree, not the kind who plants it."

Eight years later, Eve bore another child, Abel.

And she had a dream.

She dreamt that the blood of her younger son, Abel, was pouring into the mouth of her older son, Cain, who was drinking it mercilessly. Abel pleaded with his brother to leave him a little blood, but Cain refused. Abel's blood poured through Cain, into and then out of his stomach, staining his limbs with blood that could not be removed.

Eve told her husband about the dream, who suggested that they keep Cain and Abel apart and keep them well supervised.

Unbeknownst to Adam, God had already told the angel Gabriel that Cain would kill Abel. "But in order that Adam not be sad," God had said, "I will give him another child, Seth. Seth will resemble my image and teach everything of which I have a memory. But don't tell Adam."

So Gabriel and God knew what was going to happen, and Adam and Eve suspected, because they took Eve's dream seriously.

Eve's dream proved accurate. Despite Adam and Eve's best parenting efforts, they suffered another tragedy when one of their children killed the other.

Their life so far had been on a nearly steady decline. Starting in the magnificent Garden of Eden, they had knowingly disobeyed God, suffering the punishment of exile; nearly starved to death; met with the Devil; and almost separated as a couple.

Their marriage was saved when Eve bore a son, but that first child had proved to be an instigator of evil. They felt they had failed as parents, too. Even knowing that their second child's life had been in danger, they were unable to save him. They were now the exiled parents of a murderer and a corpse.

Still, they kept on. Eve bore a third son, Seth, who resembled Adam and who, Adam and Eve hoped, would take the place of Abel. Even though it was God who first suggested it, this plan to have one child replace another may have been the epitome of their denial.

Perhaps for this reason, Adam and Eve's life became routine after Seth was born. Their days were taken up with the raising of children—thirty boys and thirty girls, they say, over the course of thirty more periods of thirty years. Their children and their children's families scattered around the earth.

As Adam eventually grew ill, he gathered all of his descendants for one last visit, at which he would put his affairs in order. He divided the world into three, assigning various children to each part. And he told them he was sick.

But the children asked, "What do you mean? How does a person get sick?"

Seth—who had been intended as the slain Abel replacement—asked his father, "Are you sad because you remember the fruit from the Garden? Is that why you are ill? If so, I will go to the Garden, and beg and weep until God hears me. And maybe God will send an angel with some fruit from the Garden and then I'll bring it to you and then you'll feel better."

"It doesn't work that way," Adam told his son. "I am sick. I'm in pain."

"What is pain?" Seth asked simply.

It's not surprising, given his life, that Adam's answer to his son's question started with the Garden of Eden. Nor is it surprising that Adam's account was colored by his own experiences thereafter. He started to explain, "When God created your mother and me, he put us in a garden of delights. But there was a beautiful plant in the middle of the garden that God had told us not to eat. Then the snake deceived your mother and made her eat it. That is why we are now going to die."

Adam offered a little more detail: "When it was time for the angels to ascend to worship God, the enemy deceived Eve and she ate from the forbidden tree. Then she deceived me—for I didn't know. God divided the garden between me and your mother, entrusting me to guard the eastern and northern parts, your mother to guard the south and the west.

"There were twelve angels with us to guard us through the night, but each day they ascended back to God. It was at the moment of their ascent that the snake deceived your mother, because the snake had seen that I was no more with her than the angels were. Your mother made me eat it, too—for I didn't understand.

"After we'd eaten, God grew angry with us, warning that he would scorn us just as we had scorned his commandment. He had us suffer. God did this to me. That is why I'm going to die."

Seth was overcome with grief. Eve was, too, even offering to take half of her husband's pain upon herself, because, she said, his suffering was her fault.

With that, Adam came up with a plan. He sent Eve and Seth back to the Garden of Eden, this time not to bring food but rather olive oil from the Tree of Life, oil that would heal him.

So they set out for the Garden.

Along the way, Eve saw a beast that was biting one of her descendants. She immediately connected the event to her own life story, lamenting her reputation on the final day of judgment, when, she feared, her sins would continue to burn her since everyone blamed her for bringing evil into the world by disobeying God.

"How dare you?" she chastised the beast, condemning it for opening its mouth and sinking its teeth into no less than a human created in the image of God.

"It's not our fault that you're suffering," the beast replied. "It's your own fault. You are the one who listened to the original beast, the snake. And how dare you? You opened your mouth and ate the fruit that God told you not to. Everything changed because of you. You wouldn't be able to endure it if I really responded to your accusations."

Seth, too, chastised the beast, commanding it to close its mouth and leave them. And the beast left.

When Eve and Seth finally arrived at the walls of the Garden, they prayed to God to send them an angel. God sent Michael, who was in charge of the souls, to meet them. He told Seth to forget about the idea of oil from the olive tree, because the timing was wrong.

In five thousand years, Michael said, the beloved body of Christ would come to earth to resurrect Adam's body from his fall. Christ would be baptized in the Jordan, just as Adam had suffered in the Jordan, and Christ would anoint Adam and all his descendants, so that they would rise at the time of the resurrection.

"But now," Michael said, "go back to your father. His time is nearing its end. In three days his soul will leave his body and he'll see the wonders of heaven."

So Seth and Eve left empty-handed, returned to Adam, and told him what had happened.

Adam started weeping anew because of what the beast had done. His whole life, as he now saw it, was nothing but a source of suffering. "Our descendants will blame their parents for their misery," he lamented, begging his wife to explain what had happened.

This gave Eve a chance to provide her account of the Fall.

"We were tricked," she began, addressing all of her children.

"Your father was guarding his part of the Garden, the east and the north, while I was guarding my part, the west and the south. And the Devil came to Adam's part.

"God had also divided the beasts in the Garden of Eden, giving me the female ones and your father the male ones. So when the Devil came to your father's part of the Garden, he was able to find the serpent. The Devil flattered the serpent with praise, and promised to teach it useful words.

"The Devil explained that all of the animals bow down to Adam each day, including the serpent, even though the serpent was created before Adam. It wasn't right, the Devil said, that the older should bow down before the younger, and it wasn't right that the serpent should eat inferior food while Adam and I ate the fruit of the Garden. The Devil told the serpent that if they worked together just outside the Garden, they could have me and Adam excluded, and maybe they would still be able to reenter the Garden.

"The serpent wanted to know how, and the Devil told the serpent to be a sheath, so he could speak through the serpent's mouth.

"Then the Devil came to me on my side of the Garden, in the form of an angel, but even as I was looking at him, he disappeared. That was when he went to get the serpent. Then the Devil slipped inside the serpent and hung his head near the Garden's wall.

"'Shame on you, woman!' he cried out to me, speaking through the serpent. 'Come over here so I can tell you a secret.'

"As I approached the serpent, it called out to me, 'Eve!'

"'I am here,' I replied.

"The serpent wanted to know what I do in the Garden, so I explained that God had given me the Garden to take care of, and I guarded the Garden and ate from its fruits. Then the serpent wanted to know if

I eat fruit from every tree, so I said that I did, except for the tree that God told me was off limits, and that if I ate from it, I would die.

"The serpent told me that it was worried about me, because I was just like the animals. God was jealous of me, it said, and that was why God didn't want me to eat from that one tree. But the serpent wanted me to be knowledgeable and to see the glory that could only come from eating from that tree. At first I didn't want to. I was afraid of dying. But the serpent said that there was no such thing as death. 'Death is life!' it told me.

"I still didn't want to, but the snake kept at it. 'God is alive, so you won't die. But when you eat from that tree your eyes will be opened and, just like God, you'll know about good and evil. God only told you not to eat from that tree because he knew that eating from it would make you more like him.'

"And I still didn't want to. The snake told me to just go take a look, to see what I thought of the fruit. It looked glorious! But I was still afraid to take it. So I told the serpent that if it was telling me the truth, it shouldn't be afraid to pick the fruit and give me some.

"The serpent told me it would, but I had to open the gate that was keeping it out. So I did. And the serpent came in a little, but then it stopped. When I asked it why it was hesitating, it tricked me. It told me that it stopped because it changed its mind, because it was worried that I would eat from the tree's fruit, and become like God. But if I became like God, the serpent was worried that I would treat Adam the way God had treated me, denying Adam the fruit just as God had tried to deny it from me. So it made me swear an oath to give some to Adam.

"And here, my children, I had a problem, because I had never sworn an oath before and I didn't know the words to any oaths. So the serpent told me the right words. And I swore by the plants of the Garden and by the cherubs that form the Father's throne that if I ate the fruit, and it opened my eyes, I would not be jealous, but instead would give some fruit to Adam, too. Then the serpent gave me some fruit to eat. And I ate it.

"That's when I needed to cover my nakedness, and I looked to the trees to find leaves, and the leaves from all the trees in my portion of the Garden had suddenly fallen to the ground. I used a leaf to cover myself, and stood by the tree. And I was afraid, because I had sworn an oath to give Adam some of the fruit.

"Then your father came to me, because he heard me shouting, and thought maybe a beast had entered the Garden. He saw me and couldn't understand why I had put a leaf on myself. I said there was something I wanted to tell him, and asked him if he wanted to hear it.

"Then I said that until that moment we had been like the animals. But I had seen the glory of the fruit that we weren't supposed to eat, eaten it, and learned good and evil. I told Adam to eat some, too, so that he would become like God.

"Adam told me he was afraid to, because God would become angry if he didn't keep his commandment.

"I said that I would take the blame. I told Adam that he could tell God that I gave him the fruit and that I showed him its glory so that it was my fault.

"Adam took the fruit, and ate from it, and became like me. And he took a fig leaf and covered up his nakedness.

"Then we heard from an angel that God had blown a trumpet to convene all of the angels and announce our sentence. Adam told me that we had sinned and that God was going to judge us. So we hid. God had to come to the Garden to find us, and when he arrived, all of the leaves from all of the trees had fallen off.

"God called out, 'Adam, Adam! Are you hiding from me? How can a house hide from its builder? And why are you hiding near the tree of the Garden?' Your father told God that he was hiding because he was naked and ashamed. God demanded to know who told him that he was naked, and whether he had broken the commandment not to eat from the tree.

"Adam remembered what I had told him, and he blamed me. Then I remembered what the serpent had told me, and I blamed it.

"God told Adam his punishment: 'The earth will be cursed by your deeds. You will work the earth and it will give you no fruit, sprouting only thorns. You will eat bread only by the sweat of your brow. You will work and find no rest. You will be hungry and not sated. You will suffer from bitterness and not taste sweetness. You will be afflicted by heat and experience cold. You will be poor and not rich. You will eat but remain malnourished. You will find fire and not be warmed. You will seek water and it will withdraw. The beasts that you used to rule over will now rise up against you. You will be weak, because you didn't keep my commandments.'

"And God told me my punishment: 'You will be in pain. You will give birth to many children and when you do give birth you will suffer and despair of your life, and you'll promise yourself that if you make it through the agony of giving birth you will never return to your husband. But you will return to him, begging him to take you back. In that way your husband will rule over you.'

"And God had a punishment for the serpent: 'You will be cursed among the animals. The food you used to eat will be withheld, and you'll eat soil. The precious cross that my Son will take upon the earth will condemn you because of how you deceived Adam.'

"Then God ordered us out of the Garden. Adam asked the angels to wait until he could petition God, so maybe God wouldn't kick him out of the Garden. The angels agreed, and Adam begged God for forgiveness.

"But God chastised the angels for waiting: 'Am I to blame?' he demanded of them. 'Didn't I act justly?' The angels agreed that he was blameless and had acted justly.

"When God told Adam that he could not remain in the Garden, Adam begged for fruit from the Tree of Life. But God told him that he had posted burning cherubim and a turning sword to guard the Tree of Life, so that Adam could never get its fruit and become immortal and boast of his immortality. But God also told him that if he guarded himself from every evil after he left the Garden, then in the future resurrection he would get the fruit of the Tree of Life and then live forever.

"As Adam left the Garden he begged the angels for incense that he could use to please God. The angels gave him nard, saffron, reed, and cinnamon to take with him from the Garden to earth.

"That, my children," said Eve, "is how we were tricked. So watch yourselves, and don't stop doing good."

With that she turned her attention back to Adam, asking why he alone was dying and what would happen to her. Would she live forever? What would life be like without him? Or would she eventually die, too?

Adam told her not to worry about things like that. If she was going to die, she would end up near him, and if not, she should leave his body where it was, because God would seek out the vessel he had made.

Adam hoped he would be reunited with his creator, but couldn't be sure of it, because he didn't know if God was still angry with him. He asked Eve to offer a prayer that he be united with God.

Overcome, Eve fell to her knees and confessed everything she thought she had done wrong. She confessed to God, to the angels, to the cherubim, to the altar of holiness, to the heavens, to the birds in the heavens, to the beasts. While she was still praying, the angel Michael came and lifted her back to her feet. "Adam your husband has gone from his body," he said.

"Look," he added. "He is with his creator."

Eve and her son Seth looked upward and saw the sun and the moon petitioning God on Adam's behalf. The angels joined in, too, praying for God to pardon Adam. God eventually commanded the angel Michael to take Adam to the third heaven, where the Garden of Eden was located. This caused the angels to rejoice, praising the wonder that Adam was forgiven and the promise of the future.

With great pomp and elaborate ceremony—too brilliant for anyone but Seth to see—God came to collect Adam's body from the earth. "If only you had kept my commandments," God told Adam sorrowfully, "your enemy would never have been able to rejoice. But I will turn his joy into sadness, and put you upon his throne."

Michael took Adam's body back to the Garden in the third heaven, where they anointed it with oil from the olive tree and wrapped it in shrouds. God commanded that Abel's body—which had lain exposed since his death—be brought, too, uniting father and son in death. There they were buried.

Finally, God called to Adam, and Adam's body answered from the soil, "I am here."

"As I told you, you are soil and you have returned to the soil," God said. "But at the time of the resurrection I will raise you back up."

Eve witnessed all of this and grew weak. She wept and wished to see her husband's body and where it was buried. She begged God to reunite them, to bring them back together as they had been in the Garden of Eden, when they were inseparable. And her body gave up her soul.

With Adam and Eve dead, the angel Michael came to Seth and taught him how to dress Eve's body, instructing him also to dress every dead person in the same way. Then Michael ascended to the seventh heaven and from there commanded Seth to mourn for the dead not more than five days and on the seventh day to rejoice, because on that day God rested from the work of creation.

With that the story ends. Seth is left in charge of things—an account confirmed by the Bible and Josephus, among other sources—while Adam and Eve are pardoned and in death reunited in the Garden of Eden.

The original texts of the Life of Adam and Eve leave out explanations and background that would have originally been superfluous. The "third heaven," where the Garden of Eden is located, and the "seventh heaven" that we find at the end of the story are part of a taxonomy of seven heavens of increasing splendor that would have been familiar to an ancient reader, so the narrative doesn't explain them, just as it refers to the Garden without mentioning Eden by name. So at times this retelling of the story fills in some background to help modern readers follow the plot. For example, the Tree of Life was frequently understood to be an olive tree, which is why the original text refers to the olive oil of the Tree of Life without explaining the connection, but here it is spelled out.

Also, like most literature from the time period, the original narrative lacks the details that modern readers generally expect. What did the people look like? How did they dress? What was the weather?

In our case, what color was the snake, and how long was it? Was it a garter snake? A python? A cobra? What color were Adam and Eve's eyes, or their hair? What did the Devil's splendid clothing look like? What did his voice sound like? How did Adam and Eve build their huts? And so forth.

Without these details, the text strikes many modern readers as sparse, a little odd perhaps, and in many ways simplistic, even in the paraphrase here. But the story—in addition to any historical value it may have—is both nuanced and remarkably insightful, offering complex and valuable lessons about our lives.

In particular, it answers a general question and a subquestion.

The question is, What is it like to be human? The subquestion is, Why isn't life perfect?

We start by returning to the themes of nakedness and clothing. As we saw, Adam and Eve start off naked in Genesis, and the snake's cunning is expressed through a Hebrew homonym of "naked."

In the Life of Adam and Eve, Adam and Eve have different recollections of what happened in the Garden of Eden—a rhetorical technique that mirrors real human memory and that adds intricacy to the tale here. But one thing they agree on is that they were naked, then ashamed of their nakedness, then clothed.

Clothing of some sort is nearly universal, perhaps even universal, among humans, and seems to have been so for some time. Evidence suggests that humans started clothing themselves roughly at the same time that Homo sapiens appeared on the earth, though "roughly" in this case means only a few tens of thousands of years apart. We find contradictory and uncertain evidence for the dating of the first Homo sapiens as well as for the first clothing, but most scholars agree that both date to between 150,000 and 200,000 years ago, while other cultural artifacts only came about some 50,000 years ago.

And as fundamental to humanity as clothing is, it is equally unknown in the animal world (with the obvious exception of people who dress their pets).

Clothing thus joins language as the two most obvious differences between humans and animals. (Even though animals talk in some stories, and even though they can communicate in real life, people never observe two animals just sitting around chewing the fat, except in the most literal of senses.)

But clothing in the Life of Adam and Eve doesn't represent the distinction between humans and animals. After all, Adam and Eve are human in the Garden of Eden, and they are distinct from the animals. Yet they are naked.

Rather, the Life of Adam and Eve focuses on the transition from childhood to adulthood. Unlike adults, children are comfortable without clothing. So are young Adam and Eve.

Other elements of the text align with this same theme.

Like Adam and Eve in the Garden of Eden, children don't have to prepare their own shelter or food. They can fall asleep whenever and wherever they want, confident that they will wake up in their own house with food automatically available. (Neglected children and children in other unfortunate circumstances are obvious exceptions. Our revulsion at these cases comes in part from the way they deviate from what we expect life to be like.)

Unlike children, if adults want food and shelter, they have to take care of it themselves.

Most adults even remember the shock of the transition from childhood to adulthood, the day they realized that they were only going to have dinner if they cooked it themselves, using food they obtained on their own—either buying it with their own money or otherwise procuring it. And if they wanted a roof under which to enjoy their food, they would have to arrange that themselves, too.

The Life of Adam and Eve opens with the couple grappling with this very shift. They have left the childhood of Eden and find themselves facing the surprising and daunting task of living their lives as adults.

So the first part of the answer to, What is it like to be human? according to the Life of Adam and Eve, is that life consists of two stages, childhood and adulthood.

Modern, Western cultures have many more stages of life, of course. Children go through infancy before becoming toddlers, then schoolchildren. After grade school but before adulthood come the teenage years, and perhaps young adulthood, as contrasted with just plain old adulthood. That in turn comes before old age, with, maybe, retirement buffering the transition.

Lives in antiquity—generally only a few decades long, despite the symbolically exaggerated ages of many of the people in the texts—didn't allow for so many distinct stages of life. People who puttered through their teen years experimenting and then spent their twenties and thirties finding themselves would have found themselves dead before they lived.

But even with our proliferation of life stages, we still recognize a major break between childhood and adulthood, though the exact dividing line is fuzzy and in flux. By age twenty-one, in the United States, citizens can do anything their elders can do, with the singular exception of holding some public offices. By age eighteen, they can vote and serve in the military. By age sixteen or so they can drive. At roughly that same age, they can marry. People as young as thirteen can be processed through the legal system as "adults."

Underlying all of these ages—thirteen, sixteen, eighteen, twenty-one, or some other cutoff—is the fundamental concept that some people are children, others adults. The Life of Adam and Eve highlights this distinction and draws attention to some of the qualities that separate childhood from adulthood. Children are not embarrassed by nudity; adults are. Children have food and shelter provided for them; adults do not.

Just as there is no single age at which children become adults in the American legal sense, children progress gradually into the adulthood envisioned in the Life of Adam and Eve. For instance, they usually insist on clothing long before they are expected or even able to obtain it for themselves. But this doesn't diminish the fundamental difference.

This division is so central to Western life that we take it for granted. It is enshrined in common phrases like "men, women, and children," for example, in addition to the various legal definitions of adulthood.

According to Genesis, adulthood for men means having to work for a living, and for women means having to deal with painful childbirth.

The Life of Adam and Eve goes into further detail and also suggests that adulthood is defined in part by longing for childhood. For their whole lives, Adam and Eve try to return to the Eden of their youth. At first, it is the sole focus of their energy. Then, as they learn how to live their lives, they spend more time focusing on the present and less time thinking about the past, but we see by the end of their saga that their adult lives are defined by their childhoods.

So the Life of Adam and Eve starts by teaching us that adulthood—the bulk of our lives—consists in part of longing for what was. This is the first part of its answer to, What is it like to be human?

Most of us relate intimately to this sentiment, and not just in terms of childhood. We long for a lover who left, a dead parent, a job we once had, a place we used to live. Like Adam and Eve, we all live in exile.

And also like Adam and Eve, our longing is accompanied by regret. The Life of Adam and Eve teaches us that the regret, though entirely human, is misplaced.

In many ways, the Tree of Knowing Good and Evil was a setup. God put the tree right in the middle of the garden, where Adam and Eve would pass by it every day. By comparison, we can imagine a parent making brownies and telling a three-year-old not to eat them. But if the parent leaves a brownie on the child's pillow at night, whose fault is it, really, when the child eats the brownie?

This brings us to the second major theme of the Life of Adam and

Eve. Having taught us that adulthood consists of hard work, pain, and longing for what was, the text turns to an obvious question: Why?

The answer in the Life of Adam and Eve comes in two stages, beginning with the wrong answer.

Part of the wrong answer, as we just saw, is that it's our fault. This is where Adam and Eve start. They ask themselves what they did to deserve this, and they think they know the answer: They disobeyed God. Missing from their analysis, though, is the possibility that this was a setup and, even more, the fact that they were duped. No less than the leader of evil, the Devil himself, arranged for their fall. They were outgunned. There was nothing they could have done.

We also see an insightful detail when Adam and Eve beg to be let back into their garden. It's not just that they think that their exile is their fault. They think they can reverse it.

We, too, live our adult lives lamenting our mistakes and trying to reverse their consequences. But like Adam and Eve, there was nothing we could have done differently, and there is nothing we can do to go back.

So if it's not our fault, why do we suffer? It is among the most human of questions, and the Life of Adam and Eve offers an answer in perhaps the most important part of the text: the interview with the Devil.

Adam, as we saw, recognizes that the Devil forced him and his wife out of the Garden of Eden. "Why did you do this to us?" Adam demands to know. "Is it because of something we did to you?"

The Devil's answer, like so much else in the text, is nuanced and poignant. "You didn't do anything to me," he says, "but it's still your fault." Then the Devil explains—in his recounting of his own fall from glory—that humans earned his wrath simply by their humanity. To be human, in other words, is to rise above the animals and to be little less than divine. But equally, to be human is to suffer. Suffering is the price we pay for experiencing the joy of being human.

And the suffering is no more our fault, and no more under our control, than the transition from childhood to adulthood.

Some people hear this as a cop-out. How can the answer to, Why do we suffer? be so amorphous as, "because we're human"? But the real value here lies not just in accepting the frustrating right answer. The value lies in rejecting the wrong answer.

That is, the answer that "we suffer because we're human" is particularly powerful because it offers an antidote to our natural human tendency to think that we suffer because we did something wrong.

As if to underscore the relevance of this message, Adam and Eve endure more misery, in the form of the death of their child—widely recognized as the most painful tragedy a parent can suffer. The text here seems particularly callous, with God suggesting that a new son, Seth, will make up for the death of another one, Abel. But, even so, we see another example of the main thrust of the Life of Adam and Eve. People suffer through no fault of their own.

In this case, we don't even see any suggestion of a connection between Adam and Eve's agony as parents and their pre-exile life. One form of suffering enumerated in Genesis and repeated in the Life of Adam and Eve is that men will have to work to get food. And we see that Adam does indeed suffer as he struggles to find food. Another form is pain in childbirth. And the Life of Adam and Eve details Eve's excruciating pain. But there is no hint as to why parents will watch their children die. Cain was born perverse. That's just the way it is. (Some later Jewish biblical traditions, perhaps uncomfortable with the notion of a person who was born evil for no apparent reason, would suggest that Cain was the result of a sexual union between Eve and the serpent or the Devil.)

Before summarizing what we learn from the Life and Adam and

Eve, it's interesting to observe one huge aspect of modern life that plays no role in the ancient text: money and material goods.

In point of fact, most modern people don't work for food and don't build their own shelter. They work for money and use the money to buy food and shelter. But, especially in the West, most people use only some of their money for food and shelter. They also use money to buy things. And they amass money, as if there's inherent value in having it.

Capitalism—in essence defined by a purposeful reliance on accumulating wealth—is so ingrained in modern society that the lack of any reference to money or things in the Life of Adam and Eve is all the more striking.

This is not to say that things don't have value, or that money can't be an important way of prodding the very human productivity that ensures plentiful food. Nor can we pretend that the text was written before the invention of money and things and that its authors couldn't have taken it into account. Rather, it seems that in answering the fundamental question, What is life like? money and possessions aren't important enough to warrant mention.

Also missing from the Life of Adam and Eve are some central Jewish and Christian messages.

We have already seen that some schools of Jewish thought would assign the Devil and/or the serpent the role of impregnating Eve, which is to say, the role of creating the evil Cain. We find various versions of that theme in the Midrash, the Talmud, and a variety of later translations and commentaries, but not in the Life of Adam and Eve.

This discrepancy is more than a passing detail. If Cain was born from the serpent's seed, as some traditions insist, the Devil had an active role in creating a murderer. It not, a murderer was born for no apparent reason: Adam and Eve created Cain before they were expelled from Eden and, therefore, before they had sinned. This is a huge theological difference. Our text here insists that some people are born evil simply because that's the way the world works. And, similarly, some people (like Abel) are murdered not for anything they did but because that's how the world works. Some parents suffer tragedy for the same reason. And so on.

Similarly, the Life of Adam and Eve skips over the pivotal Christian issue of fallenness. In Christianity, Adam's sin permeates all of humanity. We are all sinners because of Adam's original sin, though the details differ among various traditions: Catholics teach (in the *Catechism of the Catholic Church,* for example) that Adam and Eve transmitted their wounded human nature to their descendants, just as Protestant tradition generally holds that all humans inherit Adam's guilt (according to Martin Luther, in the second article of the Augsburg Confession, the Lutheran Church's primary confession of faith, or John Calvin, in his *Institutes of the Christian Religion*). This doctrine—variously called "original sin," "human fallenness," "the fallenness of man," and so on—is notably absent from the Life of Adam and Eve.

Again, this discrepancy is no small matter. Human fallenness is not only a statement about all people—who, because of Adam, are sinners by their nature. It helps explain why the world is imperfect. Had Adam not sinned, there would be no sinners, and there would be no evil.

Like the Jewish insistence that Cain couldn't have been born evil without a reason, the doctrine of original sin similarly insists on a direct cause for human sin. Or, to look at things from the other side, original sin and the tradition that Cain was the Devil's offspring both answer the same question, Why is there evil in the world? This, in turn, is among the most central questions that come under the umbrella of, What is life like?

That is the question that Genesis asks, and answers only partially.

The Life of Adam and Eve completes the account of the human condition, answering the important questions in Genesis more fully. To be human is to work for a living, to endure pain, to live in exile, to long for what was, to wonder why we suffer, and—if we're lucky— ultimately to understand that our suffering is simply a part of the universe, which inherently contains both good and evil.

And yet for all its focus on suffering, the Life of Adam and Eve is an optimistic book. As we saw, it ends with a commandment to rejoice. If it addresses suffering in detail, it's only because most people, like Adam and Eve, misunderstand their own circumstances, wrongly thinking that their adult life should be as carefree as their childhood. They never overcome the surprise of living in exile and always wonder what they should have done differently. Stripped of its mystery, unhappiness becomes part of a happy life, not an impediment to it.

6

ABRAHAM: HUMANS, IDOLS, AND GODS

An image-maker never worships the gods.
—CHINESE PROVERB

The first clue came when the young child was surveying the gods at home.

Made of wood, stone, and a variety of precious metals, they formed an impressive array. Some were small, easily carried, and convenient for travel. Others were huge and too heavy to be lifted by a single man.

The gods belonged to his father and brother, but the young boy helped carve them. He also helped prepare their sacrifices.

As he looked around, the boy saw that Master of the Nations had fallen to the feet of Steadfast. Master of the Nations was too heavy for the boy to lift, so he called for his father. The boy grabbed the god's head, the father the feet. Together, they lifted Master of the Nations, and they might have managed to set him upright had not his head fallen off.

They both looked down at the headless Master of the Nations and reflected on what had happened to the god.

The boy is Abraham, a figure so important that Judaism, Christianity, and Islam are collectively called the "Abrahamic faiths." But as with so many other biblical characters, the Bible's text stops tantalizingly short of telling us what we most want to know.

Abraham is probably most famous for being the first monotheist. But was he? And if so, what made him leave idolatry behind? Genesis only tells us (in chapter 12) that God told him to leave his father's land and journey to a new land, where he would become the head of a great nation. God doesn't even mention monotheism or polytheism.

The Apocalypse of Abraham fills in the blanks. The book was probably first written about two thousand years ago in Hebrew or perhaps Aramaic, and our current copies of it come to us from much later Slavic translations, which are themselves translations either from Greek or maybe even from the original. But even though the Apocalypse has undergone a series of translations, we probably still have a pretty good sense of the original.

The first part of the Apocalypse gives us critical insight into Abraham's childhood, starting, as we just saw, with the episode of the headless god, as Abraham works in his father's god business.

Bits of the story survive in other works. The Jewish Midrash (Genesis Rabbah 38:13) describes Terah, Abraham's father, as an idol maker. So does the Quran. But here we have a detailed account.

A word about terminology is in order. In hindsight, we might call these figurines "idols" or "icons" rather than "gods," particularly in the context of Abraham's upcoming monotheism. But that's only because we already know how this part of the story ends. We know that Abraham will propose one true god (almost always capitalized nowadays as "one true God") to the exclusion of all others. But before that worldview, which he himself started, there were lots of gods. So in the Apocalypse, we'll keep calling them "gods," as he would have, not idols.

We pick up the story with Terah, Abraham's father.

"Abraham," the boy's father called out.

"Here I am," Abraham replied.

"Get me my tools from the house."

Abraham did, and his father carved a new body for Master of the Nations. He took the old head and set it on the new body. Then he smashed the rest of the old Master of the Nations.

That was the first clue.

The second clue came in the form of five gods that Abraham had been given to sell.

Abraham saddled his father's donkey, loaded it up with the five gods, and set out to the main road. There, he hoped, he would find buyers. Before long, merchants from Syria passed by with their camels on their way to Egypt. Abraham greeted them, and they stopped to talk. As they were chatting, one of the camels bleated, scaring the donkey. The donkey fled and cast Abraham's five gods to the ground, breaking three of them.

"Why didn't you tell us that you had gods?" the merchants demanded to know when they saw the broken gods on the ground. "We would have bought them from you before the donkey heard the camel bleat, so you wouldn't have had to suffer this loss.

"At least sell us the remaining gods," they continued. "We'll give you a good price."

Abraham was worried that he would have to tell his father about the broken gods, but the merchants agreed to pay him the value of all five gods, even though they were only getting two. Seeing a good deal, Abraham agreed. He sold the two unbroken gods to the merchants, who continued on their way to Egypt. Then he cast the debris from the other three gods into the river Gur, where they sank deep below the surface and vanished.

That was the second clue.

As Abraham was returning home, he reflected on what had happened. What's the point, he wondered, of everything that his father did? Wasn't his father more like a god than the "gods" he was fashioning? After all, it's his father's sculpting, carving, and skill that bring the gods into being. They are his own work. They should worship him, not the other way around.

Master of the Nations fell and couldn't even get up in his own temple. Young Abraham couldn't lift him without his father's help. Even with his help, the head fell off. But his father just made a new body for the head.

The five gods were similarly powerless against the donkey. They couldn't save themselves, and they couldn't punish the donkey. Nor could they rise up from the river.

Abraham wondered how his father's god, the Master of the Nations, with the head of one stone and the body of another, could save people or hear human prayer.

With this in mind, Abraham returned home and arranged water and hay for his donkey. Then he brought the money he had received from the merchants to his father.

"Abraham," his father said, "you honor the gods, so my work is not in vain."

"But my father, you aren't blessed by the gods, they are blessed by you. You are a god to them. You made them. They have no blessings or power of their own. They couldn't even help themselves. How will they ever help you or me? Even I am more of a god than they are. It was my cleverness that brought you money for smashed gods."

Abraham's father was furious at his son for speaking such harsh words about his gods, and Abraham stormed off.

"Abraham," his father called not long after.

"I am here."

"Go get the splinters from the wood I was using to make the gods. Use that wood to cook me dinner."

As Abraham was collecting the wood remnants, he found a small god, Master of Fire. Instead of telling his father about what he'd found, he added the other pieces of wood to the fire and started cooking dinner, and then put Master of Fire near the fire and told the god to keep an eye on things. "If the fire starts to go out," Abraham told Master of Fire, "blow on it to keep it going." And he left the fire unattended.

When he came back, Master of Fire had fallen backward, feet toward the fire, so close that his feet were actually singed. "Master of Fire," he mocked, "you sure can kindle a fire and cook." And Abraham watched as the fire completely consumed Master of Fire.

When the meal was ready, he brought it to his father, with wine and milk. After enjoying his meal, Terah blessed his god, Master of the Nations.

"Father," Abraham said, "you shouldn't bless your god Master of the Nations. You should bless your god Master of Fire, because in his love he threw himself into the fire I used to cook your food."

"Where is he now?" Terah asked.

"Dust and ashes."

"Great is the power of Master of Fire," Terah proclaimed. "I will create another one who will cook me food tomorrow."

As children so often do, Abraham grew frustrated with his father's stupidity. How could a statue made by his father ever be his helper? And why couldn't his father see this obvious contradiction? Such a foolish man as his father would just as soon put his body and soul in the care of folly and ignorance, Abraham thought.

And again as children so often do, Abraham made a mental accounting of his world.

Gods came in at least three varieties: wood, stone, and metal. His brother had a god made of gold. That god must be better than his father's stone Master of the Nations, because gold is just like money. And if a golden god wears out, it can be remade, but Master of the

Nations could not. Even silver gods, though they are obviously subordinate to gold gods, are better than wooden gods. Master of Fire, before he was a god, was a beautiful tree, with roots and branches and flowers and glory. Then a human cut him down, depriving him of his life-giving sap. It used to be a glorious part of nature, only to be turned into an insignificant statue. And then it was burned and destroyed.

His father was going to make a new Master of Fire, even though the old one had no power.

Abraham kept thinking, shifting his attention from gods to elements more generally.

Fire was the most noble of elements, with its flames that mocked and force that destroyed. But it still wasn't a god, because water could overcome it. So maybe water was more noble than fire? But when water is poured on a fire, it seeps into the earth, and the earth soaks it up. So water isn't a god either, since the earth can overcome it. Maybe earth is the most noble element? But the sun can dry it up. So maybe the sun is the most noble? But even the sun can be blocked by the clouds and by the night.

Abraham explained his thinking to his father, adding that he was going to search for the God who created all of the gods and all of the elements. The same God who colored heaven and made the sun golden, who gave light to the moon and stars, and who could dry the earth had now chosen him. "He is God!"

Not surprisingly, Abraham got no response from his father.

Undeterred, he kept thinking about these things.

Lost in thought, he suddenly heard a voice calling him, "Abraham, Abraham!" It was the Almighty, who had come down from heaven in a pillar of fire.

"I am here," Abraham responded.

"You are wise to search for the God of gods. That is me. Leave your father and his house, so that you will not be punished for your father's sins."

Abraham did leave. He was still in the courtyard when he heard the sound of thunder and saw his house and everything in it burned to the ground.

Abraham had discovered God, and lost his father.

And there the first part of the Apocalypse ends.

The Bible gives us very little information about Abraham. Genesis 11:27–28 indicates that he was born to Terah. Then, after a verse about the death of one of Abraham's brothers, the very next verse has Abraham (still called Abram) taking Sarah (Sarai) as his wife. His whole childhood is missing. That is, the Abraham of the Bible is a man apparently with an unremarkable childhood.

But his life as a husband and parent is marked by ineptitude and poor judgment. For example, he has difficulty fathering a child with his wife, so his plan (originally hers) is to give it a shot with her maid. When that attempt is successful, Abraham is surprised at the family tension that results. Then, after he and Sarah finally do have a son together, Abraham sends his firstborn child and the child's mother into the desert to die. Not long after that, Abraham takes the one son still living with him on a picnic and almost kills him.

While difficulty conceiving is without doubt painful and stressful for a couple, it was also common in antiquity, and it hardly explains Abraham's practically criminal approach to parenting. But once we read the Apocalypse, we have a better sense of the man who fathers Isaac and Ishmael: He was a child prodigy who saw folly in the very underpinnings of daily life.

Because physical idols are rare in modern Western life, it's hard for many modern readers to appreciate how tightly integrated into society they used to be, much the way, say, money or freedom are now in the West. Abraham's rejection of idolatry would be like a child now being the first to realize that we would all be better off without money, or that we would all be better off as slaves. Both suggestions—that money has no purpose and that slavery is better than freedom—are so radical that modern westerners are generally unwilling even to have a conversation about their merits. Abraham's plan to give up idols would have been perceived similarly.

Worse, Abraham's father was not just an idol worshiper but an actual idol manufacturer. The family business lay at the core of what Abraham saw as silly. Abraham's father wasn't the hero figure that most boys want in a parent, but rather a stinging reminder of how alone Abraham was. Continuing our modern analogy, we can imagine a modern boy who rejects money having a banker for a father, or a boy who rejects freedom growing up with a civil rights worker.

And worse yet, Abraham's convictions are directly connected to his own father's death. Though the text of the Apocalypse doesn't blame Abraham for what happens to Terah, the timing is suggestive. God burns Terah alive for his "sins" of idolatry immediately after Abraham challenged him. How could Abraham not feel responsible?

In the context of this traumatic childhood, it is easier to understand, though perhaps not to forgive, a man whose adult behavior seems reckless—sending one child to die in the desert (Ishmael is only saved by divine intervention) and tying up the other and nearly slaughtering him.

Up to this point, as we've seen, the Apocalypse has read like a short story about a family and, in particular, about Abraham. Now the style changes.

The next section of the Apocalypse expands on an enigmatic but central passage in Genesis 15. There, Abraham's covenant with God is connected to the splitting in half of a series of animals: a three-year-old cow, goat, and ram. Abraham also has with him a dove and a pigeon, but he leaves these whole. Then the unsplit birds descend upon the split carcasses of the other animals, and Abraham chases them away, thus cementing God's covenant with Abraham. (It's not clear from the biblical text whether the birds actually eat the carcasses or whether Abraham is able to send them off first.)

This "splitting covenant" in Genesis comes in response to God's promise to Abraham that he will inherit the Land of Israel. Abraham wonders how he can trust God, and God offers this ceremony as proof. Right after the birds leave, just as the sun is setting, Abraham falls into a deep sleep and has a vision in which God tells him what will happen to his descendants: They will be enslaved as strangers in a foreign land for four hundred years, but God will judge the nation that they serve, delivering them with great wealth. Then Abraham wakes to darkness, and smoke and fire pass between the pieces he had previously split.

Based on other evidence from antiquity, passing between split (and therefore dead) animals looks like it was a fairly usual form of swearing a covenant, the idea perhaps being that whoever breaks the pact should become like the carcasses. If so, the very next line of Genesis falls right into place: "On that day God made a covenant with Abraham," according to which Abraham's descendants would inherit the land.

The smoke and fire between the split animals represent (or are?) God, and the animals themselves are the means by which God swears, answering Abraham's concern that he can't trust God.

To a modern reader, the whole Genesis narrative here is jarring. Why did Abraham split the animals? What are the birds? What prompted the sleep-induced vision of the future? What are the smoke and fire? How is all of this related to the covenant? And why would we care?

To ancient readers, though, everything except the vision of the future would have been familiar.

The Apocalypse resumes with a narrative that parallels the biblical account.

Mirroring the text of Genesis, God again calls out here, "Abraham, Abraham," and Abraham answers, "I am here."

"Take a three-year-old cow, a three-year-old goat, a three-year-old ram, a dove, and a pigeon, and set them out for me as a sacrifice," God instructs. So far, the text looks almost exactly the same as Genesis.

But the point of the ceremony in Genesis is to cement a pact, while here the text tells us that the goal is for Abraham to know the secrets of the ages and other great things, including, importantly, "what will happen to those who have done evil and those who have done just things."

Though Abraham hears God's voice, he does not see any divine image, a contradiction that terrifies him to the point of collapsing. This obvious human reaction to hearing a voice and not knowing where it's coming from—bewilderment and terror—is poignantly absent from the Bible, as though in the Bible such a thing is so common as to be expected. Here we see perhaps a more realistic scenario. God's voice speaks, and the human hearer, unaccustomed to such things, is too stunned even to respond.

So God sends an angel in the form of a human to help Abraham. The angel's name is Yahoel, a fact that Abraham learns as he hears God send him, "Go, Yahoel, and help this man." Abraham also learns that Yahoel's name is connected—in some manner that is difficult for us to discern with preciseness—to God's own ineffable name.

Tradition holds that the four-letter Hebrew word Yud-Heh-Vav-Heh spells God's name in a way that we no longer know how to pronounce. Because the explicit name of God was too holy to use in ordinary circumstances, goes the tradition, its use was confined to priestly functions, and as the priests stopped running Judaism, God's name was forgotten. Though the historical accuracy of this common narrative is suspect, the power of God's no-longer-pronounceable name forms a consistent thread in Jewish literature, practice, and thought.

Yahoel's name seems to come from the first two letters of that ineffable name—Yud (Y) and Heh (H), combined with the common suffix -el ("God") that we frequently see in Hebrew names (like Daniel or Ezekiel).

This unique merging of two of God's names, combined with the connection the text makes to God's holiest name, suggests that Yahoel is no ordinary angel. Obviously, the appearance of such an extraordinary angel just as Abraham is reeling from the sound of God's voice might send Abraham further into shock, so God cleverly sends Yahoel in the form of a man.

Yahoel first explains that he's come to help, and then he introduces himself as Yahoel. His power causes those that are with him on what he calls the "seventh vault" of heaven to tremble. And he is the "power amid the Ineffable, who put together his names in me." Once again, we see his close connection to none other than God.

Then Yahoel presents a short CV. He was appointed by God to reconcile the rivalries among angels. He rules over serpents. And because he was ordered to unlock Hades and destroy anyone who worships dead things, he was the one who burned down Abraham's father's house. (Abraham is again confronted with the fact that his new friends are the ones who killed his father.)

Precise details of Yahoel's role are obscure, in part because of issues of translation. But he is so similar to another angel, Metatron, that a later document known as 3 Enoch equates the two. (Despite the name, 3 Enoch has very little in common with 1 Enoch, the most famous book by that name, and the topic of chapter 7.)

As modern readers, we easily skip over details like the names and specific responsibilities of the angels, but these were apparently important. A visit from the chief angel was vastly more prestigious than if a lesser angel came by. We know of Yahoel primarily from this text, but the description and nature of his name make it clear that this is an angel of great importance.

Yahoel takes Abraham on a forty-day journey, during which Abraham doesn't eat or drink, Yahoel's appearance sustaining him and Yahoel's voice quenching his thirst. Then they arrive at Mount Horeb, where Abraham is supposed to offer a sacrifice.

But Abraham has brought nothing with him, and there's no altar.

Fortunately, following behind Abraham, unnoticed, were just the right animals: a three-year-old cow, goat, and ram, as well as a dove and pigeon. The plan is for Abraham to cut the mammals in half and leave the birds alone, just as in Genesis. And two men on the mountain will serve as the altar. Abraham should give the mammals to the men and hand the birds over to Yahoel. Abraham's reward will be that Yahoel will ascend with him on the wings of those two birds and that Abraham will learn everything about the world, heaven and earth, the Garden of Eden, and more.

Abraham starts to follow Yahoel's instruction, cutting up the animals, giving the halves to two angels (apparently the "men" that Yahoel mentioned were in fact angels) and letting another angel take the two birds. Then as evening falls—just as in Genesis—an impure bird flies down to the carcasses, and (still following the Genesis narrative) Abraham chases the bird away.

But here the bird speaks.

"What are you doing," the bird demands to know, "on the holy heights, where no one eats or drinks?" Then the bird warns Abraham to flee.

Confused, and perhaps worried, Abraham asks Yahoel what to do.

"That bird is sin. That bird is Azazel!" Yahoel warns, using one common name for the Devil to refer to God's archrival. Amazingly,

Yahoel then chastises Azazel for venturing up into heaven, because, after all, he says, Abraham's portion is in heaven, but Azazel's is on earth, since Azazel chose it to be where impurity lives.

"Shame on you," Yahoel continues, "for tempting righteous men. Leave this man alone!" Yahoel tells Azazel that Abraham can't be deceived, because he and Azazel represent opposite sides of the battle between good and evil. In fact, the very clothes that Azazel once wore in heaven have now been set aside for Abraham, and Abraham's corruption has transferred to Azazel.

Yahoel seems less confident than his words would indicate, though, as he also warns Abraham never to answer Azazel, because Azazel has power over anyone who answers him. But apparently Abraham can talk to Azazel—talking is different than answering—and Yahoel even gives Abraham some words he might use to repel Azazel: "May you kindle the fires of the furnace of the earth, Azazel. Go to the untrodden parts of the earth. Because justice is anathema to you, through your own destruction vanish before me."

This particular exchange seems remarkably like how a parent might help a child deal with an imaginary evil. We can picture a small child afraid of goblins and whatnot and a parent telling the child not to worry. "Just say, 'Go away, goblins!' and they'll leave you alone." There is no indication in the text that Abraham is still a child (even though he was in the first part of the Apocalypse), and Azazel is supposed to be real, at least in the sense of representing a real threat, unlike a child's nighttime goblins. Yet the similarity is intriguing.

As presented in the Apocalypse, this is an approach to the common theme of a seductive evil force: Azazel here, the snake in the Garden of Eden according to Genesis, Satan in the Garden of Eden according to the Life of Adam and Eve (last chapter), and many more.

Later rabbinic tradition would address the temptation-inducing nature of what is usually called the "Evil Inclination," that is, the innate human tendency to do wrong. At one point the Talmud even equates the Evil Inclination with Satan and with the Angel of Death, claiming that all three are the same. In typical Talmudic style, the text follows up with another group of three. Three people were immune from the power of the Evil Inclination, which is to say, from Satan: Abraham, Isaac, and Jacob. (Another particularly troubling passage warns that one group of people is more susceptible to the Evil Inclination than most: scholars!)

This tradition of Abraham, Isaac, and Jacob's immunity from evil temptation meshes with Yahoel's claim here, that Abraham cannot be tempted by Azazel.

The facts, though, seem to present a different story. The lives of Abraham, Isaac, and Jacob are filled with what looks like Azazel's work. As we discussed above, Abraham cheats on his wife, banishes his first son to die in the wilderness, and then almost murders his second son. Isaac (along with Rebecca) openly plays favorites with his children. Then in old age he accidentally blesses the wrong child. Jacob inadvertently marries the wrong sister and (in a stunning lack of appreciation for the depth of the human soul) doesn't notice until after they've spent the whole night together. Then, continuing the family tradition of poor parenting, Jacob, too, plays favorites, giving only one of his twelve sons a lavish gift.

In the particularly vivid Joseph narrative at the end of Genesis, Jacob compounds his poor parenting when famine hits the land. He gathers his children and tells them, "I want all of you to go down to Egypt to procure food," adding, "except for Benjamin."

Why not Benjamin?

"Because I love him," Jacob explains.

In what way are these people immune from temptation by the forces of evil? Rather, Abraham, like his son and grandson, is an entirely human hero. Traumatized in childhood, torn between his past and his future, and ever frustrated by the mundane disappointments of his life, he still manages at times to transcend his circumstances as he forms the people of Israel and brings monotheism into the world.

The Apocalypse focuses on Abraham's heroic side, the ways in which he is larger than life. He has just spoken with none other than Satan and has even prevailed against the leader of evil.

Now the Apocalypse continues in a similar vein.

Having sacrificed the split animals and repelled Yahoel, Abraham in fact ascends to heaven, not—as most people do—as a result of his death, but rather during his life, carried on the right wing of one of the birds, with the angel on the left wing of the other. (It's not clear why the angel needs the bird for transport.) The birds in Genesis serve no obvious practical purpose. Here in the Apocalypse, they literally escort Abraham out of this world.

Abraham sees the sky and an indescribable light with a fire burning inside, and inside the fire a crowd of people, men, changing in appearance, running this way and that, transforming, bowing, and shouting words Abraham can't understand.

Abraham wants to know where he is. He feels like he can't see. And he feels weak.

Yet again, the angel reassures Abraham. "You will soon see the Eternal going before both of us amid the great sound of holiness. I am with you. And you will be strong."

Both the "great sound" and the "holiness" (*kedusha* in Hebrew) that we see here would have been familiar phrasings to ancient readers. One instance comes from the famous repetition "holy, holy, holy is the Lord of Hosts" from Isaiah 6:3, included in both Jewish and Christian worship services and technically known as the Trisagion. There the prophet Isaiah reports that he saw the Lord sitting on a throne on high with six-winged seraphim in attendance. It is these angels who call out "holy, holy, holy." The prophet Ezekiel, too, hears a "great sound," then the sound of the wings of angels brushing against each other. Then he is lifted by a spirit to see the Lord and attending angels. So the ancient reader would have recognized these common symbols as indicators of an imminent audience with God.

But it turns out that the meeting is still a ways off.

What Abraham does see is a fire coming toward him, and inside the fire he hears a roar like many oceans.

The angel sees it, too, and bows.

Now Abraham has a problem. It was his custom to prostrate himself on occasions such as these, kneeling or lying on the ground in a sign of respect. But here there is no ground on which to lie.

Instead, Abraham bows and sings a song the angel taught him.

Both Jewish and Christian ancient sources refer to the Song of Abraham or Poem of Abraham, but the words don't appear in the Bible or in any other currently mainstream religious work. (These sources were written in languages that use the same word for "poem" and "song," so we have no way of knowing for sure if the original intention was a poem or a song.) Apparently the text here is the lost Song of Abraham.

The poetic words praise God for power, might, glory, and for hearing prayer. One particularly interesting line addresses God as "Most Glorious El, El, El, El, Yahoel." "El" means "God" in Hebrew, and fourfold repetitions are rare, so this may be a way of referring to the four-letter name of God.

Even as Abraham is singing his song, the intensity of the fire increases, and Abraham hears a voice as loud as the sea. The flames rise. The voice roars. The flames rise higher. And then Abraham sees a throne, itself made of fire. And he sees wheels.

The exact nature of these "wheels" isn't clear. Called *ophanim* in Hebrew (singular, *ophan*), they are known mostly from Ezekiel, where, like here, they are both the wheels of God's divine chariot and living angels. Ezekiel himself seems confused by them. Their construction, apparently, is like "a wheel within a wheel," and they follow the "living creatures" (which are also part of what Ezekiel sees). But even more, "the living creatures' spirit was in each wheel," and each wheel "was full of eyes all around." So to call these "wheels" is to follow normal convention, but they are certainly not normal wheels. They are akin to angels, akin to other living creatures, and they have lots of eyes.

Here we'll call them Creatures of Wheels. And we'll use Creatures of Life for the "living creatures" that go with them.

So Abraham sees that the Creatures of Wheels have many eyes and that they are singing his song. Under the throne are four fiery Creatures of Life, each of which has four faces: of a lion, a man, an ox, and an eagle. This mirrors Ezekiel's vision exactly, though Abraham helps the reader here by clarifying that four angels times four faces equals sixteen angel-faces.

The Creatures of Life each has six wings, extending in pairs from their shoulders, their sides, and their middles. Their shoulder wings covered their faces, their middle wings their feet, and they stretched out their side wings to fly.

Just as the creatures finish singing the song, they start threatening each other. So Abraham's angel, alarmed by this potentially violent turn of events, leaves Abraham and runs to the creatures. The angel turns the creatures' faces so that they can't see one another (not an easy task when four-faced creatures are involved). Then the angel teaches the creatures a "song of peace," telling them that the whole earth belongs to the Eternal One.

Behind the Creatures of Life Abraham sees a chariot with fiery Creatures of Wheels, each one full of eyes. The throne, he now sees, is above the Creatures of Wheels, covered with and surrounded by fire, which in turn is surrounded by an indescribable light.

Amid the throne and the fire and the sealike roar and the Creatures of Life with their four faces each and the Creatures of Wheels with their many eyes, Abraham hears the sound of praise as though from a lone man.

The voice, in typical biblical fashion, calls out, "Abraham, Abraham!" And Abraham answers, "I am here!"

"Look at the levels that are under you," the voice instructs, referring to the typical-of-the-time cosmology that posits a universe built like a multistoried building, "and you will see that the one you are searching for is the only one there." Just then the levels open up, and Abraham sees the heavens under him.

This vision introduces the first of two lessons that Abraham will learn about the world. This one deals with the cosmic nature of the universe. The next will deal with good and evil.

On the seventh level—the one Abraham is standing on—Abraham sees fire, light, dew, angels, and the power of the invisible glory from the Creatures of Life, but no one else.

Beneath that, on the sixth level, he sees incorporeal angels carrying out the orders of the fiery angels from the eighth level. (This "eighth" level is surprising, because the tradition of "seven heavens" is so familiar now. But other sources also suggest that there might be another level above the usual seven. For instance, the Talmud [Hagigah 13a] posits an eighth level based on an interpretation of Ezekiel 1.) On the sixth level, too, Abraham sees only angels.

In order for Abraham to see farther down, to the fifth level, the sixth level has to open up. And that's what happens, letting Abraham see the stars there, along with the elements of earth, carrying out their respective orders.

"How many stars are there?" God asks Abraham.

"How could I possibly count them? I am just a man," Abraham replies.

"The number of stars will be the number of your descendants, whom I have set apart for me in my lot with Azazel."

The ancient reader might have noticed three things.

Most obviously, this claim that Abraham's descendants will be as numerous as the stars mirrors Genesis 15:5, "Look up toward heaven and count the stars, if you are able. . . . That is how numerous your descendants will be."

Second, an ancient reader may have appreciated the literary beauty of connecting Abraham's revelation—the vision, the creatures, the fire, the sound, the song, the levels, etcetera—to the main narrative of the Bible.

Third, the ancient reader—along with modern readers—would be shocked by the last line, added seemingly as an afterthought: Abraham's descendants are set apart for God "with Azazel." Azazel is the Devil. Why are they together?

Modern and ancient readers aren't alone in their surprise. Abraham, too, responds to this promise of innumerable progeny by asking God, "Azazel abused me. Why then—now that he's not before you—do you still set yourself with him?"

This question, and God's answer, lie at the heart of the Apocalypse of Abraham. We have already encountered Azazel—in the form of the bird who tempts Abraham. And we have already seen two incompatible descriptions of Azazel's power.

Yahoel—the angel who accompanied Abraham on his vision—chastised Azazel for trying to tempt Abraham because, after all, Abraham is untemptable. Abraham and Azazel represent opposing sides in the battle between good and evil. But we also saw that Yahoel had to instruct Abraham not to answer Azazel, because Azazel has power over anyone who answers him.

Here God expands on the nature of good and evil in response to Abraham's question. Not surprisingly, the information comes in the form of a vision.

Continuing the theme of looking farther and farther downward from his perch on the seventh level, Abraham sees all of creation: the heavens; the earth and its fruits, creatures, people, etc.; perdition; the sea and its islands, animals, fishes, etc.; rivers; and so on. Abraham also sees "the tree" in Eden, along with other parts of Eden. And Abraham sees a multitude of men, women, and children, half of them on the left, and half of them on the right.

The people on the left, Abraham learns, are the various other tribes and nations that would come before and after him, while the people on the right are the people set apart for God from among the people of Azazel. The people on the left are destined to be judged in the end of days, while the people on the right are destined to be born of Abraham and to be called God's people.

Unfortunately, reading the text now it's hard to know if the original intention was that all of the people on the left would be judged guilty, and therefore punished, or if only some of the people on the left were guilty.

Regardless of the details, this punishment at the end of times introduces an entirely new element of the nature of good and evil: evil is eventually punished. Most modern readers are familiar with some variation of this idea precisely because ancient literature made it so well known. In this case, the most common version is heaven and hell. Good people go to heaven and bad people to hell. Modern Judaism doesn't adhere to this standard (Christian) approach, but it does suggest that good deeds in this world are rewarded in the next.

At their core, belief systems like these are built around three connected notions. The first is a desire for fairness. Our actions should have consequences, with good behavior rewarded and bad behavior punished. The second part is the observation based on our day-to-day experience that not all actions have consequences, because lots of good people suffer and lots of bad people thrive. So the third part reconciles the first part and the second: Bad people eventually suffer, and good people eventually thrive, if not before their death, then after it.

With the introduction here in the Apocalypse of Abraham of a system of ultimate reward and punishment, we can note that the Life of Adam and Eve has only ultimate reward, for both Adam and Eve, despite any mistakes they may have made. Adam and Eve's punishment comes in the world before death: They have to work for a living, endure pain, etcetera. But after death they return to the Garden of Eden.

Here we see death treated differently. It is a time of ultimate judgment. The people on the left—the "other" people—will be judged for their actions, while the people on the right are destined to be God's people. (Similar language and imagery in Matthew 25 has the Son of Man dividing people the way a shepherd might divide sheep and goats, with the sheep on the right and the goats on the left. The sheep are the righteous, and they will earn eternal life. The goats are the accursed, destined for eternal punishment.)

And though it is slipped in here—again, almost as an afterthought—the people Abraham sees on the right are God's people "with Azazel."

So until now, we have a system with God on the side of good and Azazel on the side of evil. Additionally, there are two sets of people: the other nations, who will ultimately be judged, and Abraham's descendants, God's people with Azazel. This double division of the world—into good versus evil and into us versus them—provides the framework for the rest of the Apocalypse.

With this mind-set, and with God having already addressed what will happen to the other people, the obvious question is how good and evil are distributed among God's chosen people.

To answer this question, God directs Abraham's attention to the Garden of Eden, which he can see as part of his view of the entire world. A huge man and an equally huge woman are standing under a tree, whose fruit is like a bunch of grapes.

Most people now imagine that the fruit from the Tree of Knowledge—whose full name is the Tree of Knowing Good and Evil—was an apple. But that tradition arose because the Latin word for "evil" is *malum,* which happens also to mean "apple." In Latin, therefore, the tree was both the tree of "evil" and the tree of an "apple." But the Talmud records an ancient debate about the nature of the fruit, with possibilities ranging from the grape to the fig to wheat. The Book of Enoch agrees that the fruit looked like grapes.

So the combination of a huge man, a huge woman, a tree, and fruit that looked like grapes obviously described Adam and Eve in the Garden of Eden, with the added nuance that the people were huge. We are not surprised to read that behind the tree was a serpentlike form with humanlike hands and feet and, in addition, six wings on either side. Again, this twelve-winged creature is obscure to modern readers, but ancient tradition describes an evil angel, Sammael. This is the one who, according to one ancient document (Targum Pseudo-Jonathan), impregnated Eve in the Garden of Eden. According to another ancient document (Pirkei d'Rabbi Eliezer), Sammael has twelve wings. So even though the reference to twelve wings is obscure for modern readers, in antiquity it may have been as familiar as the horns that we now use for the Devil. Abraham sees the twelve-winged snakelike creature with human hands and feet feeding the grapes to the huge man and the huge woman, who are "intertwined." Though the reader understands exactly what's going on, Abraham asks God who the intertwined people are, who is between them, and what the fruit is. Unsurprisingly, God answers that they are Adam, Eve, and Azazel and, furthermore, that Adam represents reason, Eve represents desire, and Azazel represents impiety.

Abraham is now set to ask the obvious follow-up on Adam and

Eve's question from the Life of Adam and Eve. They wanted to know why Azazel had focused his ire on them. Abraham wants to know why God gave Azazel the power to hurt humans in the first place.

Abraham's question comes in response to part of God's answer about what will happen to Abraham's descendants. We can infer from this that the text is particularly concerned—at least here—with why evil continues to plague God's chosen people.

God's answer is that God only gave Azazel power over those who desire evil. This is in huge contrast to the Life of Adam and Eve, where the serpent himself explained that he had chosen to injure humans through no fault of their own. Here the fault lies entirely with the humans who choose evil.

Abraham recognizes that God's answer isn't really an answer. "Why did you make people who desire evil?" Abraham, along with the reader, naturally wants to know.

The answer comes in a vision by way of a return to the theme of us versus them. Abraham sees the entire history and future of the other people and, in particular, a litany of sins, starting with those of Adam, Eve, Satan, and Cain—who here murdered Abel "because of Satan." Abraham sees fornication, defilement, jealousy, corruption, theft, and so on. (It is particularly interesting to see fornication listed among the sins here. It's the first time we've seen an explicit connection between sex and sin.)

And Abraham sees the entire history and future of his people to be. He sees a statue of jealousy, similar to what his father might have made; a man, worshipping the statue; and an altar opposite the statue, where children are slaughtered before the idol. In the same question-and-answer format that we've seen throughout the Apocalypse, Abraham asks God what he is seeing. What are the idol and the altar? Who are the children and who is killing them? And—though the text doesn't explicitly mention that Abraham sees them—what is the beautiful temple, the art and beauty that lie beneath God's throne?

God tells him that the temple and the altar and the beauty are the sanctification of God, including the future kings and prophets and including the sacrifice that will be established among Abraham's descendants. The statue is God's anger. The slaughterer is the one who angered God. And the slaughtered children are those who are testimony to God's judgment and who are being murdered.

It is hardly an optimistic picture. God's chosen people are slaughtered in service to the idolatry that Abraham rejected and for which Abraham's father was killed. Abraham parted ways with his father and forged a new path, only to learn now that his descendants will be slaughtered for his choice.

Until now Abraham has asked God for explanations. Now, distraught, he goes a step further and begs God to take back this vision.

The reader may recall that all of this was in answer to Abraham's question about why God gave people the power to choose evil. If anything, the "answer" has only intensified the urgency of the question. If choosing evil can have such disastrous consequences, why did God include it in the grand plan for humanity?

More generally, we might ask—just as we did with suffering—why living life on earth involves dealing with people who, it would certainly seem, choose evil. And, like the newly enlightened Abraham, we know the stakes can be higher than mere personal tragedy. The question is not just why a criminal chooses to steal or even to murder. The question is why people are able to wage war, to demolish whole civilizations, to abide mass starvation.

And—again as in the Apocalypse—we are forced to grapple with the apparent reality that, as often as not, it is the righteous who suffer at the hands of the evil. What point is there in being good or in siding with the force of good?

God finally turns to an answer, at least in part, this time in the form of a question to Abraham, "Why didn't your father listen to you and abandon his demonic idolatry? Why did he perish?"

Contemplating such matters must have been overwhelmingly emotional for Abraham, as it would be for us. This is hardly a mere theoretical discussion. To drive home the point, God couches the question first in terms of Abraham's father's idols, which served as the force of God's anger, and now explicitly in terms of his father's death.

In a fit of rationality, Abraham responds that his father did not want to listen to him, any more than Abraham wanted to listen to his father. Or, in more modern terminology, Abraham and his father, Terah, both had free will. They could do what they wanted.

That is God's answer, which Abraham has discovered for himself.

The conversation started with the nature of the world: What is the world like? It contains good and evil. Why does it contain evil? Because of Azazel. Why does Azazel have power over people? Azazel only has power over people who choose to give him power. Why can people choose to give him power? Because they have free will.

As with so much else, the answer seems intensely dissatisfying to many modern readers. It seems like a cop-out. Millions of people died because of free will? Starvation is rampant across huge swaths of the earth? And it was on purpose? God *planned* it this way?

But again, the value of the answer lies in its nuance. Though the conversation in the Apocalypse has been between God and Abraham, and though it has dealt primarily with God's overwhelming power, the answer is that God is powerless in this regard. God did not plan it this way. The world is built in such a way that free will is incompatible with absolute good. We live in a world where we have free will, which means we do not enjoy absolute good. (One wonders if there isn't a parallel universe in which the reverse is true: its inhabitants are just like us, but they have no suffering and are therefore powerless to choose anything for themselves. They are automatons, who cannot choose to hate but neither can they choose to love. Interacting with them is no more interesting than interacting with any other mechanical device. Would we choose to live in that world? They, of course, cannot choose to live in ours, because they cannot choose.)

The notion of free will opens a segue to the next part of the Apocalypse. Just as Abraham and Terah have free will, so, too, God's will is inevitable. Then God shows Abraham the future.

The prose in this section of the Apocalypse is detailed and sometimes obscure, but the arc of events is simple: God's great Temple will be destroyed, leading to the exile of God's people. During the exile a leader from the other nations and a leader from God's people will each present themselves. This will precede a time of final reckoning, during which the other peoples will be punished and God's people will be rewarded.

What Abraham sees is people from the left (the other nations) capturing the people from the right and variously killing or imprisoning them—all because Abraham's descendants enrage God, just as Abraham saw at the statue and the altar. Abraham wants to know how long this state of affairs will last.

God provides a symbolic accounting of years and answers that a man will emerge from the left side, with Azazel immediately behind him, and that people from the right will either worship or denounce the man. During the same period, a man will emerge from the right, whom the people from the right will follow. Mimicking the confusion that the appearance of two leaders might create, the text itself shifts attention back and forth between the two men—one from left and one from the right—to the point that it is possible to mix them up even when just reading about them. The passage ends with admonition that, "He will tempt those of [Abraham's] descendants who have worshiped him." But it is not clear if "he" is the man from the left or the man from the right.

Because the man from the right sounds a lot like Jesus, this is obviously a matter of some importance. Some scholars, noting that nothing else in the text alludes to Christianity, assume that the passage about the man is a late insertion into the text, added long after the original was composed. Others reject the idea that the man is anything like Jesus, because the man doesn't promise redemption or otherwise do the things that Jesus did. Still others point to the judgment and salvation that are about to come and see evidence of a figure very much like Jesus. Vexingly, we cannot solve this mystery here. And although we may care about the details, they do not seem important in the context of the Apocalypse.

By contrast, the final passages are the key. As we saw briefly above, they describe a time of final reckoning.

Still as part of an answer to Abraham about the unknown man we just saw, God describes an age of justice, which will include ten plagues on the earth, but from which Abraham's descendants will emerge to bask in the glory that is their destiny. Then they will rejoice forever in God, victorious over their former enemies.

"Go," God tells Abraham. "I am with you forever."

With that, Abraham's journey to the seventh heaven ends, and he finds himself back on earth. But he has one final question: What about those ten plagues?

God details their nature and then tells Abraham that he will "sound the trumpet from the sky" and "send the chosen one," who will gather all the evildoers. God will then burn them, casting them into the underground depths, there to rot in Azazel's belly. God explains that he waited for those people, but they did not want to come to him.

The final judgment is thus complete. Abraham's people have emerged victorious, and the other nations have been punished. The text ends with an apt summary of the key theme.

"I am the judge," says God.

Like the Life of Adam and Eve, the style of the Apocalypse of Abraham has the potential to hide its message from modern readers. While the Life of Adam and Eve was simplistically written by modern norms, the Apocalypse is both simplistic and overcomplicated.

What was Abraham wearing? What color were his eyes? Had his father's hair started to recede? Was his text a poem or a song? And if it was a song, what was the melody like? And so forth.

Equally, the imagery of the angels, the heavens, the levels, the creatures (and their wings), and so forth are so foreign to modern readers as to be overwhelming. This is why the presentation here actually omits myriad nonessential details and skips over things like the accounting of time toward the end of the Apocalypse. For the same reason it spells out some of the imagery, as for example turning the original phrase "people from Padan Aram" into "merchants," because the ancient reader but not the modern one would have known that Padan Aram specialized in international commerce.

More generally, an ancient reader would have recognized much of the imagery as familiar (such as the levels of the universe, the Creatures of the Wheels, the hierarchy of good and bad angels, even the apocalyptic narrative style) and then given thought to the details that were new, while the modern reader is left to synthesize everything at once.

But this should not detract from the thrust of the Apocalypse, which, like the Life of Adam and Eve, fulfills two functions. It contains details that were left out of the Bible, and it answers a question. The Life of Adam and Eve told about the first humans, and addressed the very general question, What is our life like? The Apocalypse, in addition to giving us insight into the forces that shaped the founder of monotheism, refines the question about life by positing a right path and a wrong path in life. The question here is, What is life like if we choose the right path?

In this particular case, naturally, the right path is the path of monotheism, even though, as we saw, it is not clear which variety the text has in mind: pre-rabbinic Judaism, Judaism, Christianity, or some other option. Because most people in the West are monotheists (to the extent that they are theists at all), there is a natural connection between the right path and monotheism. But the questions in the text are not, fundamentally, limited to monotheism. The question is more general, even if the circumstances are not.

Choosing the "right path" may mean choosing a life of integrity, devoting time to charity, supporting one's family, or fighting for one's country. Choosing monotheism over idolatry is not the only way people see themselves as consciously taking the right path when others do not, though certainly most people continue to see religious leaders as the epitome of people who have chosen the path of God.

The fundamental problem is that life for the people who strive to do well seems to be pretty much the same as it is for everyone else. There doesn't appear to be any particular benefit to choosing the right path over the wrong one. In this sense, nothing has changed in two thousand years.

Now, as in the waning days of Jerusalem's glory, evil people appear to flourish, just as the righteous appear to suffer. The tyrant Herod the Great by all accounts lived a pretty happy life, just as our modern newspapers report on successful criminals. Conversely, God's chosen people suffered under Herod just as priests and rabbis are subject to violent crime today.

The Apocalypse has a twofold answer as to why this is so.

The first part of the answer builds on the message of the Life of Adam and Eve, that life involves suffering. In the Apocalypse we see that suffering can come not only from God but also from other people. The reason is that people have free will. This valuable attribute—perhaps one way in which people are different from the animals—may make life worth living, and it certainly makes it interesting and challenging: Would an act of kindness mean what it does if the actor had no choice but to act? Would falling in love be as satisfying? But free will also makes life harder.

The second part of the answer is that things even out in the end. The wicked ultimately suffer, and the righteous ultimately triumph. This is the kind of answer that rarely evokes indifference. Modern people tend to love it or hate it. It gives some of us the strength to continue through difficult times: If the descendants of Abraham could keep faith through their exile, goes one modern argument, we can get through our suffering, too. For others, the absurdity of the answer proves the folly of the premise. There is obviously no right path or wrong path, and the proof is in the proverbial pudding.

In this regard, the Apocalypse is a bravely optimistic text. Written at a time when there was no objective reason to believe that things would work out well, it boldly ignores the troubling evidence about the various conquerors of Jerusalem: the prosperity of the Greeks, the power of the Romans, the influence of the Egyptians, the aspirations of the Syrians, the empire of the Babylonians, and more. Rather, the text focuses on hope for the future.

Only in retrospect do we (perhaps) marvel that the Greeks, Romans, Egyptians, Syrians, and Babylonians are all gone, while Abraham's descendants, the monotheists, remain strong.

7

ENOCH: THE BEGINNING OF THE END

You will live poorly if you do not know how to die well.
—SENECA

On one thing the record is clear: He never died.

Both the Old Testament and New Testament say so. The historian Josephus and the philosopher Philo agree, as do the Dead Sea Scrolls, along with such books as the Wisdom of Sirach and Jubilees, among many others. And just in case there was any doubt, he tells us so himself.

As modern readers, we are, therefore, hardly surprised that he was so famous in antiquity or that his work influenced so many Jewish and Christian books, among them the Gospels. We are surprised, though, that he has become so obscure in modernity, particularly in light of the extraordinary way in which the Bible describes him.

His name is Enoch—*chanoch* in Hebrew—and we first encounter him in Genesis 5:18, as Jared's son, descended from Adam through Seth, Enosh, Cainen, and Mahalalel.

The family tree is complicated, though, less like a single tree and more like two trees of the same species whose branches are intertwined. Another passage in Genesis 4 lists different people, including an Enoch descended from Adam through Cain. And though this is not the same Enoch, it's interesting to note the similarity between the lists in Genesis 4 and Genesis 5: Cain in the first and Cainen in the second, Enoch in both, Irad and Jared, and Mehujael and Mehalalel; then we have Methusael and Methuselah, and Lamech in both lists. But because Cain's descendants will not survive the flood, it is the line of Seth that ends up being more important. That's why Seth's descendant Enoch is "the" Enoch.

Genesis 5 gives us the genealogy and life spans of these people, using a standard fourfold formula for each successive generation. First we get the age at which each man became a father. Then we get the name of the first son. After that comes the number of years during which the man "fathered more sons and daughters." The fourth bit of information is the age at which the man died.

For example, Adam, according to Genesis, lived 130 years and fathered Seth; after Seth, Adam lived 800 years, fathering sons and daughters; the days of Adam's life came to 930 years; then he died. The four parts are: 130 years, Seth, 800 years of "sons and daughters," and death. Similarly, Seth lived 105 years and fathered Enosh (Enosh is not the same as Enoch); after Enosh, Seth lived 707 years, fathering sons and daughters; the days of Seth's life came to 912 years; he died. Again, the key parts are 105 years, Enosh, 707 years, and death. For Enosh we have 90 years, Cainen, 815 years, and death. For Cainen, 70 years, Mahalalel, 840 years, and death. And so forth.

But when we get to Enoch, we find two fascinating variations.

Enoch lived 65 years and fathered Methuselah. So far, his life follows the pattern. But then, instead of just living out the rest of life "fathering sons and daughters," Enoch "walked with God for 300 years, fathering sons and daughters." That's the first departure. The more significant surprise comes right at the end. The days of Enoch's life came to 365 years and then . . .

. . . "God took him."

He didn't die.

What he did do is lend his name to the Book of Enoch, which was among the most well-known religious writings throughout the ancient world, even though it isn't in our Bible today. Jude in the New Testament, though, quotes the book directly (in verse 1:14), and the theology and general worldview from the Book of Enoch permeate other parts of the New Testament.

Enoch himself appears in genealogies in 1 Chronicles and Luke, along with his ancestors and descendants. Hebrews (11:5) expands on Genesis 5, explicitly telling the reader that Enoch was taken so that he would not see death and adding, in the context of what faith means, that Enoch was taken up "by faith."

These are only some of the reasons that such influential church fathers as Origen (an early Christian scholar and theologian born in the second century A.D. in Alexandria) thought so highly of Enoch and why we are not surprised that fragments from Enoch were found among the Dead Sea Scrolls.

Yet for all its fame, popularity, and influence, the Book of Enoch moved into near obscurity after it fell out of favor around the fourth century A.D. The Book of Enoch was rejected by Saint Jerome (the influential Christian theologian of the third and fourth centuries A.D. who translated the Bible into the Latin version called the Vulgate), for example, and by Saint Augustine (another influential Christian thinker from about the same time period), as well as by great rabbis who wrote the Talmud and shaped rabbinic Judaism.

In fact, we might not even have the Book on Enoch had it not been preserved in Ethiopia, where it remained central to religious thought. (Though the Ethiopian church is tiny in the United States, and equally marginal in most Western nations, Ethiopian Christianity, like Catholicism and Eastern Orthodoxy, is a mainstream church with a rich history and its own traditions and theology. It is also one of the six major denominations that control the Church of the Holy Sepulcher in Jerusalem—the others being Roman Catholic, Armenian, Greek Orthodox, Syrian Orthodox, and Coptic.)

Our most complete texts of the Book of Enoch, then, come from Ethiopia, in the form of manuscripts from the fifteenth century onward. These are, naturally, in the local language, variously called Ethiopic or Ge'ez. We also have some fragments in Greek and some Dead Sea Scroll fragments in Aramaic. The Aramaic texts from the Dead Sea Scrolls are almost certainly the original. These were probably translated into Greek, then into Ethiopic.

There are actually three books called the Book of Enoch. Scholars number them one through three. Our topic here is the first, that is, 1 Enoch, parts of which date back probably to the third century B.C. The second book, 2 Enoch, was probably composed later and deals with similar themes, while 3 Enoch is only vaguely related to the first two and comes from the middle of the first millennium A.D. But it's 1 Enoch that was so influential, so we focus on that book.

Because it survives primarily in Ethiopic, some people prefer to call it Ethiopic Enoch or the Ethiopic Apocalypse of Enoch instead of 1 Enoch. Following the same pattern, 2 Enoch, which survives in a language called Slavonic, is sometimes called Slavonic Enoch, while 3 Enoch is Hebrew Enoch.

Just to confuse the terminology further, our Book of Enoch here—1 Enoch—actually contains five books: the Book of the Watchers; the Book of the Similitudes, also more conveniently called the Parables of Enoch; the Book of Astronomical Writings; the Book of Dream Visions; and the Book of the Epistle of Enoch. We use the word "book" to mean any complete set of writing, so a book can contain lots of smaller books. 1 Enoch contains five books in exactly the same way that the Bible contains lots of books.

These five subbooks were not all composed at the same time, and even within books we find passages from different time periods. The earliest parts date to the third century B.C., and the latest parts were apparently written before the destruction of Jerusalem in the year A.D. 70.

So in many ways the contents are diverse, ranging from the fascinating account of the mysterious Watchers to details of the ancient calendar, from allegorical history to the coming of the Messiah, the Son of Man. But, as we'll see, the accounts, questions, and answers point the reader in a unified and bold direction.

Even before the book begins, we know from Genesis that Enoch was a most extraordinary man, because he didn't die. Genesis also tells us that he was a good man who walked with God. But Genesis is curiously silent on the details. What was it like to walk with God? What does that even mean? Why was Enoch chosen? Why didn't he die? Is he still alive? What did he learn from his time with God? And why should we, as readers, care?

Against this background, the Book of Enoch begins.

Enoch has composed blessings for the righteous people, who will be present at the difficult time when the wicked and ungodly people are removed. But his message—based on a holy vision that the angels in heaven showed him—is not for his own generation. It's for generations yet to come.

Having taunted the reader in this way, Enoch explains the distant future in familiar biblical terms. The Eternal God will appear on Mount Sinai. All will be afraid, and the Watchers will shake. The high mountains, too, will shake, and the high hills will be made low, melting like honeycombs. The earth will sink, and everything upon earth will perish. The Lord will arrive with ten thousand holy ones in order to execute judgment upon everyone, with reward coming to the righteous and destruction to the wicked.

Ancient readers would have recognized the themes, and even

much of the language, from Numbers, Micah, Isaiah, Daniel, and Jude, all of which appear in the Bible, as well as from the Psalms of Solomon, Ascension of Moses, and the Wisdom of Solomon, which ended up on the cutting room floor.

Then Enoch turns to his view of the universe. The luminaries in the sky follow their paths with predictable precision, rising and setting at the right times, never straying from their appointed order. So, too, on earth, with God's work manifest in the unchanging order of the seasons and in the way that the trees' behavior matches the seasons. In the winter the trees lose their leaves, and in the summer they grow them back.

Furthermore, Enoch notes, the leaves show up just when we need them, because in summer we need shade from the sun. God has planned everything out, from the paths of the sun, moon, and stars to automatic seasonal parasols. (Enoch actually goes into more detail, correctly limiting his observations to some kinds of deciduous trees.)

Yet even as all parts of the natural world follow their proper paths, there are people who have strayed, deviating from God's commandments and ignoring God's will. These are wicked people, and in the end they will be punished, while only the righteous shall prosper with their happiness multiplied forever.

It was in this context, after the children of humans had multiplied, that they produced beautiful women who caught the attention of the children of heaven, the angels. These angels decided to go down to earth to choose wives for themselves from among the human women.

Their leader was named Semyaza. The idea was his, but he was afraid that he alone would dare to go down to earth and take a human wife, so that he alone might be blamed for committing this grave sin. He convinced the others that they should all swear an oath to join him, which they did—swearing upon a curse instead of a blessing.

Then, two hundred strong, they descended to Ardis at the peak of

Mount Hermon, a mountain located one hundred miles north of Jerusalem between Damascus and the Mediterranean Sea and known from various mentions in the Bible. Enoch connects the name of the mountain to the curse, or *herem* in Hebrew, that they swore. The angels Ramiel, Kokahiel, Daniel, Ezekiel, and others each took one wife apiece and mated with her. The angels also taught the women magical medicine, spells, and the nature of roots and plants.

The women got pregnant and gave birth to giants nearly five hundred feet tall. These giants devoured everything humans had created, then the humans themselves, then birds, reptiles, fish, and other animals. Finally the giants turned on one another, drinking each other's blood, until things got so bad that the very earth itself filed a complaint against these lawless ones.

While this was going on, the (evil) angel Azazel taught people how to make swords and daggers, shields and breastplates, as well as bracelets, ornaments, makeup, and jewelry. This changed the world, bringing about evil behavior such as adultery and other corrupt conduct. The angel Amezarak taught people how to cast spells and cut roots. The angel Armaros taught people how to resolve those spells. The angel Barakiel taught astrology; the angel Kokabel, portents; the angel Tamiel, more astrology; and the angel Asradel, the path of the moon and human deception.

Amid this massive destruction, the people of the earth cried out, and their voice reached heaven.

The angels Michael, Gabriel, Suriel, and Uriel looked down from heaven and saw the earthly bloodshed, lamenting to one another about the sorry state of the earth and the way human voices had reached the gates of heaven. And they didn't know what to do.

They petitioned God, who, after all, knows everything before it happens and before whom everyone and everything is naked, with nothing hidden. Surely God has seen how Azazel had taught humans every form of oppression and had revealed heaven's eternal secrets, just as God has seen how Semyaza had taught people how to cast spells. The same Semyaza to whom God had given the power of angelic leadership had led the angels to take human wives and defile them, fathering giants who had caused the whole earth to be filled with blood and sin so that the cries of the souls of the suffering humans had ascended to heaven, where surely God could hear their misery. "O God," demanded Michael, Gabriel, Suriel, and Uriel. "What should we do?"

God sent the angel Arsyalalyur to Lamech's son Noah with instructions to tell Noah to hide because the world was going to come to an end in a great flood that would destroy everything. God also directed Arsyalalyur to teach Noah how to escape so that he would save himself and his children.

And God sent the angel Raphael to bind the angel Azazel by his hands and feet and throw him into darkness. Raphael made a hole in the desert and threw Azazel into it, covering him with rocks. Raphael covered Azazel's face so that he could no longer see any light and so that he would eventually be sent into the fire on the great day of judgment. God also tasked Raphael with restoring the earth that the angels had ruined and with announcing the restoration of the earth, because God planned to restore the earth, not letting humanity be destroyed by the mystery of everything that the Watchers had taught. "The whole earth has been ruined by what Azazel taught," God lamented. "Record all sin as coming from him," God told Raphael.

God told the angel Gabriel to destroy the adulterous children and to expel the children of the Watchers from humanity, setting them against each other so that they destroy each other. God warned Gabriel that the Watchers would plead for their lives—which would have been eternal because angels never die—but Gabriel was forbidden to listen to them.

God told the angel Michael to deal with Semyaza similarly, locking him away in darkness until he and the angels he convinced to join him are ultimately punished. Then good would replace evil, with the earth producing plentiful food and the heavenly storehouses of blessing descending to earth to spread peace and truth forever.

We met Enoch right at the beginning of the book, when he told the reader that he had a message for the future, explaining that everything in the world followed its set path, except for people, who sometimes strayed. But Enoch has remained hidden from view since the beginning of the saga with the Watchers.

Based on its style and content, and because Enoch doesn't play a role in it, some people suspect that the passage about the Watchers is either based on or even a direct copy of a now-lost Book of Noah, rather than an original composition. Either way, it meshes seamlessly with the biblical narrative. Starting in Genesis 6:1, we read about the time when "people multiplied . . . and daughters were born to them, and the sons of angels took wives for themselves" from among the humans. That's why, in those days, there were "the *nephilim* upon the earth . . . when the sons of angels entered the daughters of humans, who in turn bore children to them."

The "sons of angels" are sometimes translated "sons of gods," and, in addition, we find various renderings of things like "sons of humans." The Septuagint translates the Hebrew *nephilim* as the Greek *gigantes,* that is, "giants." Whatever the terminology, the point is clear: Male divine beings mated with female humans, the result of which were the giants.

The phrasing in Genesis—and, in particular, the use of "the" in "the giants"—suggests that the ancient reader was expected to be familiar with the story and that Genesis was just providing a summary to remind people of what they already knew. With Enoch, we, too, have access to that prerequisite information.

We now call the angels that mated with people the "fallen angels," a nomenclature that matches the literal meaning of the Hebrew *nephilim* ("fallen ones") but only partially accords with the text. The Hebrew "fallen ones" are the giants themselves, while the English "fallen angels" are their angelic parents.

Interestingly, Enoch spends more time on what the fallen angels teach humans than on their misguided procreation. We get detailed lists of which angels taught what, and toward the end God tells Raphael that "the whole earth has been ruined by what Azazel taught," not by who Semyaza chose for a wife.

In passages that people often skip over, Genesis also sometimes indicates who taught people what. For example, Genesis 4:21 tells us that Jubal invented music, and the next verse indicates that Zillah's son Tubal-cain was the first metalsmith. Similarly, we saw in the Life of Adam and Eve that the angels had to teach Eve about childbirth and, later, Seth how to dress Eve's body. This kind of information answers the implicit general question, How did humans ever figure that out?

(A much later rabbinic tradition, continuing in the theme of metal-working, wonders about the metal tongs used in forging metal. The tongs are used to move metal into and back out of fire. But those tongs have to be annealed, a process that involves pushing the tongs themselves into fire and pulling them back out. It's easy to make new tongs with the help of old tongs, but how, the Rabbis wonder, were the first tongs made? They must have come directly from God.)

The inventions in Genesis are presented neutrally. They are neither specifically beneficial nor detrimental. But the etymology of many music words in Hebrew suggests that people were suspicious of this new artistic technology. The Hebrew word for "harp" (or something like it) is *nevel,* and the related *n'vala* means "disgrace" or "disgust." The Hebrew for word "flute" (or, again, something like it) is *chalil,* whose root we also find in the word *chalila,* which means roughly "God forbid!" This pattern may reflect a specific suspicion of the power of music, or more generally a fear of new things. (As modern people, we may find it hard to think of music as something that could once have been considered "newfangled technology." But it was.)

This brings us back to Enoch's criticism of what Azazel taught people how to do. The details of what Azazel taught and the consequences of humans having that knowledge are particularly interesting and astonishingly relevant. He taught people how to make bracelets, ornaments, and jewelry, but apparently the same technology could be used for swords, daggers, and shields.

More generally, Enoch expresses the sentiments that we were better off when we were ignorant and that knowledge will lead to evil. Though Enoch's words date back over two thousand years, they are eerily reminiscent of the modern debate over such things as nuclear technology, which, it would seem, helps us power lights but which also led to horrific deaths in Japan. Even cell phones and other modern conveniences have earned a reputation as both helpful and harmful, with fears that they are corrupting young minds.

Going back a little further, in the 1800s the son of a European builder wanted to make it easier to perform such construction tasks as excavating rock and drilling tunnels. To this end, he tried to form a flexible, stable, easy-to-use explosive. Nitroglycerin was already around, but it was so volatile that it was considered too dangerous to produce and use. This particular man, Alfred Nobel, thought there must be a way of taming nitroglycerin. In 1864 he found it, calling his new invention dynamite. And it did make it easier and safer to excavate rock, drill tunnels, build canals, and much more. Nobel paved the way to success for untold numbers of public works projects. But Nobel's invention, like Azazel's craft millennia earlier, proved to be not only productive but also destructive, because the dynamite could be used to kill.

Enoch might say that Azazel taught Nobel how to blow things up.

Except that so far Enoch hasn't been involved, save for his brief appearance in the introduction. The Book of Enoch picks up by recognizing this fact, even telling the reader that Enoch had hidden before the whole mess with the Watchers. No one knew where he was, though apparently in some unclear way he was actually with the Watchers and other holy ones. This is how it was possible for the good Watchers—the ones who didn't go down to earth to take human wives—to petition him to send a message to the fallen angels.

Enoch complied, starting with Azazel, telling the archangel of evil that a grave judgment awaited him and that he would know no peace. He would be put in bonds and have no opportunity even to offer a prayer of supplication. Enoch sent a similar message to the rest of the fallen angels.

The angels begged Enoch to write prayers of remembrance and forgiveness on their behalf, because they would no longer be able to speak, and they would have no way of praying for themselves. Enoch did this, recording their prayers for forgiveness from sin and for long lives.

He took the prayers to the waters of the Dan River, to the southwest of Mount Hermon, and started reciting them. And there, by the Dan, not far from Mount Hermon, with prayers on behalf of the fallen Watchers in his mouth, he saw a vision.

Clouds and fog. Stars. Lightning. Winds hoisting Enoch high into heaven. Then higher. White marble. Frightening tongues of fire. Fiery cherubim. A house hot as fire yet cold as ice, and nothing inside. But wait! An inner opening leading to another house even greater than the first one. A floor of fire and a ceiling of fire, with stars and lightning beyond.

A throne! Crystal, and Wheels like the shining sun. The voice of the cherubim. Streams of flaming fire supporting the throne. Upon the throne His Great Glory, in clothes brighter than the sun, whiter than snow. The Lord!

The Lord called Enoch with his own voice: "Come near to me, and hear my holy word. Do not be afraid, Enoch, for you are a righteous man, a scribe of righteousness. Come near and hear my voice.

"Tell the Watchers that they should petition on behalf of humans, not humans on their behalf. Ask them why they abandoned the high, holy, and eternal heaven to become unclean with human women, emulating the behavior of humans of the earth. They used to be holy, spiritual creatures. They used to be immortal.

"Tell them that humans have wives and children because they are mortal. Immortal beings need no wives.

"Now," God continued to Enoch, "the giants produced by the union of spirits and flesh will be called evil spirits. Spiritual beings live in heaven, but the evil spirits will live on earth, neither eating nor drinking, but eventually opposing each other, and wreaking havoc on Earth. They will rise up against the humans and in particular against the women, because they came from the women.

"And they will keep causing problems but not be punished, until the great conclusion, the great age.

"And tell the Watchers that they used to be in heaven, but even so, they were not aware of all of the mysteries of heaven. They only know the rejected mysteries. Those are the mysteries they broadcast to human women, and those are the mysteries that will cause women and men to multiply evil on the earth. Tell the Watchers they will never know peace."

As with the Apocalypse of Abraham, Enoch's vision involves the usual visual elements: fire, snow whiteness, and, in particular, seraphim, Wheels (which we called Creatures of the Wheels there), and a throne, and then God's voice. These signal the reader that the important theology is coming up.

Here we see that it has a few particular claims. Perhaps the clearest is the point that mortals need marriage and children precisely because they don't live forever, while angels, who live forever, don't need marriage or children. This is in keeping with the opening theme. The world was constructed in just the right way so that everything works out. In the introduction, Enoch noted how the trees sprout leaves only in the summer, because people need shade in the summer. Now he learns that only mortals have sex, because only mortals need to have children.

But there's a huge catch here. The immortal angels did have sex. And they did produce children. The universe was planned in a certain way, in fact, in a perfect way, but things have gone wrong.

Two mystical journeys continue this theme.

Enoch's vision took him next to a mountain of precious stones in the west. There was a pit inside, and atop the pit a place that lacked both the usual sky above and the usual earth or water below. It was empty, desolate, and terrible. Inside were seven stars like great, burning mountains. An angel told Enoch that the pit was a prison for fallen stars and that the seven stars were stars that had transgressed God's commandments by not arriving punctually. God was furious with the stars, so he bound them in the pit-prison. And the angel Uriel told Enoch that the same pit would hold the fallen angels who had united with human women.

Then, after recounting a list of archangels, Enoch journeyed on, ending up (for unexplained reasons) at the same place, where he saw the same star prison with the fallen angels.

Next he saw another mountain, this one with four hollowed-out chambers, each one a way station for four different categories of human soul, a place where the souls would wait for the final day of judgment.

Enoch heard the voices of the souls, and, as it happened, the first one he heard was the voice of a soul lodging a complaint. "Whose voice is that?" Enoch wanted to know.

Rufael, the angel who was now with him, explained that it was the voice of Abel's spirit, whom Cain had murdered, and that the voice would continue against Cain until all of Cain's descendants perish. This is Enoch's way of starting to address a familiar question: Why do good people suffer?

We already saw that the Apocalypse of Abraham addresses this question, coming to the not uncommon conclusion that good people get an eventual eternal reward, just as bad people are eventually punished. This is part of the equity that people demand from the universe.

Enoch notes that right off the bat, as it were, as soon as we are born, we find unfairness in the world. Did Abel do anything to deserve his suffering? No. In this sense, we all know an Abel—someone who, it would seem, did nothing wrong but nonetheless suffered.

One common modern answer is that everyone is a sinner, having been born with original sin from the original sinners Adam and Eve. Abel was their immediate child. You don't get closer than that to inheriting original sin. Another common modern answer is the non-answer: "God works in mysterious ways."

Enoch's answer is to probe the issue further, coming up with four categories of people, which he sees in his vision and which are explained to him by the angel Rufael.

The first category is righteous people. Enoch doesn't make it clear if these are all righteous people, or just the righteous people that live happy lives, but the third category makes it pretty clear that this first category is just a subset of the righteous people.

So we jump to that third category: people who lodge complaints (or perhaps even "engage in lawsuits"). These are people, like Abel, who were unjustly wronged. Enoch here gives them a voice after their death, in the form of the cries that continue to complain against their assailants.

The second category is the flipside of the third: sinners who were not punished on earth. Taken together, these two categories of people— good people who get punished and bad people who don't—epitomize the difficulties in the classical doctrine of reward and punishment, which insists that good things come to good people and bad things come to bad people.

Like Enoch here, parts of the Bible insist on this classical reward and punishment. Just for example, Deuteronomy 11 is clear that crop-nourishing rain is a reward for following God's commandments. "If you listen to my commandments . . . then I [God] will grant timely rain." But "be careful not to turn away and worship other gods," for then "God will stop up the sky and there will be no rain."

It's a simple, compelling thesis, and one that most people believe at some level. It has amazingly broad appeal. We might summarize this theology—prevalent in the Bible as well as among believers and apparent nonbelievers to this day—as "fairness."

This demand of the world seems almost hardwired into the brains of children, which is why children repeatedly complain, bitterly, that "it's not fair." Children don't like to be punished, but they usually accept punishment as part of life. On the other hand, they hate it when adults dole out undeserved punishment. And, curiously, they also can't abide people who get away with evil. The world should be fair.

Most adults remain children in this regard. When tragedy strikes, even people who don't believe in God usually find themselves wondering what they did to earn God's wrath. And these same people sometimes ask of good fortune, What did I do to deserve this?—bypassing the inconvenient facts that they don't believe in a God who might answer the question any more than they believe in good fortune coming as a reward.

The problem with this intuitive and pervasive theology, of course, is that it doesn't work. The world is full of good people whose crops have failed, and it is equally full of despicable people who have, apparently, thrived.

The Bible does address this glaring problem, most notably in the book of Job, where the answer is that the question is beyond our comprehension. "You don't even know how I created the ocean," God chastises Job when he asks why he, a good man, is suffering. *What makes you think you can understand something as complicated as suffering?* is God's point. But in a sense, this is a nonanswer answer.

Rufael tells Enoch that sometimes sinners die and are buried even though judgment hasn't been executed upon them. These people will suffer in the end of days. This lets Enoch skip Job and return to the point, if not the details, of Deuteronomy. Sinners are always punished, just not always in this world. For Enoch, as for Abraham in his Apocalypse, final judgment seems to be a matter of rectifying the apparent lack of fairness in life.

This explanation took care of Enoch's second category, sinners who escaped punishment. And Enoch was grateful, praising the "Lord of righteousness." But what about the third category, people like Abel whose spirits' voices continue to complain?

To find the answer, Enoch journeyed on.

He saw a mountain of fire and, as he approached, seven mountains, each different from the other, each made of unique beautiful stones. The mountains, situated among ravines, formed the shape of a throne surrounded by trees. And one of those trees was unlike anything Enoch had ever experienced: unique in fragrance, adorned with eternal leaves, and graced with beautiful fruit.

The angel Michael, who was now with Enoch, explained that the mountains did in fact form a throne, the throne on which God will sit when he comes to earth for good. And the tree—which was off-limits to humanity until the great judgment—was reserved for the righteous and the pious. Those select few would eat its fruit of life.

Above, Rufael explained that bad people eventually suffer. Here Michael completes the picture by adding that good people eventually earn eternal reward.

The basic questions are similar to what we saw in the Apocalypse of Abraham: Is there a reason to be good? Is virtue rewarded? Is evil punished? And the answers are similar: Life is fair, but—as it were—only because life doesn't end at death. Rather, life after death eventually evens things out. But as we'll see below, the superficial similarities mask fundamental differences. Enoch draws very different conclusions about the world than Abraham does, and has a very different lesson to teach us.

Additionally, Enoch insists on more detail regarding these matters. We get it in books 2–5.

But book 1 is not quite over. He takes one more mystical journey first, traveling to the center of the earth to a blessed place shaded with branches. There he finds a holy mountain. We know from the way it matches descriptions in Ezekiel (5:5, 38:12) that this is Jerusalem, and Enoch provides exquisite detail of what he sees, both there and in the surrounding areas. But we skip those details here to move on to book 2, the Book of the Similitudes, or the Parables of Enoch.

The Parables are so rich in imagery, and so detailed in content, that they deserve a book of their own. So rather than proceed chapter by chapter, we focus on the particularly relevant themes.

In addition to the judgment of the wicked and the reward of the righteous in general, Enoch now turns his attention to the details: Who is righteous? Who is wicked? And what will judgment look like?

We are hardly surprised to find believers listed among the righteous and nonbelievers among the wicked, even though that theme was practically missing from Book 1. God in Book 2 is frequently the "Lord of Spirits," and nonbelievers are the ones who deny his name.

But there are other groups of evildoers, too, most notably the ruling class, which Enoch enumerates into categories that we might translate as, "governors, kings, officials, and landowners." They are all evil. Enoch spends two full chapters on the pain these people will experience in the end of days and on the class reversal that will rectify the situation. For example, the downtrodden will wear garments of glory while the rulers will be stripped of their power, and kings of the earth and mighty landowners will be humiliated on account of what they did.

Much of the rhetoric comes in terms of what the upper class will finally learn: "We now know that we should glorify the Lord of kings, who rules over all kings." "We had [wrongly] put our trust in our scepters." "God's judgment comes regardless of status." And even, "We have gorged on financial exploitation."

Enoch also rails against the Parthians and the Medes to his east, who had occupied Jerusalem. (The Parthians' occupation of Jerusalem in the year 40 B.C. was in fact short-lived, but their reputation as a mighty force was not limited to the duration of that occupation.)

Though couched in language that is largely inaccessible to today's readers, Enoch's themes sound remarkably modern, representing not just lofty matters like belief in God but everyday practical matters like financial equality and political skirmishes.

Alongside these day-to-day realities, Enoch includes Azazel and the other fallen angels among those who will be punished. In this way he connects his mundane observations about the world's woes to their cosmic solutions as he describes them.

According to Enoch, God existed even before time began—during the before-time. Enoch caught a glimpse of that before-time and saw the One to whom that before-time belonged (God, presumably), with a head white like snow. Enoch also saw another one there, with a human face: the Son of Man.

This Son of Man was, apparently, created by God and named before anything else came into being—before even the sun and the moon, before the stars. The Son of Man is the one who will bring about the final reckoning.

In particular—and reinforcing some of the themes we just saw—the Son of Man will dethrone kings, loosen the stranglehold the mighty have on the downtrodden, and crush the teeth of sinners. When that happens, everyone who dwells on earth will praise his name. He will be a staff for the righteous. He is the Messiah.

As it happens, the English phrase "Son of Man" is actually a pretty bad translation of the text here. "Human one" would be better, because "son of" was used in the original language of the text to indicate membership in a group, and the group was "humans," not just "men." But we keep "Son of Man" here both because it is so well known in connection with Enoch and because it reinforces the obvious connection to the "Son of Man" in the New Testament. ("Son of Man" is a bad translation there, too, for the same reasons.)

In fact, we find the phrase "son of man" frequently throughout both the Old Testament and the New Testament, but translations often hide that fact by using "human," "human being," or "mortal" in the Old Testament, and "son of man" (or, capitalized, "Son of Man") only in the New. For example, in Isaiah (56:2), God commands people to maintain justice, noting the joy that doing so will bring "to a person," that is "to the son of man." And God frequently addresses the prophet Ezekiel as "son of man."

Yet it's only in the New Testament that the Son of Man is clearly identified with the Messiah, just as he is in the Parables of Enoch. This makes it tempting to equate the two.

But though they are similar, they are also different. Enoch's Son of Man was waiting at the ready from before the universe was created, unlike Jesus. Even more to the point, Enoch's "Son of Man," Enoch tells us, is himself!

This Son of Man will be instrumental in bringing about the final judgment, which will include resurrection of the righteous in addition to everything that we've seen.

Though we've barely touched on the beauty and intricacy of the Parables of Enoch, the second of the five books in the Book of Enoch, we leave it for the moment and skip to the fourth book to continue the theme of politics that we saw just above.

The fourth book, the Book of Dream Visions, details two visions that Enoch sees. The first portrays how the sky literally fell onto the earth.

In the second vision, a snow-white bull emerged from the earth, soon to be followed by a female calf along with two other calves, one dark and the other red. The dark calf gored the red calf after pursuing it all over the earth, and then the red calf disappeared so that Enoch could no longer see it. By contrast, the dark calf grew up to be strong and took a female calf. After that, Enoch saw lots of calves that were similar to the dark calf.

The first female calf looked all over for the red calf but couldn't find it. And she was distraught, but she kept looking. So Enoch helped her look, at the same time consoling the female calf. Thus quieted, the female calf bore another snow-white bull and, after that, many more cows, some of them dark.

That snow-white bull grew up to be big and strong, and from him came many more snow-white cows, all of which resembled him. Then those cows in turn gave birth to more cows, all resembling each other, each one following many others.

Then Enoch again saw a vision with his own eyes. From the lofty heaven a star fell down to earth but managed to rise and eat and pasture among the bulls. Then these big dark cows altered their pens (in some way that isn't explained), their pastures, and even their calves. And they started to complain to one another. Then many more stars came down from heaven, joining the first star among the cows in their pasture. And the stars brought out their sexual organs and mounted the cows, so that the cows all became pregnant and bore elephants and camels and donkeys. The other bulls were terrified of them, because they bit with their teeth and swallowed and gored with their horns, eventually eating the cows. And all the children of the earth trembled and shook and fled before them.

Amid the violence of their goring and devouring each other, the earth itself began to cry aloud. And Enoch saw another vision: A snow-white creature descended from heaven in the form of a human, along with three others like it. They took Enoch by the hand and lofted him high above the earth, so he could see what would happen to the elephants, camels, and donkeys.

One of the four creatures from heaven took the first star, bound its hands and feet, and threw it into a deep, empty, dark abyss. Then the creatures turned to deal with the other stars.

Enoch's vision progressed, with more animals joining the fray, everything from great cats like lions and leopards to farm hunters like wolves and foxes, along with sheep, raptors of various sorts, and more.

The wolves oversaw the sheep, an arrangement that, not surprisingly, led to trouble, but the sheep, with the help of the Lord of the Sheep, managed to escape, eventually building a glorious house in a beautiful land. Things were going so well for the sheep that their eyes were opened. With the help of a series of particularly strong rams, the sheep repelled various attacks by all manner of wild beasts.

But as time progressed, the sheep strayed, and attacks by the other animals grew more successful. The lions and the leopards feasted on the sheep. So did the wild boars. The sheep were evicted from their glorious home, and Enoch couldn't see if the sheep would be let back in.

Eventually the sheep returned to their house, rebuilding it and repelling the wild boars.

Nonetheless, before long the sheep mixed in with the wild beasts. They were so intermingled that most of them could not be rescued from the onslaught of attacking animals.

Then the raptors came—eagles, vultures, kites, and ravens. The eagles led the pack and started devouring the sheep, gouging out their eyes and then feasting on their flesh.

The ravens would circle over the sheep, swooping down to snatch a lamb, throwing it back to the ground, and feasting on it. Some of the lambs grew horns, but the ravens ate the horns, too, until one day a particularly strong lamb grew an especially strong horn. The eagles, vultures, kites, and ravens kept attacking that one sheep. The ravens in particular turned their united attention to the sheep, now a grown ram, with the horn. A vicious battle ensued, but the ravens were unable to remove the ram's horn.

Yet the animal violence continued.

Finally another snow-white cow was born with huge horns. This cow united all of the animals, transforming them, too, into snow-white cows. At this the Lord of the Sheep rejoiced, and, with him, Enoch.

We now understand this intriguing vision to be a detailed history of all time. White represents goodness, darkness sin, and redness innocent bloodshed. The first snow-white bull is Adam, who, as we saw, is followed by a female calf (Eve) and two other calves, one dark (Cain) and the other red (Abel). The dark calf kills the red calf, and the female calf scours the earth looking for it.

Our English rendition here is hindered by the paucity of animal terms available to us. We do have technical progressions like "calf, heifer, cow" and "calf, bullock, bull," which, in the United States, represent three stages of the female's life (weaning, before childbirth, and after childbirth) and three stages of the male's life (weaning, young, and old). But these terms vary from place to place. Some communities use "bullock" not for a young bull but rather for an old one. More important, most nonfarmers call all of these a cow, not reserving "cow" only for female bovines that have given birth. Similarly, for the transition from young male sheep to adult male sheep, the best we can do is "sheep to ram." So our text is of necessity a little awkward and vague.

Other translations prefer other terminology. Sometimes Adam, Eve, Cain, and Abel are a bull, a heifer, and two bullocks. Other times they are all "bovids."

If we use the English word "cow" to represent any sort of cow, bull, etcetera, then the cows are the line of Adam. The sheep are the people of the Lord.

In a scene we skipped before, Enoch sees one of the stars (the good angels) teach one of the cows how to make a boat. Then the cow becomes a person who uses the boat to survive a flood, while the other animals—the other cows along with the elephants, camels, and donkeys—perish. This is obviously the story of Noah's ark.

The wolves, who ended up overseeing the sheep, are the Egyptians who enslaved the Israelites. In another scene we skipped, the sheep escape from the wolves as a great lake parts, letting the sheep through but drowning the wolves in the face of the Lord of the Sheep.

The sheep establish a great house (the Temple) in a beautiful land (Jerusalem), only to be expelled by the lions and leopards, or, in other translations, the lions and the hyenas, or the lions and the tigers, etcetera. These are the first conquerors of Israelite Jerusalem—probably the Babylonians and the Assyrians. And this matches the history of Jerusalem as we know it, as described in detail in chapter 1.

The sheep in Enoch's vision reestablish their great house, just as we know that the Israelites returned to Jerusalem.

We also know how various peoples conquered Jerusalem over the next few centuries: including the Macedonians, sometimes called the Greeks (eagles); the Syrians, also sometimes called the Greeks or the Greek Syrians (crows); and the Egyptians, also more specifically called the Ptolemies (kites).

The great ram whose horn is so strong that the ravens cannot eat it is one of the Maccabees, and the battle is the one recorded by Josephus and in 1 and 2 Maccabees and celebrated by the Jewish holiday Hanukkah.

The end of Enoch's vision is perhaps the most important. A snow-white cow (technically, a calf, then a bullock, then a bull) was born with great horns to unite all the animals. This is, of course, the Messiah, from the line of Adam.

Enoch's intricate animal vision reinforces his understanding of history as starting with Adam and Eve and ending with the coming of the Messiah. He highlights the important events, including the fallen angels, the flood, Israelite slavery in Egypt, the Exodus, Israelite presence in the promised land, the building of the First Temple, the first exile, assimilation of the Jews, the Second Temple, the battles for Jerusalem, and the Messiah.

The most important part of this vision, though, is what's missing.

Enoch doesn't include any sort of final judgment. And this omission epitomizes Enoch's fundamental struggle.

On the one hand, he believes—or, at least, would like to believe—that God has established a perfect world, down to the tiniest detail. As we saw right at the outset of the book, even the trees sprout leaves only in summer, because that's when people need shade. Similarly, humans have children because they are mortal, while angels, being immortal and therefore having no need of children, do not marry.

But Enoch's world is one that has gone awry. Even God's holy angels deviated from his perfect plan when they mated with human women and, it would seem, caused suffering that no one deserved and that he didn't intend.

Similarly, the sheep (Israelites) in the animal history repeatedly suffer. In one particularly poignant passage, the Lord of the Sheep even rejoiced as he fed the sheep to the wild animals, remaining silent as the sheep were devoured.

Above we saw how Rufael taught Enoch that bad people eventually suffer and good people eventually earn eternal reward. And we saw how this seemed, at least superficially, to match Abraham in the Apocalypse. But the difference is that Enoch doesn't seem to fully believe it.

Enoch—like many of us in modernity—seems unable to reconcile what he sees around him with his idea of what a universe with God in charge should look like. Enoch's world is, in the end, not the perfect world of God but rather a world marred by unplanned circumstances and unforeseen events. According to Enoch, we are not living in the world destined for us but, rather, in a faulty and imperfect substitute.

A bold interpretation even suggests that Enoch feels a personal responsibility to make things better. After all, the only messiah coming to fix things, he sees, is himself.

Either way, Enoch is certainly skeptical of God's power to deliver on an ultimate plan. At times Enoch even denies that we are living according to God's will.

In light of the physical suffering and emotional angst that marked the final decades of the first millennium, we are not surprised that the Book of Enoch was so highly esteemed two thousand years ago. The book offered precisely what readers needed: affirmation that their suffering was undeserved and was not the will of the God they felt either had abandoned them or, worse, had never cared for them in the first place.

And we similarly understand why later generations of Jews and Christians wished to squash this seemingly heretical work. Their postexilic theology and worldview had no place for anything but God's perfect plan. The reason to be Jewish was because it was God's desire and because God favored those who believed in him. The reason to be Christian was, again, because it was God's desire and because God not only favored those who believed in him but also severely punished those who did not. God had a perfect plan, in other words, and you either got on board or got left behind.

But Enoch had the audacity to suggest that our world was imperfect, in spite of God. Perhaps some people suffer for no reason at all. Perhaps sinners don't get punished in life after death, or, in a more nuanced interpretation, perhaps they do but it doesn't matter.

Enoch's message is a timeless expression of the human condition.

We have all felt that something has gone awry in our lives: childhood dreams that never materialized or unforeseen nightmares for which we couldn't even begin to plan. Like Enoch, we generally find that life is a mixed bag, and our daily existence consists of balancing the good and the bad, trying to appreciate and augment the former, hoping to endure and mitigate the latter.

And also like Enoch, we are often unconsoled and unconvinced by claims that our suffering—be it temporary or permanent, meager or substantial—is God's will. Indeed, we are often infuriated by the suggestion.

We are, therefore, lucky that the cutting room floor has preserved this counterpoint to what has become traditional theology, just as we are fortunate that earlier attempts to erase the Book of Enoch were thwarted by a circuitous path from Hebrew and Aramaic through Greek and Latin to Ethiopic and now English, bolstered by fragments from the Dead Sea Scrolls.

Against all odds, the book, like Enoch himself, never died.

8

THE BIG PICTURE: FINDING
THE UNABRIDGED BIBLE

There is nothing new under the sun.
—ECCLESIASTES

New friends are always surpassed by old ones.
—BEN SIRA

"There is nothing new under the sun," according to the philosopher Kohelet in Ecclesiastes. But ironically, Kohelet may have been the first person to pen those words. There was a time when that very observation was new.

Perhaps more than anything else, this tension between old and new defines the modern role of the Bible. Our Bible today is tens of centuries old, while the Bible of antiquity was new. So even to the extent that it was the same Bible back then as it is now, it was also completely different.

The Bible used to be a representative sample of a larger set of favorite texts, while now it's perceived to be the full collection.

It was as though we'd built a sacred museum for our treasured documents. Some of them went on permanent display in the main lobby (dubbed the Bible), others in back rooms, and others yet in the archives. Even in the main lobby, some texts were more showcased than others—Genesis over Habakkuk, for example.

Rabbinic Judaism and Christianity became the curators and the docents of this invaluable resource.

As long as the texts were new and fresh in everyone's mind, it was easy to keep track of the complete collection. A document didn't have to be in the main lobby for it to remain prominent, and the curators could enthusiastically tell visitors that their museum was bigger than what a cursory glance might indicate. No one could possibly forget the Book of Enoch, they must have thought, even though it wasn't in the main lobby. But then, over time—lots of time—people did start to forget. Fortunately, the texts were written down.

But keeping up the museum proved to be painstaking work. Parchment grew brittle and ink faded, so the manuscripts had to be restored and recopied. The first to receive attention, naturally, were the ones in the main lobby, starting with the most centrally featured texts.

That's why the Five Books of Moses have survived nearly intact, with only a letter or two having changed over two thousand years (as we saw in chapters 2 and 3). Those books were in the center of the lobby. The Book of Samuel, still in the lobby but not so central, survived, too, but a few of its passages got lost over time (again, as we saw in chapter 2).

It was the back rooms, though, and the archives that really suffered. Lights went dim. The collections grew musty. And documents went missing.

What started as an entranceway to the complete collection ended up as the collection itself. The Bible of modernity is that abridged collection, newly perceived to be the whole thing. But we now know that there was once a whole museum's worth of documents.

To explore it, we started with Jerusalem, because that city's waning days were undeniably among the most productive and influential the world has ever seen. Hardly a spot on earth is untouched by the ideas and writings from that tiny hill two thousand years ago, just as we continue to ask the fundamental questions of human existence that were so central back then: Why is my life like this? What is my life supposed to be? Is there something I'm expected to do? Is there a right and wrong path for me? Do my actions have consequences? Does anyone care what I do? What happens after I die? Am I fundamentally alone?

We saw how the advent of the codex, or book, ended up distorting the nature of what was written in and around Jerusalem. Before the codex, there were lots of holy scrolls, arranged in a loose hierarchy of importance. Not everyone agreed which ones were most important, just as disagreement abounded regarding the details of the texts.

So the Dead Sea Scrolls contain not only the text of the Bible but also lots more. It's also why the Dead Sea Scrolls don't cleanly divide the texts into "the Bible" and "not the Bible." Lots of texts were holy. None of them were "the Bible" yet. And it is why the Dead Sea Scrolls don't agree word for word with the Bible. Though in places the Dead Sea Scrolls contain errors (like our standard text of the Bible), sometimes the differences reflect disagreement about the original holy words.

The Septuagint reinforces this pattern of different textual traditions, because sometimes the text as translated in the Septuagint doesn't mean the same thing as the original Hebrew. Equally, we see that the custom in Jerusalem was to accept the different versions rather than to choose among them. That's why Matthew in the New Testament was able to quote the Greek version of Isaiah instead of the Hebrew. The two texts may have disagreed, but, to Matthew, they were both holy, just as different understandings of the text would be holy for the Rabbis who created rabbinic Judaism.

Josephus's writings further amplify our view. Like the Dead Sea Scrolls and the Septuagint, Josephus shows us different ideas about what should be in the Bible and different textual traditions about those writings. He also shows us that some of the material required for us to understand the Bible wasn't actually included in the Bible. It's impossible to understand the impact of Matthew 2 without knowing who Herod was, but the Bible doesn't tell us. The Tower of Babel was waterproofed against a potential future flood, but unless you're an expert in the ancient role of bitumen, you'd never know it from reading the Bible.

In general, we see an ancient culture that welcomed different opinions rather than focusing on one right answer. This flexibility was important when it came to details of the text and even more important in terms of broader concepts.

Accordingly, we see contradictory ideas in our current version of the Bible. Deuteronomy shouts traditional reward and punishment, insisting that people only suffer if they disobey God, but Job differs and vehemently maintains that we will never know why people suffer.

In the same spirit of diversity, we looked at three documents that serve a dual purpose. They fill in significant gaps in some of the Bible's most well-known passages: what happened to Adam and Eve after they left the Garden of Eden, how Abraham discovered monotheism, and why Enoch was so important. In addition, these texts offer three different answers to the same questions that are addressed in Deuteronomy and Job: Why do people suffer?

According to the Life of Adam and Eve, people suffer simply because that is the nature of being human. Having to work for a living is the result of Adam's transgression, but only because—we clearly read—Satan tricked Eve into tricking Adam. And Satan did this not because of anything that Adam or Eve did but simply because they were human. The text teaches that part of being human is to work for a living, to endure pain, to be mortal, to mourn the dead, and so forth. Those are inseparable from being nearly divine. The short answer to why people suffer is that that's the price of being human. Life is fundamentally a mixture of joy and pain lived in no small part in exile.

The Apocalypse of Abraham disagrees. There, actions come in two varieties: good and bad. Furthermore, people are able to choose for themselves which path they take, and they will be rewarded for taking the right path in life just as they will be punished for taking the wrong. So far, this is similar to Deuteronomy. But the Apocalypse deals with the obvious objection to Deuteronomy, namely, that it doesn't seem to be true. So the Apocalypse posits an afterlife that evens things out, eventually punishing evil and rewarding good. The short answer to why people suffer is that they either did something wrong or their suffering is temporary and they will be compensated later by much-longer-lasting reward. Life is fundamentally fair.

Enoch agrees with some of these details but disagrees about the conclusion. For Enoch, God's world was originally designed with perfection. Trees sprouted leaves just when people needed them, for instance. Part of that perfection is the eventual reward and punishment that we see in the Apocalypse of Abraham. But things didn't work out the way God planned, so for Enoch, the short answer to why people suffer is that something is wrong with the universe; they shouldn't suffer. Life is at times fundamentally flawed.

These three positions complement Job, which suggests that life is fundamentally impossible to understand, and also Deuteronomy, which insists that anyone currently suffering has done something wrong.

So according to the five texts, our life on this earth is: good if you do good, bad if you don't (Deuteronomy), enigmatic (Job), a mixed bag no matter what you do (Adam and Eve), only part of a bigger scheme of fairness (Abraham), or imperfect (Enoch).

Though we get this complete picture only from the cutting room floor, the Bible does allude to many of these views.

Deuteronomy and Job, of course, are full books in the Bible. Clearly the philosophies represented by these two works—fairness and mystery—are mainstream biblical positions. And of the two, Job seems more narrowly focused on answering the question of why people suffer. Deuteronomy contains all sorts of other material in addition to its answer about good and evil. We find the other three philosophies, too, even without a full or partial biblical book devoted to them.

The life after death that serves as a reward, as in the Apocalypse of Abraham, is a major theme in the New Testament, for example in Matthew 25:31–46, which details eternal life as a reward for the righteous and eternal punishment for the accursed. Similarly, the Rabbis read this tradition into the text of the Bible, referring to the "world to come."

In terms of the sometimes-surprising lack of justice in the Life of Adam and Eve, we see that after Cain murders his brother, Abel, God doesn't punish Cain but rather protects him.

Biblical passages supporting Enoch are harder to come by, because later tradition minimized their importance or purposely misread them, but they do exist. Among the most famous quotations from Isaiah, for example, is that "nation will not lift up sword against nation" (2:4). But in contrast to the popular interpretation, Isaiah's message wasn't antiwar, because he wasn't talking about reality as he knew it. He was referring to God's future house, that is, a time when God would eventually make things better. Similarly, the detailed passage in 1 Corinthians 15 about the nature of Christ's resurrection promises a future time when things will be made right.

Christ's resurrection was like the first fruits of a harvest, with the best yet to come. So just as the Apocalypse of Abraham promises a future when injustice will be corrected, texts like these predict a future when life's flaws more generally will be corrected. Both the fundamental Jewish notion that we live in an "unredeemed world" and the Christian (and Muslim) hope for the Second Coming are, therefore, consistent with Enoch.

Despite the biblical support for the divergent viewpoints from the Bible's cutting room floor, successive generations—sometimes by accident, sometimes on purpose—have selectively discarded parts of the original message, so even though we in the West generally live in a biblically oriented culture, ours is but one possible such culture. We focus on original sin but not on Satan's responsibility for it. We focus on the battle between good and evil, not on the way God and Satan are the same (which is expressed as God's portion "with Azazel"). We focus on God's perfect world, not the frightening possibility that things have gone awry or Enoch's intriguing vision that we are the ones who have to fix things. We focus on finding the right answer instead of asking the right question and learning that it has more than one answer.

Our journey together here has obviously not allowed for a complete examination of all of the Bible's supporting evidence, lost passages, deleted scenes, and background information that fell to the cutting room floor. There are dozens of major documents we didn't have room for here, and hundreds of minor ones. Equally, a full analysis of any one of the sources here could fill a complete book by itself. But by choosing our texts carefully, we have gained a good sense of the broader picture that the Bible was supposed to represent.

In this regard, we may return to the observation from chapter 1 that little has changed geopolitically in two thousand years. Similarly, despite all of our scientific advances, technology, world discovery, music, art, space exploration, philosophy, and the overall march of time, we are essentially just like the denizens of ancient Jerusalem: trying to make sense of things as we live through uncertain times, whether in our personal lives, the lives of our families, our larger social groups, or even the life of our planet.

Like Adam and Eve's son Seth, we struggle to understand illness. Like Eve, we wonder how to cope with loss. Like Enoch, we ask if our lives have purpose. Like Abraham, we hope, sometimes in vain, for an elusive fairness. And in terms of more day-to-day matters, we still insist on the distinction between right and wrong, the central concept that underlies so much of what we've seen here.

Many people continue to find the Bible hugely meaningful. Others do not, perhaps because they let the ancient rhetoric get in the way of the message. The atheist or agnostic or antireligionist who doesn't care what God did to Adam may nonetheless be interested in the intrinsic connection between living an adult life and working to survive, or in the universality of exile.

The texts of the Bible's cutting room floor bring both believers and nonbelievers closer to the original breadth, beauty, and insight that made the ancient unabridged Bible into the most influential collection of words the world has created.

Because of the overarching centrality of that collection, our modern life is in many ways a continuation of a dialogue that began over two thousand years ago. Some of the conversation was carefully recorded, still available for us to review whenever we like. But some remarks were off the record, as it were, and never officially written down. Some comments were even stricken from the record, often by overzealous editors who wanted to hijack our conversation.

Our journey together here has peeled back the layers of history that hide some of the most important parts of this millennia-long dialogue, helping us get reacquainted with our ancient interlocutors. And for this we should be grateful. For just as Kohelet tells us that there is nothing new under the sun, Ben Sira reminds us that new friends are always surpassed by old ones.

APPENDIX:
SUGGESTIONS FOR FURTHER READING

The ancient writings that make up the Bible's cutting room floor are, for the most part, well known within the halls of the academy, so there are plenty of scholarly essays and books about them. Equally, as with most matters connected to the Bible and religion, there's no shortage of popular books that overcome the stiffness of typical academic prose but at the expense of accuracy; they end up easy to read but wrong.

And the deficiencies of both kinds of writing are only exaggerated on the Internet.

This puts the reader looking for more information in a bind. On the one hand, the sheer volume of readily available material means that it's easy to find a book or essay about almost any of the topics I've presented here. But that same quantity, coupled with the grossly uneven quality that these works achieve, makes it much easier to find bad information than good. (I try to counteract this trend on my site, The Unabridged Bible, at www.TheUnabridgedBible.com. There, you'll find a comprehensive list of the documents from the Bible's cutting room floor, along with links to quality online writing about them, an expanded glossary of the people and places connected to them, and a variety of additional supporting material.)

My hope is that the following suggestions will guide the reader to some sources that strike me as helpful. Surely there are many other valuable works that don't appear here, though. By excluding them, I don't mean to imply that they have no value. And I offer my apologies to their authors in advance, for not recognizing their work, and to my readers, for my inadvertent complicity in keeping them in the dark.

Translations

The first thing the reader will want is full translations of the material from chapters 2–7. Here there is both good news and bad.

The good news is that translations are readily available.

The bad news is that they tend to be outdated, because many of them were composed some time ago. And they tend to be overly literal, partly for the same reason, partly because the texts are sometimes obscure, and partly because the scholars who translate the texts are usually not professional translators. So we end up with renderings of Josephus like "Nay, Nicolaus of Damascus, in his ninety-sixth book, hath a particular relation about them; where he speaks thus: . . ." for what could more simply be, "Even Nicolaus of Damascus, in his 96th book, has this to say . . ." Or we find translations along the lines of, "he died a death" for what should just be "he died." And so on.

Still, with a little work the modern reader can find the gist, if not the nuance and poetry, of most of the ancient texts, as follows:

Almost all the Dead Sea Scrolls are available in translation from Florentino García Martínez and Eibert J. C. Tigchelaar's *The Dead Sea Scrolls Study Edition,* published in 2000. It comes in a reasonably priced two-volume paperback edition, and it contains a comprehensive summary of transcriptions and translations of the nonbiblical Dead

Sea Scrolls. You'll find the original Hebrew or Aramaic text alongside a fairly good word-level English translation. So start here to read the Dead Sea Scrolls for yourself.

The Septuagint is available in English in Sir Lancelot C. L. Brenton's 1851 translation, called *The Septuagint,* now in the public domain. You can find it online or in the 1986 reprint by Hendrickson Publishers. Oxford University Press has a more contemporary translation by Albert Pietersma and Benjamin G. Wright, published in 2007 under the name *A New English Translation of the Septuagint.*

The standard eighteenth-century translation of Josephus, by William Whiston, is also in the public domain and readily available online and in various print and e-book compilations. It's not ideal, but it's the best there is.

Translations of the Life of Adam of Eve, the Apocalypse of Abraham, and Enoch are available in volumes 1 and 2 of *The Old Testament Pseudepigrapha,* edited by James H. Charlesworth and available from both Yale University Press and from Doubleday. The books are expensive, but affordable used copies can often be found. The Life of Adam and Eve is in the second volume (published in 1985), the Apocalypse of Abraham and Enoch in the first (published in 1983). This is a compilation you'll want to own anyway, as I describe below, so start looking for your copies now.

My *And God Said: How Translations Conceal the Bible's Original Meaning,* published in 2010 by Thomas Dunne Books/St. Martin's Press, explains why translating ancient texts is so hard, details how modern translations distort the original text of the Bible, and explains what modern readers can do to see past these mistakes. Though focusing more narrowly on the Old Testament, it will give readers a sense of what they get and what they miss when they read translations of the material from the Bible's cutting room floor.

I've referred to three Bible translations in these pages.

The JPS (Jewish Publication Society) translation is the most popular Jewish translation, and it comes in two versions, the first JPS translation from 1917 and a newer one, sometimes called the NJPS translation, published in 1985. The NJPS has two editions, the original translation and a revised gender-inclusive text. The 1917 version is no longer in copyright, so it's widely available for free online, but it's outdated. The 1985 version is also widely available in print and e-book editions. As a Jewish translation, it only covers the Old Testament.

The NRSV (New Revised Standard Version) translation is, in my opinion, unsurpassed as an English translation of the Old and New Testaments, for the reasons I describe in *And God Said*. It is widely available in print and e-book editions and available online.

The KJV (King James Version), though outdated as a translation, remains influential and, in addition, helps us understand what people four hundred years ago thought the Bible meant. Though technically still in copyright (in perpetuity, the copyright being held by the Crown), Her Highness Queen Elizabeth II graciously allows its use almost without restriction.

General

The same two-volume edition we just saw, *The Old Testament Pseudepigrapha*, is an excellent way to continue studying the Bible's cutting room floor. It is a remarkably comprehensive compilation of ancient writings, offering scholarly analysis in addition to translations of dozens of major and minor works from antiquity. Both volumes also contain three forewords (indicated as being for the general reader, for the Jewish reader, and for the Christian reader) and a general overview of the material.

The way that edition treats the individual works is also typical of what's available. You'll find short summaries of what's in each work, when and where it was written, how we know about it, why it's important, and where to find more information. Equally, the edition does a good job conveying the degree to which we have confidence in our information, helpfully noting when scholars themselves disagree. It's not easy reading, but (unlike some scholarly publications), at least it's almost entirely in English; only the footnotes assume that the reader can keep up with French, German, Russian, Greek, Latin, Hebrew, Aramaic, and more. The only major deficiency I've found when using the two-volume set is that the fourteen-page list of abbreviations is sorted by type, so if you see an abbreviation, you often have to look through more than one list to find out what it means. Though *The Old Testament Pseudepigrapha* is comprehensive, even that edition is not complete. Additional material can be found in a more recent 2013 publication of almost the same name: *Old Testament Pseudepigrapha*. Consisting of two volumes (one of which is still forthcoming as I write this), the subtitle—"More Noncanonical Scriptures"—describes its nature exactly. It's edited by Richard Bauckham, James Davila, and Alexander Panayotov, and published by Wm. B. Eerdmans.

The Secret Book of James that I mention in passing in chapter 4 is part of the collection of fourth century A.D. codices found at Nag Hammadi in Egypt. Thanks to Elaine Pagels's excellent book *The Gnostic Gospels* (available in a 1989 paperback edition from Vintage), these, along with some other manuscripts, are widely known as the Gnostic Gospels. Pagels's book about them is a great place to start.

Because most of these Gnostic Gospels come from Nag Hammadi, they are also called the Nag Hammadi Scriptures, and a book by that name, edited by Marvin Meyer and published in paperback in 2007 by HarperOne, has translations of them with commentary by the translators. Another option, also from HarperOne, is *The Nag Hammadi Library in English,* edited by James Robinson and published in 1990.

History

The history from chapter 1 is fairly well known, and histories of the first millennium B.C. are easy to come by, though most of them do not indicate the tentative nature of some of the information—particularly when it comes from only one or two sources, like the Bible or Josephus.

For following up on what you've read here, start with H. W. F. Saggs's *Civilization before Greece and Rome,* published in 1989 by Yale University Press. It's one of the best books I've ever read, and a beautiful example of how to combine scholarly research and accuracy with engaging prose. As the title suggests, it's about what happened before Greece and Rome. I'm not aware of any better introduction to the forces that shaped the first part of the first millennium B.C.

J. M. Roberts has a 1976 volume—since reprinted many times—from Oxford University Press with the only slightly pretentious title *History of the World.* It's obviously not as detailed as a single book about, say, Alexander the Great or King Herod, but it's better than an encyclopedia and is a marvelous addition to any bookshelf. Only some parts overlap with the history that concerns us here, but those parts make the book worth it.

For the specific period from about 200 B.C. to A.D. 200, a great place to start is A. R. C. Leaney's *The Jewish & Christian World: 200 B.C. to A.D. 200,* published by Cambridge University Press in 1984. It's the seventh volume of their Cambridge Commentaries on

Writings of the Jewish & Christian World 200 B.C. to A.D. 200, and it expands on much of the historical narrative I've presented.

Dead Sea Scrolls

I've already mentioned that the best way to start reading the Dead Sea Scrolls is García Martínez and Tigchelaar's *The Dead Sea Scrolls Study Edition*. It contains everything except the biblical material. You can get that from the 2002 paperback edition of *The Dead Sea Scrolls Bible*, by Martin Abegg, Peter Flint, and Eugene Ulrich. While their work doesn't give you the original Hebrew, it does tell you where the Dead Sea Scrolls differ from the Masoretic text of the Old Testament.

My presentation in chapter 2 of how the Dead Sea Scrolls were discovered and brought to light is fairly comprehensive. For another take on the riveting story, you can try the introduction of Florentino García Martínez and Wilfred G. E. Watson's *The Dead Sea Scrolls Translated*, published in 1996 by William B. Eerdmans.

Because the Dead Sea Scrolls are the oldest significant manuscripts we have, you'll want to see some them. Start with Ayala Sussmann and Ruth Peled's *Scrolls from the Dead Sea*, which contains some lovely full-color photos. Then plan a trip to Jerusalem to see them in person at the Shrine of the Book.

Septuagint

A good next step in learning about the Septuagint is Karen H. Jobes and Moisés Silva's *Invitation to the Septuagint*, published in 2000 by Baker Academic. It gives you a concise history of the Septuagint, some interesting photos of various manuscripts (sadly, in black and white), and a series of increasingly narrow essays about the content and importance of the Septuagint. For some parts of the book it helps to know Hebrew and Greek, because those languages appear in their native scripts, rather than in English transliteration, but readers can equally skip over those parts and still get most of the main thrust.

You'll also want a translation, as indicated above.

Josephus

Many people's first instinct when they first become interested in Josephus is to try to read what he actually wrote. Unfortunately, this is a daunting task. His complete works, as translated by William Whiston, run about half a million words, frequently in complex, almost archaic English. And while the notes help a little, the reader still has to know a fair deal about the ancient world to keep up.

Steve Mason has a better place to start. His *Josephus and the New Testament* (second edition published 2003 by Hendrickson Publishers) is an excellent guide to Josephus in general and, in addition, accomplishes the author's more specific goal of exploring how Josephus and the New Testament overlap. It is a natural place to follow up on the issues from chapter 4. It is a fine example of what I might call the "new scholarship": it is well researched and footnoted though still generally readable by lay audiences, and you only need to know one language to read it: English.

Adam and Eve, Abraham, and Enoch

It is easy to find books about the Life of Adam and Eve, the Apocalypse of Abraham, and especially Enoch, and most of them are not very good. Rather than searching around at random, a good place to follow up on these three books is Charlesworth's comprehensive two-volume series, mentioned above. It will take some work to read through the scholarly presentations there, but it's worth it.

How the Bible Became a Book

In addition to the documents and writings themselves, one of my major themes here has been how those texts turned into what we now call "the Bible," along with related themes like why some texts were included, others excluded, and others yet modified. Unfortunately, the simple question, How did the Bible become a book? defies any simple or even widely accepted answer.

William M. Schniedewind has a book published in 2004 by Cambridge University Press. Its title, *How the Bible Became a Book,* suggests that it might offer an answer. It does not, because, as Schniedewind explains, he primarily addresses the writing of the individual scrolls, not their compilation into one book. Still, it's a great place to start exploring these issues. In particular, his first chapter, "How the Bible Became a Book," provides a succinct and clear overview of the issues surrounding the written texts that we now call the Bible.

Schniedewind correctly points out that the nature of writing in antiquity is closely related to the writings that became the Bible and its cutting room floor. My own belief is that writing was widespread among at least some of the Jews (and, therefore, early Christians), for the reasons I explain in detail in my *In the Beginning: A Short History of the Hebrew Language* (NYU Press, 2004). Unfortunately, Karel van der Toorn in his excellent *Scribal Culture and the Making of the Hebrew Bible,* published in 2009 by Harvard University Press, presents evidence that points toward much more limited literacy. But he doesn't refute any of my evidence. So we're left with two convincing but contradictory explanations about the very nature of writing that underpins all the ancient manuscripts that were available for inclusion in the Bible. If you figure out which one of us is right, please let me know.

Finally, all of the sources I've mentioned here have their own suggested reading lists.

Happy reading.

INDEX